Unwin Education Books

EDUCATING ADOLESCENT GIRLS

Educating Adolescent Girls

E. M. CHANDLER

School of Education, University of Exeter

London
GEORGE ALLEN & UNWIN
Boston   Sydney

First published in 1980

GEORGE ALLEN & UNWIN LTD
40 Museum Street, London WC1A 1LU

© George Allen & Unwin (Publishers) Ltd, 1980

British Library Cataloguing in Publication Data

Chandler, E M
    Educating adolescent girls.
    1. Adolescent girls – Education
    I. Title
    376'.63   LC1421   80-40404

    ISBN 0-04-370096-9
    ISBN 0-04-370097-7 Pbk

Set in 10 on 11 point Times by Red Lion Setters, London
and printed in Great Britain by Billing and Sons Ltd.,
Guildford, London and Worcester.

Contents

To my students past and present in gratitude for all their help, and to my Art Teacher, Sister Florence, who taught me how to enjoy my adolescence.

Preface

Learning, 'if she has a real taste for it, will not only make her contented, but happy in it', wrote Lady Mary Wortley Montague some two hundred years ago. This advice on education was for the benefit of her little grand-daughter. She warned, however, that it would be 'most absolutely necessary' for her to 'conceal whatever learning she attains with as much solicitude as she would hide crookedness or lameness; the parade of it can only serve to draw on her the envy, and consequently the most inveterate hatred, of all he and she fools'.

This is a book for those who, considering themselves to be neither he nor she fools, believe that it is possible for girls to have a real taste for learning. To some it might seem that all teachers, by their very profession, must hold to such a belief; the evidence, unfortunately, does not support such a view. In a society in which the pre-eminence of feminine beauty over feminine intelligence has diminished little since the eighteenth century the temptation for females to be intellectually able is still easily resisted. That the temptation to take seriously girls' intellectual ability is also easily resisted by many educators is likewise sadly evident.

Dr Guido Brunner, when European Commissioner responsible for Education, issued a report which is damning in the extreme in its criticism of the education being given to girls throughout Europe. Pointing out that one woman in five in the UK is the family bread-winner, he goes on to show how little help she is given by her education to reach a position in which she can earn enough to support herself, let alone a family. Girls, he says, are suffering from 'inequalities which should not be allowed to exist in our community'. Girls everywhere are under-achieving, even those who are being successful at school. They are likely to be discouraged from a too-ambitious attitude towards further education. Far more than twice as many boys as girls go to university; far fewer girls than boys continue schooling after the minimum leaving age and hardly any girls get into technical training or apprenticeships. The lot of those who start out with only limited intellectual potential is even worse: their education often finishes long before they have left school.

Dr Brunner puts all this boldly at the door of 'discrimination and sex stereotyping'; yet there must be few teachers who would accept such an accusation with ease. Although there are undoubtedly prejudiced people in the teaching profession, as in all other walks of life, there are far more who are simply unaware that they are perpetuating an unsatisfactory state of affairs, and who are all too aware that many young girls appear to be perfectly content with things as they are.

Alas, there will always be girls who will have no need to hide their learning, having none to hide. How easy it has been therefore to dismiss them as ineducable and to relegate them to the ranks of the foolish which they have graced for so long. Whilst the prevailing model for the ideal woman is the pretty, silly, acquisitive but submissive dolly-girl who decorates most of our advertisements, or the man-hunting adventuress who dominates the magazines, we might well doubt the need for educating girls. Girls who believe that their only hope for the future is to find a man who will support them do not respond too well to pressure to involve themselves in the work that is currently offered to them in many schools. Obviously in an insecure world they will put their best efforts into those aspects of life that promise to bring them the desired reward. Teachers have the job of trying to show them that this is no adequate aim in life. To do so teachers need to know why it is not, if they are to carry conviction. It is all too easy for staff, infected by the boredom and resentment of their adolescent students, to resign themselves to the belief that these girls' interests lie outside the school and should be left to lie there.

Ivan Illich and other de-schoolers propose freedom to choose to absent oneself from school. There is a case to be made for allowing young adolescents to leave if they find school intolerable and have work to go to which would be more interesting and rewarding. There is an even better case to be made for making the acquisition of knowledge more interesting and rewarding than any other work. Currently there is little work that uneducated and not very intellectual girls can do in our society that is more rewarding than the studying that they could be doing at school. Unfortunately, what they are doing in school is often neither meaningful nor useful; too many are merely keeping themselves occupied and sometimes they are not even doing that. They are biding their time until they can leave.

Indifference to learning is easily nurtured, albeit unwittingly, by those who expect to find it; and there are still teachers whose behaviour suggests that they do not really believe that girls will ever want to learn. Quite a number doubt, for example, that many girls can have any ability in such subjects as maths, science, engineering and the like; girls respond by showing little interest.

The notion that there is a specific entity known as a 'Man's Mind' can be discouraging to those who by birth are excluded from the possession of such a luxury. Indeed it can create even today the kind of bitterness that led George Eliot in the last century to write: 'A man's mind – what there is of it – has always the advantage of being masculine, as the smallest birch tree is of a higher kind than the most soaring palm – and even his ignorance is of a sounder quality.'

It is not suggested for one moment that there are no differences between men and women, nor that those which are perceived are either all artificially engendered or necessarily bad. What is important is to become aware of those practices which stem from stereotyped ideas, and which react to the detriment of girls' education. There is a need for us to adjust our thinking so that we can adjust our behaviour. To the extent that we type-cast girls into the social role of the intellectually inferior, we limit their ability to develop their own personalities.

We have to thank Miss Beale and Miss Buss and all the other excellent nineteenth-century reformers for their magnificent work in bringing to light the damage that was being done by such thinking. They improved beyond measure the educational lot of upper-class and middle-class girls. To this day such girls suffer from somewhat fewer handicaps than do their less fortunate sisters.

In their day these reformers were determined to ensure that girls would have the same opportunities as boys, which they perceived in terms of upper-class boys' schools. They did not wholly succeed because they were under pressure to demonstrate that girls deserved, let alone needed, such opportunities. It became, in fact, incumbent on women who wished to be educated to prove that they were as good as men. Where Lady Mary had accepted the status quo her successors decided to fight it. As a result, from these nineteenth-century reformers we inherited an educational system based on the implicit assumption that the needs of girls must be shown to be identical with those of boys. Since then, apart from the addition of a few feminine subjects to the timetable, of their nature forbidden to boys until the Sex Discrimination Act, no real thought has been given to the idea that there might be other aspects of feminine life which should be taken into account by those who are educating girls.

A school system in which girls' education has aped that of boys, even to the extent of a uniform that was originally an adaptation of male attire, reinforces this commitment on the part of girls to prove their worth in male terms. Underlying the education that we give to children from the earliest age is this assumption, therefore, that boys and girls are coping with the same tasks. Fortunately up to the age of puberty this is a reasonable working hypothesis. By and large primary schools cater well enough for the needs of all children; it is in the secondary schools that the disadvantages of being a girl begin to take on more significance. Not surprisingly, therefore, it is in these schools that girls begin to be difficult and that teachers begin to lose heart.

Attempts to look at the education of girls separately from that of boys will always be hampered by the danger of implied corroboration of prejudices; different is assumed to mean inferior. Whilst this is the case we need first of all to tackle those areas in which perception of differences is irrational and then those where it is not only rational but helpful. We need at the same time to recognise the disadvantages to both boys and girls of these prejudices.

Any segregation of society into two extreme groups is inevitably damaging to both. To concentrate, as I am doing, on the difficulties that girls experience is not to suggest that boys are not also victims of this invalid dichotomy. Whilst girls undoubtedly suffer from prejudices and misconceptions which their brothers have been spared, they have also been permitted freedoms that have not been so easily available to boys. A sound education system would redress these wrongs.

Girls have, in the past, been allowed to be gentle and sensitive, quiet and passive, to care for the weak and the damaged and to admit to frailty. Boys, on the other hand, have been asked to be masterful and strong whatever their inclinations, to conceal their feelings and to condemn weakness in themselves and others. Girls have been free to live in the privacy of their own inner worlds of imagination and fantasy, to take the small matters of daily life into serious consideration and yet, if they wish, to be frivolous. Boys in contrast have the virtues of extraversion and reality-testing firmly put before them.

Girls are allowed to adorn themselves and to enjoy their own physical beauty; even now, after a decade of unisex, boys are governed by strict rules of attire far more limiting than those applying to girls. Girls are more likely than boys to be encouraged to discover creative pursuits which do not necessarily lead to careers; they may cook and sew, although they are not expected to see themselves as future chefs, and they rarely dominate the world of haute couture. In fact their inner imaginative worlds and their creative tendencies have been given some freedom to develop, so long as they have kept them to themselves; it is only when they break Lady Mary's strictures and allow their intellectual interests to be known, or venture with their ideas into the outer world, that they bring down opprobrium on themselves.

The more that women demand to partake of the external world, the more disapproval they expose themselves to. This unfortunately pressurises a great many girls into rejecting all the positive aspects of their sexual caste, in their attempts to redress the balance. We are seeing frightening signs of this in the brutality that some of them practise in their determination to demonstrate some fantasied equality of physical strength.

Members of women's movements have drawn attention to the number of ways in which girls have been educated to see themselves as subsidiary to boys: as help-mates rather than initiators. Boys become surgeons and business tycoons, girls become nurses and secretaries. Helping has become synonymous with relegation to a secondary role, yet in rejecting the picture of themselves as helpers girls can turn their backs on some of the most valuable contributions that anyone can make to society.

The demands of motherhood, exaggerated by one section of society so that nothing short of total servitude by the mother to the family is accepted, can be too easily relegated to a minor position by those who would throw off these shackles altogether. Meanwhile for too long boys have been virtually excluded from taking part in the enjoyable aspects of child-rearing. The sense of inferiority expressed by so many house-wives does not come from the role of helper or mother, but from the poor value set by society on house-centred work. When all boys too are brought up to be helpers, to find the pleasures that have been so long denied to them in child-care and to feel no shame in taking part in running a home, the menial aspects of such essential work may dis-appear. At present it is for the most part only the privileged middle- and upper-class men who dare risk abdicating the traditional male role in this way.

A world full of helpers who saw themselves and were seen by others as pillars of society, instead of second-class citizens, would surely be a splendid place. In such a world we could trust to a secure future undreamed of in our present war-torn, warrior-dominated lives. Schools could make a start in creating such a world.

This book is not, therefore, dedicated to the idea that girls always get a worse deal than boys. It is concerned with those aspects of the treat-ment that they receive in schools that undoubtedly hampers their development in some essential areas, and with the behaviour that so many of them are beginning to show which can only be detrimental to their own happiness, as well as to that of others.

There is no doubt then from the evidence presented in Dr Brunner's report and Eileen Byrne's *Women and Education* that girls receive less help than boys in gaining benefit from the education that is offered to them, and that they therefore have less breadth of career choice. There is no doubt also that girls are beginning to cause more and more concern to their teachers when they reach their teens. It is equally certain that there are ways in which the distinctive needs of girls are not being met.

This should not, by any means, all be blamed on schools. Teachers may want girls to learn but powerful forces from outside school, even sometimes from their own homes, will persuade them otherwise. Never-theless there is a great deal that can be done through the education system.

I am concerned with such of the anomalies as can be rectified by the work of individual teachers, rather than those which require a reform of the whole structure. Whilst we live in hope of exciting new ventures, the majority of teachers are concerned with their day-to-day task of educating the next generation. My aim is not, therefore, to preach revolution but more modestly to look for solutions to immediate problems.

In 1963 the Newsons produced their report *Half Our Future* which alerted us to our failure to provide for the less able children in our schools. Some notice was taken of their excellent advice. Now we need to examine what is happening, not so much to half our future as to far more than half, since girls will be the future mothers of families.

If I appear to criticise the teaching profession in my attempt to put the case of the girls they teach I would offer in mitigation my recognition that teachers perform a desperately demanding and, in some schools, an excessively difficult task; and that as a former teacher I take it for granted that we all know how much strain this work causes. In my experience some teachers fulfil their role with a skill that often amounts to heroism, and get precious little recognition for it from the outside world; they realise this and ignore it because their concern is for the children they teach.

Teaching, requiring as it does concern, involvement and unremitting concentration, besides academic ability, patience and almost unlimited energy, is hard and relatively poorly paid work. There are easier and more financially rewarding ways of earning a living; but those who take up any profession have to remind themselves from time to time that the essence of professionalism is to put the needs of others before ourselves. The fact that other professionals do not always have such a pure outlook on their responsibilities should not be of consequence to a teacher.

Only the teaching profession has the responsibility for developing the minds of the young. Those who deal with their bodies, their teeth, their eyes or their feet might be better paid but they do not do such important work. Teachers who develop the thinking faculties of the young are dealing with something that can affect the future of the world; developing the thinking faculties of the mothers of the next generation, done well, might go some way towards saving us from Armageddon.

If their education helps them to enjoy learning, girls can pass to their children, and to their children's children, the possibility of being happy in learning. Teachers can create this enjoyment if they can find it in their hearts to like the girls they teach; liking people requires getting to know them. I hope in this book to help some of you to get to know your girl students better and so like them better.

I am concerned in particular for those new or aspiring teachers who may have been intimidated by some of the stories that are put about concerning adolescent girls. I would like to encourage them to have trust in the girls they teach, and to embark on their careers with enthusiasm.

Enthusiasm has to be tempered with reality, but not crushed by it, so I present some of the realities of everyday life in ordinary schools attended by ordinary girls. Without dwelling to excess on those few who present problems that are manifestly beyond the skills of the ordinary teacher, I hope to increase understanding of some of the more intractable behaviour that may at first seem incomprehensible. I write from my own experience of thirty years' work both as a teacher and as a psychologist. I have also drawn on the knowledge of the many teachers whom I have met in the course of my lecturing and research. My most valuable source of information has been girls themselves, in particular those who have helped me recently by giving generously of their time to talk to me and to my colleagues. Around four hundred girls from all types of school have been given an interview structured by a questionnaire. Others have had a longer term of contact in the form of counselling or therapy with either myself or a school counsellor. Most of these counsellors have been in training with me at Exeter University, where I have tried to inculcate into them a commitment to listening to what adolescents have to say themselves, as an essential preliminary to embarking on any programme for their reform, improvement or even entertainment.

All names and some details have been altered so as to retain anonymity, and for the sake of convenience I have taken adolescence to begin in girls where it very often does begin, with the onset of menstruation. I have used the term 'pupil' more often than the increasingly preferred 'student' so as to avoid confusion with student teachers.

Chapter 1

An Introduction to Adolescent Girls

Let me introduce you to adolescent girls first through the eyes of a man:

> that dubious quality of young feminine life which is so fleeting and so easily destroyed. The presence of a man destroys it in a second, introducing a different element altogether. Totally unconscious of what is happening to their young bodies and souls, girls, when they are thus alone together, give themselves up to all manner of little gestures, movements, abandonments, which not only the presence of a man but the presence of an older woman could drive away. Certain filmy and delicate essences in young girls' beings come to the surface only when they are alone like this with one another. When any of them is alone by herself it is different again; for then her own thoughts are apt to play the part of intruders and cause those fragile petals of her identity to draw in and close up.

John Cowper Powys wrote this nearly half a century ago; does she still exist, this wisp of a girl? Or was she only ever a figment of male fantasy? It would certainly be hard to identify her amongst the strident hoydenish young ladies who dominate some of our third and fourth year groups. Does the girl who waits outside the school gate to attack physically and brutally the friends she shared her lunch with only yesterday have a fragile petal of identity? Oddly enough, I believe she has: an identity whose fragility is such that it is even more liable for destruction nowadays than it was in 1933; an identity which is in fact in danger. It is her teachers who are in the best position to help her to find it and preserve it.

If we are to make any sense of the behaviour of young people we have to begin by believing in them; this means believing in the possibility of something in their essence. Goethe tells us that there is a basic goodness in all human beings. Without some such faith it must be hard, if not impossible, to find the patience and tolerance that is the prerequisite for coping with so much of the incomprehensible behaviour that characterises adolescence. Patience and tolerance are not all that is required, they are simply fundamental necessities. Beyond them we need other qualities like toughness, consistency and the ability to bear with being disliked. Sometimes it seems that we need to have the qualities of saints, but I do not believe that this is really the case. No human being, however much in need, can demand sanctity from another as a right. The tolerance to be extended to the young need only be reasonable. Should it spill over into sanctity, or something of the kind, it might actually be bad for both the young and old alike.

Why then this need for tolerance? Adolescents seem always to have made excessive demands on the patience of adults. Perhaps it is true that the condition known as adolescence is a function of society or indeed, as has been suggested, an invention of our culture. Certainly researchers like Margaret Mead have given convincing evidence that there are societies which show few, if any, of what we recognise as typical adolescent behaviour patterns. But in the Western world for many centuries it has seemed that only in those societies which have kept the young in submission, by rigid protocol or by malnutrition, do we see no signs of disruption or revolt during the years between 10 and 20.

In our society, for every one young person who goes through these years in peace and tranquillity there appear to be at least three who cause havoc and chaos. No doubt this is an exaggerated perception but it is common amongst teachers and the general public alike. Throughout our history, the transition from childhood to adulthood has been seen as a time for testing out the limits of freedom by the young, and struggling to define them by the old. There is a common belief, and a good deal of evidence from statistics on delinquency to support it, that this rebelliousness is on the increase. Alan Harrington in his book *Psychopaths* quotes Robert Lindher: 'A profound and terrifying change has taken over the character of that time of life we call "adolescence"', suggesting that young people are not only 'conventionally rebellious' but in a state of 'mutiny against Life itself'.

Whether or not this syndrome is really on the increase overall, there is no doubt that of late the impact of the adolescence of girls has been making itself felt in new and very concrete ways. Whereas in the past delinquency and crimes of violence were the province of boys, nowadays girls too are making bombs and hijacking planes. The ratio of female to male delinquents, until recently remaining pretty constant, now appears to be changing, and girls, though still well behind boys, are responding rapidly to the violence of the times. In schools they are also making their presence felt by bolder and more assertive behaviour. Headteachers who once thought of girls as the stabilising influence in their schools have been known to quail at the sight of some of their new-style female adolescents clad in what is still thought of as masculine attire and expressing their opinions as forcefully as any boys do. At the same time, girls are still undertaking their confrontation with the adult world along the established lines: by being generally defiant and obtuse; by indulging in proscribed sexual practices; by taking whatever forbidden drugs are fashionable, in particular by taking an overdose; and, perhaps most frustrating of all, by running away. Along with this in school we continue to find the startling drop in work output that accompanies the arrival of more serious interest in the opposite sex for so many girls.

What then has happened to these girls that makes them deviate so much from the still-established concept of the feminine ideal? Perhaps it is this question that we must answer before we can begin to deal with the girls themselves. We need to examine what we do to them before we can understand what they do to us.

What we do to a girl, first of all, is define femininity for her. We then present her with a world in which she is supposed to cope in a feminine way whilst being bombarded with messages that contradict, for her, almost everything that she has been taught. In adolescence she tries to redefine femininity for herself. It could be that this redefinition, that is so painful for all of us nowadays, is the inevitable outcome of the changes that have been taking place all over the world, throughout the last century or so, in attitudes to women. Perhaps these changes are coming to some sort of climax in the second half of this century through which we may be able to see what girls really need to learn about being female.

If we look at a girl's life-history up to adolescence, we see a similar pattern now to the one which has been with us for at least a hundred years. As a baby she is cared for, protected and controlled by adults. She is given to understand what is expected of her in the way of behaviour as a little girl by adults who are often totally unaware that they are providing any such information. As a young girl she goes out into the world usually feeling strong enough to cope because of the stability that her family has provided. She learns now to deal on her own with external reality. She can rely on some kind of support from the adults at home whilst she is taken up into a world of work and play which in all probability she attacks with zest and success, and with very little question as to its significance to herself. She is quite possibly more approved of than the boys with whom she associates and in many ways more successful and content than they are. She rarely doubts the rightness of what is happening to her and in any case she has no say in the matter.

Then almost overnight she is transformed. She reaches puberty. It is not possible to exaggerate the significance of this event for a girl, though it is frequently played down, if not totally ignored, by the adult world. The education that she has received in school has been identical with that of a boy in its demands that she be competitive, assertive and success-oriented. Now with the arrival of puberty she finds herself in a world radically different from that of the boys, and changed for ever. Although in school her education continues along the same lines, every other aspect of her life becomes dominated by ideas which are pushing her into the traditional 'feminine' part that she will be expected to play; the compliant unassuming role which requires her to charm boys with her dependent docility rather than compete with them with her independent intelligence. The reason for this? Motherhood has become a possibility, with all its attendant demands. From now on, whatever else she may do with her life, she will in some way be dominated by this fact, whether or not she ever actually produces a child.

The comparatively recent developments which have made it possible for her also to decide with some degree of certainty not to become a mother have not only not diminished the importance of this event for her, they have made it even more of a problem. There is no doubt that the coincidental arrival of an age of virtually untrammelled sexuality with reliable contraception has heightened the effect of sexual maturation for girls.

Together with this have come the political changes that are bringing women into some sort of equality with men. Somewhere within the response to these changes, which the adult world has imposed upon her, are to be found the roots of the girl's new adolescent attitudes. For boys, however great the significance of puberty, these changes have not made such a dramatic impact. The freedom to make sexual experiments is nothing like as novel, and, in the young, the possibility of becoming a father is a distant and relatively insignificant event. This sometimes makes it hard for men to understand the quality of a girl's reaction to the onset of adolescence. Laurens Van der Post, who has an unusual capacity for awareness of the feminine spirit, suggests that every schoolboy should be taught about the feelings of women. He quotes an Ethiopean woman who lived in the eleventh century AD as saying: 'How can a man know what a woman's life is? . . . the woman from the day of her first love is "Another".' Even today, nine hundred years later, perhaps all teachers, male and female, should remember that from the first day of her menarche, of her true femininity, the girl is already and for ever 'Another'.

Although she is not by any means consciously absorbed in these matters at all times, for many a young girl no other aspect of her life will ever equal in importance the reality of her potential as a wife and mother. School curricula do not seem to take this into account; nor do some teachers. Yet somehow the attitudes of educational planners must change if girls are really to receive the education that they need. It might be helpful for those who find it hard to bear with what looks like a silly obsession with the trivialities of boyfriends to remember these facts. The trivialities are there but they can be a cloak or a substitute for something much more profound. A young girl in school is now in a position to undertake the momentous task of bringing another human being into the world.

When she sees adulthood on the horizon she sees also a world of potential ready-made commitments which she may enter without further thought or preparation. In spite of all the social upheavals that are taking place, marriage and motherhood are still expected of her and to some extent she will always be judged on the basis of how or whether she fulfils these expectations. She knows this. The title 'wife and mother' will always bring automatic approval, that of 'spinster' never. 'Husband and father' has no such obvious status and 'bachelor' is quite acceptable. So besides the natural physiological attraction to the opposite sex which is likely to dominate her feelings, she is also driven by these sociological factors which will have an effect on her thinking Increasingly she will be preoccupied with thoughts that lead her away from school and studies and towards what she will often conceptualise as settling down, and having a home of her own. These ideas include, less consciously, taking on the role of the mother with whom she is usually still closely in touch. The fact that she is ill-prepared makes little difference. If she has captured a male, she has fulfilled society's expectation. She has a place in the world.

The temptation to accept the imposition of this life without question is very strong for a young girl, to whom the world can seem a turbulent and threatening place. Unlike the boys with whom she has grown up she will often not feel encouraged to consider too wide a variety of alternatives. In many schools only lip-service is paid to the notion that girls need careers as much as boys; in many more homes not even lip-service is paid to such a revolutionary idea. Because of the paucity of her expectations, the girl exercises little judgement about what should happen to her.

In this way, a large number of girls preserve themselves from the too-great pressures of future decision-making and settle, before they have begun to mature, for a style of life in which they believe that they will never again feel the need to exert their own personal initiative. Their identity, having been subtly undermined by an indifferent society, is virtually atrophied. Being allowed to drift, or sometimes to run, into a scarcely understood role of colossal responsibility, they lose any sense of themselves. If, on this road towards stagnation, mindless protests are made in the form of violence to society's rules, who is to blame?

When a simulated maturity in the form of early sexual development is promoted with conscious intention by those with only commercial interests at heart, what chance of survival has the insecure personality of a silly young girl without some kind of firm adult support? What hope have the young when, unprepared by any solid ethical standards at home, they are bombarded by advertisers with encouragement to believe that material goods are the greatest reward that life has to offer? What can we expect from a girl other than obsession with her appearance when she is constantly reminded that her sexual attractions are her greatest asset? Only the strong who have equally strong adult support can hope to resist these blandishments. If a girl's family cannot supply this support teachers have no option but to try to fill the gap. They might not see this as their role, but society does so increasingly, and they are in a unique position to take on the responsibility of presenting a different and better viewpoint.

There is no doubt that this part of a teacher's work is one of the most difficult when, for example, even the most carefully reared child is subjected to pre-teen magazines that offer opportunities to chart the number of times she has intercourse as a measure of her self-worth. Others with less careful rearing can receive much more dramatically stimulating encouragement to see themselves primarily as sex objects and only secondarily as human beings. Although there are plenty of girls who do not follow this pattern, there are few who do not somewhere in their adolescent years experience some of the bitterness that the dishonesty of our social mores arouses. Always they will have heard the contradictory messages which tell them at one moment to be competitive, to aim to defeat others in the battle for honours, to study and head for a career; and the next that they must be submissive, yielding, sweet and, above all, attractive to the opposite sex. Too many give way and follow the dangerous route of easy submission, subscribing themselves to the belief that a girl does not need an educated mind, only an attractive body.

Kierkegaard has told us that philistinism tranquillises itself with the trivial. At times society seems to be involved in a vast conspiracy to trivialise women and to push them into philistinism. That they allow themselves so easily to be pushed is a function of generations of trivialisation. Young girls, bombarded with propaganda which it is very hard for them to resist, avoid confronting reality by accepting the trivial role. Should they attempt to take part in a real world they would find themselves in the position of having to make moral decisions. There are no doubt some teachers who think that, because so many of them are inarticulate, adolescent girls do not have the ability to see the world as an arena for fighting moral or ethical battles. Perhaps this is because those teachers have not really met the girls with whom they are dealing. The outer shell may well be one of ill-expressed indifference to the world. Beneath it, in the most obtuse adolescent, is someone who is struggling with genuine and serious problems of an ethical nature.

We may forget that we went through those struggles ourselves, or we may prefer to forget, having failed to resolve them. By the time they have reached their early twenties many of these girls will have forgotten them too, some much earlier. They are then well set on the path of a trivial and unrewarding life. But adolescence is a time of hope. It is a time for altruism and for coming to terms with your own egocentric and amoral self in relation to the rest of the world's egocentricity and amorality. If these matters are not dealt with, what is left for girls is to slip, perhaps into overt delinquency but, more likely, into what I would call covert delinquency. To allow yourself to be pushed into a trivialised mode of life is as dangerous to yourself and to society as to go in for a life of crime. What lies ahead for such people is at least a life of resentment and waste in which no serious work will be undertaken.

In too many schools teachers, having been delegated the task of bringing into the second half of the twentieth century girls from an environment still rooted in the nineteenth, have themselves so little idea of what these girls are going through. They do not recognise the fact that the adolescent girl is singularly available to encouragement by sympathetic adults to find her own unique 'petal of identity'. Yet at this time of life she is open in a way that may never be possible again: to ideas, to feelings, to learning about the meaning of the world and to discovering what she herself can give to it.

At no other time in her life will she be in the position to deal so sensitively with her own development. No longer entirely ruled by others, she still has the chance to avoid becoming immersed in responsibilities and customs before she is ready. She has now, with her increased capacity for thought and for self-awareness, a chance to discover a world of her own, one in which she can blossom as a person. She can, with only a little encouragement, dream great dreams and even fulfil them.

Once she has left her adolescence behind she can so easily leave, too, the ability to make that very unusual intuitive response to life that is so significant and so fleeting, that is of inestimable value to the maturing young person, but so terribly easily crushed and so difficult to recapture once it has been lost. If, during these years, we do not feed her spirit, we deprive her and future generations for whom she will be responsible of the enjoyment of a rich and fruitful inner life which is everyone's birthright and which should especially be the prerogative of mothers of young children. If those who educate her do not recognise the spirit of excitement and wonder that is available to her, they will have failed her, and society, by allowing something irreplaceable to be crushed.

What, then, is this intuition you may ask? It is the ability to live where reality is not. It is the possibility of responding to the world of feeling, of knowing that a primrose by a river's brim is something more than a simple primrose and of not needing to make sense of this. It is the realisation that the world is a wonderful and awesome place where everyone has a right to be. To adolescents there are no frontiers of science to be pushed forward, they themselves are at the front; they can believe that everything is possible even to themselves. If we do not dash their hopes or systematically quench their ardour, they can reach out to life with confidence. Their instinctive response gives them the possibilities of immense depths of feeling, flashes of astounding perception and moments of intense awareness.

This is not a description of a conscious nor of an intellectual process. Even the dullest, least speculative or academic adolescent goes through this phase of subtle psychological enrichment. At some level all the young, by the nature of their humanity, have the capacity to be artists, scientists, maybe even mystics. They also carry within them the possibility of being murderers, destroyers and rapacious materialists. If we do not give them the opportunity to develop their creative selves their destructive side will surely take over.

Adolescents of the lowest intelligence can show concern for others, can delight in making and giving. They can also, under different circumstances, show nothing but self-centredness, destruction and greed, or at least brashness and a crass insensitivity to the needs of anyone but themselves. They may clam up and take no apparent notice of anything that is presented to them in the way of learning. They can defend themselves with a protective armour which will prevent any intrusion by the adult world.

For some young people the intuitive side of their being is hardly allowed to reach consciousness, so it is not easy for their teachers to discover and nourish it. It is crushed by experiences that make sensitivity a liability rather than an asset. There are frightening people in the world who produce and bring up children in unremitting contact with evil, so that by the time that they reach adolescence they seem already beyond hope. There are children whose parents neglect or ill-treat them, and there are others whose living conditions are such that it is almost impossible for the adults to provide a decent upbringing, however good their intentions.

In a world where children are daily presented with an idealised picture of what life should be like on a screen in their own homes, this kind of life may indeed produce a cynical indifference to other human beings. So damaged are some by their experiences that as a form of self-protection they inhibit their natural human responses to life. Having lost touch with their inner nature, they behave in a manner that is destructive to themselves and to the rest of the world.

This is not a new phenomenon; it has been described by socially conscious writers of all ages. Such children need the greatest sensitivity on the part of the adults who deal with them. Unfortunately they often elicit the least sensitive response because their conduct is so threatening to other people. They are a minority, but a powerful and disruptive one. Some of them show behaviour of such a level that teachers should not even be expected to cope with them in the ordinary classroom. Yet teachers frequently find themselves being blamed for this behaviour although, manifestly, they suffer from it far more than does any other section of the population.

There is, however, a dangerous temptation for some teachers to assume that all badly behaved young people belong in this extreme category and so to abdicate from the responsibility of dealing with them. In fact, of course, the majority of them have not had to suffer these more obvious assaults on their being, and even those who have are not always so damaged that their behaviour in school is affected beyond change. Human beings are adept at surviving in even the most adverse circumstances. Apart from this, large numbers of young people from perfectly reasonable homes show from time to time signs of storm and stress if this seems an apt response to life; they are not beyond the powers of any reasonable teacher to cope with.

These negative aspects of adolescent behaviour are as valuable clues to their inner world as are the positive; if we recognise them for the defences that they are we understand better how to deal with them. We, the adults, decide in the end which aspects of their personalities will be allowed to flourish. The decision comes about through the education that we give them.

For many adolescents this time of life is one of excitement, even delirium, when everything seems possible and so much worthwhile. Most of them will lay a sound foundation, having established their identity and defended it, in all its fragility, from the attacks of the world. This is the time of greatest openness to change, to new ideas and the excitement of very existence. From it they will move into the adult world as reasonably accepting or sometimes over-conforming human beings; they will leave behind the turbulence and the stress. In protecting them from the turbulence we need to see, however, that they do not also leave behind a great part of the joy too. There is always the danger that too many will settle for a mundane and safe approach to new ideas and experiences, rejecting the less secure and more rewarding fields that were so tempting in adolescence. This can happen to those who start off in life full of excitement and good cheer, but come up against intransigent and unimaginative authority.

Civilisation exerts its pressure at an early age. Those who encounter no undue personal difficulties still have to contend with the demands of society. There is encouragement on all sides to conform to the lowest common denominator of thought and feeling, to abandon the sensitive intuitive approach to life in favour of more acceptable group norms. This is where teachers can, if they choose, exert influence. They can add to the growing pressures from the outside world or, if they have the courage, they can resist them and help the adolescent to do likewise. It is in school where the materialism and brutality of the world can be must successfully kept at bay. It is there, therefore, that adolescence should be cherished rather than destroyed. This would involve teachers in encouraging an inquiring and challenging approach to life. By the time that school has been left behind opportunities for changing attitudes are fewer. Once a way of life has been adopted that provides security, it becomes increasingly difficult to contemplate the risks that are involved in changing either attitudes or behaviour. This becomes progressively more obvious as we grow older.

There is no doubt that societies, if they are to remain stable, need a modicum of settled and contented adults who will maintain the status quo. What we do not need is a majority of the population who are dull and apathetic. Certainly societies run by people who have not outgrown their adolescence can be horrific. We cannot but regret, however, that so much of the fire of youth is damped down, so much energy squandered and so much sensitivity crushed in a few short years, never to return. Far too many have their spontaneity destroyed by schools that have not been able to cater for it. When we limit the encouragement that girls are given to explore possibilities, both practical and intellectual, we limit also the adventurousness in ideas that they could pass on to their children.

I do not aim to make girls into intellectual giants and I do not suggest that there is anything wrong in their hoping to be married and in expecting to find relationships with the opposite sex more rewarding than those with books. Likewise I do not believe that there is anything inherently virtuous in enjoying academic studies. But there is value in intellectual activity for everyone, however slight their ability may seem. What teachers can offer is an experience that will encourage their pupils to think.

For girls there is a need to think about themselves in terms of their own future. If we can give all girls an education that will encourage them to believe in their own worth as individuals, not solely as one half of a partnership, and to value some aspects of themselves other than their sexual attractions, we will have given them a reasonable start in life. If we can go further and help them to find out how exciting it is to cope with new ideas and to think for themselves we will have given them the means to make their own lives and those of their children really worth living. If we can go even further than this and help them to see how much they can contribute to the world in the way of work that is satisfying to them and useful to society, we will have effected a peaceful revolution. We will also have brought more peace into our classrooms.

Above all, what a young girl needs from the adults around is a response to her inner life of imagination; to her altruism, her genuine sensitivity to the world, her concern for other people and for nature; to her capacity for deep feeling about the suffering of others and her search for meaning in her own life. It requires tough as well as sensitive adults to recognise, and to continue to believe in, the possibilities of this going on under the raucous, uncouth or merely foolish behaviour of many an adolescent. Those who fail to recognise it, however, or to believe in it, will fail to nurture it, and it will die.

Chapter 2

The Adolescent in Conflict

I met Henrietta, a rather sophisticated young lady of 16, during my first year of teaching. She came from a family of artists and writers and knew her way around the psychology books. She was a good student, intelligent, friendly and enthusiastic about life. She commented to me one day that she had heard that adolescence was a time of conflict: 'I don't feel any conflict,' she said. 'What do they mean?' I was, I think, too close to my own adolescence to be able to answer her question adequately. Eight years later I read a report in a local paper about a court case in which Henrietta was being charged with receiving stolen goods. Notices taken from railway sidings and other railway paraphernalia had been collected by her boyfriend and used by Henrietta to decorate her Chelsea flat. This was described by her solicitor as an adolescent prank. It occurred to me that at around 24 Henrietta was a little old for adolescent pranks and that maybe if she had let herself admit to some of her conflicts during her teens she might have grown up rather sooner.

At any stage of human development, from infancy to old age, we meet and deal with crises of varying degrees of significance. If we face up to them and cope successfully, we grow in maturity; if we ignore them we lose out, denying a part of ourselves and perhaps stunting some of our personal growth. The crises that characterise adolescence have particular impact because they encompass the last of our childhood experiences and the first of our ventures into the world of adult responsibilities and adult rewards. The adaptation from one mode of being to another can be difficult for some more than for others. Hence the conflict that Henrietta had heard about.

There are undoubtedly young people who go through adolescence without anxiety or difficulties. This perhaps gives rise to the belief that the notion of adolescence is itself simply an invention of the adults. Those however who have worked with secondary school children or reared their own young know how often the apparently contented and acquiescent teenager will suddenly show another aspect of personality, startlingly different from the familiar facade. Sometimes the facade is only let down when the young person feels secure enough to reveal real feelings; sometimes it it not let down at all during adolescence, but is forced down later in life when the strength of the feelings that it has been hiding break through.

The inability to recognise that there are any conflicts to be resolved can indeed produce a smooth untroubled adolescence. Although by no means all contented adolescents are concealing a sea of turbulence beneath a calm surface, certainly some of them are. The young will hide, even from themselves, the true nature of their feelings, because of the pain and anxiety that these feelings would cause if they were faced up to. They do not hide them so easily from the more experienced adults.

Mostly they will give some indication of their anxieties and adults can learn to interpret the evidence. The temptation, however, is to ignore it and accept the facade that is presented, as I did when I failed to recognise that Henrietta might have been trying to talk about something quite important to her when she opened up her discussion about conflict. Though by no means a deeply disturbed adolescent, she could well have been looking for an understanding adult who would help her to straighten out her ideas. She did not find one in me.

The majority of troubled adolescents, however, leave us in no doubt about their miseries, making their problems only too evident to all who cross their paths. Alison was one of these; she will be familiar, with slight variations, to many a parent and most teachers. Unlike Henrietta she saw life as one continual conflict, both at home and at school, and the adults in her life saw it that way too.

She came with her mother to see me at a child guidance clinic presenting something like an archetypal adolescent syndrome. Aged 14, she had spent the first twelve years of her life being the darling daughter of a doting father, pretty, clever and well behaved. Overnight it seemed she had changed into a termagant, rejecting schoolwork, family beliefs, acceptable standards of behaviour and everything that represented the middle-class culture in which she was being brought up. She had used terrible language, been rude to old friends and ancient aunts; had stopped going to church; invited wholly unsuitable boyfriends to the house in her parents' absence and raided, with them, the family liquor cabinet. She had visited forbidden cafes with the wrong class of boy instead of accepting the invitations of the nice boys with whom she had grown up; furthermore she wore terrible clothes and quarrelled with her impeccably behaved little sister. To her parents the only explanation could be that she was taking drugs. Meantime her schoolwork, which had been excellent, had deteriorated disastrously; she was refusing to work at maths and physics and insisting on doing drama and art. Her teachers complained that she would only work at what she was interested in. After a year of quarrels, tantrums and rages on both sides, in despair her parents had sent her to a boarding school. There, it was hoped, she would be once more inculcated with the parental values that she now rejected at home. She ran away. What is more when she was found she was in a cafe with a man.

This was the story that her mother regaled me with whilst Alison sat looking disdainfully out of the window. When, at my request, her mother left us alone together Alison continued to look in the opposite direction, but agreed grudgingly to my suggestion that she might like to give me her own version of the story. She gave it: she didn't care; she didn't want to know; she hated them all; teachers, parents, good little sister, nice boys, aunts and old ladies: the lot. I said that I could appreciate how she felt having listened to such a catalogue of crimes, but added that I would be interested to know which piece of behaviour she thought her parents objected to most of all. 'Going to cafes', she replied promptly. I wondered aloud what danger they thought might befall her there: did they, I ventured, think she might get raped? She swung round and looked at me in amazement: 'How did you know?' From then on I became acceptable; she had decided that she could talk to me. I had used the dread word which Alison believed lay just below the surface of all their disputes. In those far-off innocent days of the sixties rape was still an unknown impossible fantasy in the genteel suburbs where she lived. For Alison it represented all that was forbidden and, therefore, exciting about sex. What she was dimly aware of was that, for her at any rate, the argument was really about whether or not she was to be allowed to grow up into a sexual being. She did not yet recognise, however, that she herself was perhaps as ambivalent about this prospect as were her parents.

She told me all about what had really happened, how she had found a perfectly nice boyfriend (only he was rather dull); true he had been working as a labourer for two years and was not very well educated, but she was going to help him to improve himself. She had stayed up all night with a girlfriend who was a bit wild; Alison had really wanted to go home, but didn't dare because it was too late and she was afraid to face her parents' anger. She was in no danger of being raped; the infamous cafe was a dreary little place on the High Street wide open to the public gaze. The man she had been found with was her 17-year-old boyfriend.

As she talked Alison's belligerence flagged a little and a more pensive mood took over. No doubt her version of the story was as emasculated as her mother's was over-dramatised. As she heard herself tell it some inkling of the truth that lay somewhere between the two might have dawned on her; she started to examine her behaviour more objectively. She was not sure why she had absconded from school and was already wishing that she had not done so. She did not want to be alienated from her family, but she did not either know how to stay in touch with them. She wanted to have boyfriends, but ones of her own, not her parents', choice. She was not yet ready to recognise that her present boyfriend was probably chosen as much for his value as a provocation to her parents as for his own sake. To her parents this seemed like a rejection, but in reality what Alison was trying to provoke was not rejection but recognition and acceptance.

For any young girl just emerging from childhood, as Alison was, parents are still of enormous importance. Alison needed them to support her and stand by her whilst she made her first tentative steps into adulthood the only way she knew how. She was testing the limits, to see how far she could go in this new-found life. When she found the limits did not seem to be too distinct she ventured farther. As time went on she began to make the mistake of believing that, because her parents did not appear to stop her, they did not really mind what she did. They in their turn were standing by anxiously, not sure what was to be done.

Then suddenly, so it seemed to her, they exploded into incomprehensible rage about some trivial matter that she was hardly aware of. Alison could not understand what was happening to her. She felt miserable and lost. She had in fact a desperate need to keep in touch with her parents, but was in despair about ever being able to reach them again because 'They don't understand the first thing about me'. What, I asked, did she want them to understand? 'That I want to be FREE.' How free? 'Free to be myself.' I suggested that this might need some further elaboration since, perhaps, to her parents she did seem to be pretty free and to be being herself, but her self appeared to them to have changed somewhat. She then revealed that she was as frightened as they were by the change. 'They think I'm mad,' she said. 'Do you know my mother threatened to take me to see a psychologist?' When I confessed to the awful truth that I was a psychologist she gained confidence enough to admit that she also feared that she might be mad.

The feelings of adolescents are often so powerful, so disturbing and so far beyond their own control that the fear of insanity is not uncommon. She found it reassuring to learn that a psychologist did not consider her to be mad and from then on I received the accolade that the young so thankfully bestow on anyone who will listen to them: 'Mrs Chandler's the only person who understands me.' I did not, of course, understand her; who ever really understands another human being? But I could help her to make sense of some of her experiences. What she was expressing was gratitude for the fact that I had had time to listen to her and try to see her point of view; that I had recognised that she was unhappy as well as badly behaved and had seen that these two aspects of herself were interrelated.

I had not done much more than any sympathetic teacher might have been able to do. However, as a result she was able to let me help her towards understanding her own behaviour. This meant both recognising those aspects of herself that were contributing to her misery, and admitting to some responsibility for what was happening. It meant no longer seeing everything in terms of cruel parents and indifferent teachers. This kind of reassessment takes time. On its own it will not be adequate because the adults too need to look at their contributions. Alison's parents and some of her teachers were exacerbating the tensions; in particular her headmistress, who was obsessed by the need to turn clever girls into scientists whatever their own inclinations.

What Alison's parents were contributing quite unwittingly was all too obvious to someone outside the family. It would be easy to dismiss this mother as an unimaginative middle-class lady whose snobbery was being deservedly punished. Truly she and her husband did appear to have a great investment in their class values and, as a result, to give equal weighting to trivial and to important issues. They seemed not to be able to distinguish between the significance of a minor disagreement about Alison's refusal to go to a socially desirable party and a major one about her failure to tell them where she was going, or whom she was meeting, when she stayed out until 2 o'clock in the morning. They also showed an inconsistency in their demands that looked to Alison like a lack of conviction.

For example, sometimes when she arrived in at 2.00 a.m. there they would be, sitting up waiting for her with a smile; they would ask her nothing but invite her to join them in a drink. Another time if she was not in before midnight they would become enraged and a family row would ensue. It seemed that they hovered between extremes of permissiveness at one moment and rigidity at another. To Alison's parents this behaviour was not so much inconsistent as desperate. They were, in her father's words, 'trying to be tolerant'. As this was not their normal mode of being they were incompetent at it. They treated her at times like the grown-up that she wanted to be, but then, responding to their natural inclination, they would revert once more to their former habits and try to put limits on her behaviour. Not feeling sure, however, that setting fixed limits and abiding by them would work, they never tried it for long enough. They could not, anyhow, decide what was a reasonable limit to set. When they treated her like the child that they wanted her to be, Alison responded with frustration and rage; equally problematic was their attempt at tolerance because, not coming naturally, it seemed to Alison like a new kind of control. As they were working according to moods rather than to any real plan they had little hope of success.

These parents, like so many parents and teachers, were as confused as was Alison herself. They had lost their grip as a once-friendly and cheerful child had become almost an enemy. Life seemed to be made up of battles about trivia, yet passions were aroused that were strong enough to tear a happy family apart. They did not know what had happened to them.

What had happened, historically, was that adolescence had arrived in the family. They felt stunned by its implications and, not being able to conceptualise them, they expressed their feelings in terms of class values and rules. They could not see that they themselves were unwilling to let Alison grow up; they could only see that the person that she was growing into was indeed terrible. In objecting to this they failed to recognise that they needed to offer her a viable alternative that was not just a return to her childhood self, however lovable that had been. What they were afraid to look at was the problem of their adaptation to Alison's burgeoning sexuality. This had taken them all by surprise and had not yet been admitted to. Schoolwork, religion, cafes and class distinctions all had their relevance, but they were of minor importance compared to the major problem which they were being used to screen. The problem of adolescence is how does the adult world adapt itself to the admission of a new member to the club? and how does the new member adapt to the club without losing her hold on her own unique personality? The solution is found eventually when the adolescent discovers an identity and settles for it.

At school Alison's teachers were suffering from the spin-off from the family rows and were little better able to adjust to her needs than were her parents. This was partly because they knew hardly anything about her home life and its troubles, and partly because they saw such matters as of little concern to them anyhow. Their task was to get Alison through her O and A levels and get her to university. Schoolwork is important; schools are places for working in and it was important for Alison that she should get down to work again. Adolescents, though they need to be able to waste some time in their own way, need also to have an objective which they can work towards and achieve. They need teachers who will be enthusiastic about helping them towards this achievement, but they also need ones who appreciate that life has other aspects to it. Neither in her new nor her old school had Alison come across any teacher who could make the necessary response to her needs or who could recognise the oblique cries for help that she was making.

A clever girl, seen in terms of future examination successes, all too easily arouses wrath instead of sympathy when she appears to lose interest in her studies. Alison complained that no one at school would listen to her. It is possible that no one had the time to do so, but it is also quite likely that there was no one in either of her schools who had given enough thought to why a girl should so suddenly change in this way. It was only when she ran away that anyone appeared to realise that her unhappiness needed to be taken seriously.

Meanwhile other problems were emerging. Her involvement with the drug scene was essentially at a level of protest. Whether or not she was really taking anything dangerous, there is no doubt that illegal drugs of some sort were around in those days in great quantities. Looking back now at the scare that they caused, and looking at the sane and successful young adults who went through that era taking the mandatory doses of amphetamines and marijuana, one is tempted to wonder what all the fuss was about. But it was about a very serious matter that is with us to this day. Those adolescents who did not come through so successfully are still, some of them, causing heartache and anguish to parents who have looked on helplessly for years. Drugs of all sorts, from the legal but often lethal alcohol to the truly terrifying illegal heroin, will always be a temptation to the unstable. The young are unstable. Alison's friend who was a bit wild was quite possibly more than a bit high, and Alison, too, in all probability.

Nevertheless drugs need not have been, in this case, a major issue. Her parents could have talked her into sense if they had only been able to keep in touch with her. Religion, another battleground, was significantly a more important problem for Alison. She defied family mores by refusing to attend church, which she found dull and uninspiring. She offended everyone by openly jeering at her religion and teasing her 10-year-old sister for being conformist, yet she was by no means without religious inclinations. She did, however, reject the rigidities that she felt overlaid any true feeling in the religion in which she had been brought up. Adolescents, who are often interested in matters of the spirit, need so much to have support and encouragement, rather than demands for conformity, if they are to find their way towards any true convictions.

Social class, that other ground for dissension, can for parents be a matter of importance because it represents what they stand for, but to an adolescent often it means nothing more than prejudice. Parents can reasonably be expected to want their children to make friends within their own group at whatever level of society they live. Sometimes there is tolerance of upward mobility, less frequently of downward, but children anyhow need the freedom to test these matters out for themselves. Usually such problems are only part of a wider area of disagreement: the child feels that the parents' views are too fixed and therefore that her chances of developing into her own kind of person are being too curtailed. Girls, who are customarily given less freedom than boys, suffer from this struggle in particular.

Another perennial matter for disagreement between young and old is, of course, the choice of boyfriends. These have to be noticed and, indeed, often vetted by concerned parents. Alison's boyfriend to whom her parents objected so much was openly rejected by them because of his class, though they also complained that he was much too old for her. In fact at 17 he was not unusually old for a 14-year-old girl, if she had been someone of more maturity. He was, however, doubtless more experienced than Alison and possibly quite as determined to seduce her as her parents imagined he was. It is unlikely though, that they would have had such suspicions if he had been the 17-year-old son of one of their own friends, from whom the danger could have been equally great. Alison recognised the irrationality in her parents' prejudices, but in rejecting it she also rejected their real concern based on real fears.

Overall her parents had good reason to be scared because Alison in her innocence was flirting with danger in several directions. She did not recognise the pitfalls in her new way of life, only its frustrations. She did, however, recognise that the list of crimes reported by her mother were not central to the issue. She knew that it was not that kind of problem. Her parents did not. They did not feel safe enough to let themselves look beyond these rigidly defined areas, but they recognised that if Alison left their group she would be lost to their way of life, perhaps for ever. It had not occurred to them that she was now about to find her own group which might not in the end prove to be too different from theirs. She needed to make it her own, not just a carbon copy of theirs, and the process was as problematic for her as it was for them.

It was problematic for Alison because she was fighting the battle both with her parents and with herself of wanting to grow up, yet at the same time wanting to remain secure in her childish dependence on them. She needed their love and support, but at the same time she needed to stretch her own wings. She made the common mistake of blaming her parents for her own resentment about her continued feelings of dependence on them. She therefore set about rejecting overtly everything that she felt they stood for. Standards and rules, beliefs and prejudices, were all thrown out in a heap. The result was inevitably a vacuum that had to be filled frantically with another set of ideas and prejudices, not necessarily worse or better than those of her parents, all that mattered was that they were different.

This is where the parents' ability to adjust was put under greatest strain. Parents and teachers, not unnaturally, find it tiresome to have every aspect of their carefully thought out and sincerely held philosophies of life dismissed as useless and outmoded by callow youth. Those adults, however, who are not able to stand this strain should beware of tangling with adolescents. When arguments on theory arise wise parents will sit tight and ride the storm rather than enter into interminable disputes about insoluble problems. Wise teachers too will give a wide rein to adolescent philosophising; it is not all bad and it is all necessary as part of the growing process.

Adolescent behaviour, however, is another matter. Wise adults do not always in my view, sit back and watch it happen. Alison's parents, fortunately for her at least, refused to do this. There are those who disagree with me on this matter and I hold in great respect many people, such as A. S. Neill and his followers, who believe that left alone the young will find their own, satisfactory, level of behaviour. Given ideal conditions from an early age this might well be the case, but ideal conditions are rare. Parents and teachers who over the last thirty years or so have tried conscientiously to put these noble aims into practice, whilst continuing to live, work and educate their children in the ordinary style of ordinary people, have all too often come to rue the day when they first heard of child psychology. Alison, whilst at one moment crying for freedom, at another made the same plea that I have heard made by dozens of adolescent girls, 'If only they would tell me what to do'. Not that these girls necessarily always intend to follow the advice, but they do need some certainties to measure themselves against.

I asked Alison what she wanted her parents to tell her to do. 'Tell me when to come in at night; say, 10.30.' 'And would you be in by 10.30 then?', I asked. 'No, of course not.' The point was not just that she needed to defy them, but that she needed to know where they set the limits so that she could get some idea as to where to set her own. Ultimately most adolescents get around in time to setting limits at much the same point as that of their parents, and not all of them need the same kinds of limits. They all do need, however, adults who have the courage to abide by their own convictions and who have prepared themselves in advance by recognising what their convictions are, and whether they are worth fighting for.

In this both Alison's parents and her teachers failed her to some extent. Their complaints about her behaviour were not that it did not accord with perfectly reasonable and necessary moral standards, though quite obviously some of it did not, but rather that it did not accord with their perception of how they wanted her to behave. Her teachers perceived her desperate attempts to find her own intellectual interests as refusal to work. They did not recognise her need to get out of the rut of reproducing received information that was beginning to hold less attraction for her once she had reached her teens.

Schools, trapped by the demands of an examination system that is ultimately aimed at sorting out that 6−7 per cent of the population that will have some pretensions to scholarship in later life, are under almost intolerable pressure in devising curricula for adolescents. The responsibility to help intelligent children to achieve results in examinations that reflect accurately their intellectual capacity is one which every teacher feels strongly. Much more difficult for them is the equally important responsibility to allow people to find themselves intellectually during adolescence; to discover and develop their own interests irrespective of the demands of examiners. Because some students, especially girls, in their early teens show signs of sloppiness, lowering of standards and lack of interest in the more repetitive side of learning, the tendency for teachers to dismiss them as lazy is very strong. With large numbers to guide through heavy syllabuses it is only too easy to let the weaker go to the wall when they show little evidence of interest.

Alison's teachers made the mistake that is commonly made in examination-oriented schools of underestimating the capacity that young people have for work in subjects that interest them. They limited her timetable, therefore to a number of useful subjects that should get her into university, unable to realise that the enjoyment of working at a subject of your own choice generalises to all work and that a self-selected course is far more likely to produce good results than an inflicted one, quite apart from any other considerations of education.

The narrowness of interest that is caused by curricula restricted to useful subjects that fulfil some university's or employer's requirements spells destruction to the adventurous spirit that is latent in every young human being. Girls, whether through endowment or upbringing, have a strong attraction to the expressive arts which, for the most part ignored by our universities and often totally unappreciated by our materialistically minded employers, tend to get deleted from the syllabus after the third year in far too many schools. This is in spite of the pious platitudes being uttered about the need for family life. Families are, at least at first, under the influence of mothers whose education during their adolescence will considerably affect the attitudes of their children. That mothers whose own adventurous spirit has been thwarted might not make the best guides to the next generation's creativity and inventiveness, is worth a thought from teachers. Alison's teachers saw her as a drop-out, a lady good-for-nothing who was wasting her intelligence demanding to take easy options like art and drama. They compounded the problem of her unhappiness at home which was causing her work failure in subjects in which she had shown promise by frustrating her further at school by failing to meet her needs for creative self-expression.

Meanwhile both teachers and parents confused the issues of custom and convention with the more serious ones of ethics and morality. This is easily done as the two aspects of life become almost inextricably entwined for everyone at times. There are glaring examples in many homes and most schools of where this confusion really militates against the adolescent's developing sound ethical standards. Schools which have teachers who define minor infringements of the rules as crimes come into this category. Students will learn to treat all rules with contempt when they perceive, for example, that a failure to wear the correct shirt is treated as seriously as a failure to be courteous to another human being. Similarly when parents like Alison's condemn to the same degree her choice of a working-class boyfriend and her unkindness to elderly people, they demonstrate a lack of values that the young feel justified in condemning. Alison did not, in fact, reject either her school's values, her class or her parents' standards of behaviour, but she had a sense of values of her own which told her what was truly important to her, although she found it difficult to put into words. Her behaviour was a clumsy attempt to convey this to the surrounding world.

Alison's disagreements with both her parents and her teachers covered a wide spectrum of typical adolescent conflicts, none of which was beyond the reach of some reasonable discussion. What she needed from school was more recognition as a person. This is a most important aspect of an adolescent girl's demands on her teachers and one that is often the hardest to respond to. She was asking for help but no one heard her request; they saw only her nuisance value. The help she needed was most of all someone to listen with real involvement to what she was trying to say and someone to give her clear-cut guidance as to what was expected of her, with reasonable explanations as to the basis of this guidance. Teachers cannot solve home problems but they can go a long way towards alleviating them if they recognise that they exist.

The signals that Alison was giving at school that all was not well were not being picked up. Her teachers had perhaps an excessive anxiety about achievement and an insufficient awareness of the other aspects of life. They were presenting her with a point of view that was so inflexible that she did not feel valued as a person at all, merely as a cog in an exam-passing machine. How she did or did not adapt to being an emerging adult with a potential sexual life did not enter into their consideration, nor did her need to express her own ideas and tastes. Teachers who question their responsibility for these aspects of a girl's life are liable to fail in the end in giving the education that is needed.

What was happening to Alison was that instead of being educated she was being steadily undermined largely by ideas emanating from outside both home and school. Neither home nor school was able to withstand these outside pressures so she was left floundering. Her family could not stand up to the attacks because it had already half sold out to the material-istic world. In spite of being good and concerned her parents were inconsistent; unable to listen to her real needs; keen for her to abide by their mores yet not strong enough to uphold them. Her school could not stand up to the pressures of the league tables that, published annually, assess achievement on the basis of university places gained. Between two sets of institutions bent on their own interests, Alison's spirit was being crushed.

The positive side of her behaviour was that she was making a protest. Unlike Henrietta she knew that she was having conflicts and she was able to work through them at the appropriate time in her life. Properly responded to, protests like Alison's can be fruitful because they are healthy. Given more attention her natural tendency towards worth-while and rewarding activities would reassert itself. The poetry which she wrote and the pictures she painted were an important part of her life to which her school would give no recognition and for which it would allow her no time.

Probably, filled with facts, she would ultimately have gained some A levels but she would have paid for them with her sensitivity, with her more gentle humanity and with all those essential and valued 'feminine' qualities that we need so much in this world. Schools run the risk of crushing the spirit of too many of their girls when they sacrifice their inner life for the sake of maintaining good academic reputations. Teachers faced with protests like Alison's run the risk of losing out if they do not respond to the girl as well as to the student.

Chapter 3

The Coming of Puberty

Adolescence came upon Emma whilst she was still in primary school. Over the last few decades the number of girls who reach puberty before secondary school age has increased considerably, though there are signs now that this increase in numbers is slowing down. Emma came to my attention because she had stopped working at school. This had come as a surprise to everyone because she was a bright little girl. She had been expected to pass her 11-plus with ease, but for a year now she had hardly put pen to paper or done a scrap of work. She was a happy friendly girl who was delighted to be brought to see me at a clinic and to receive so much attention. She used her time with me mostly in painting pictures of explosions and bombs.

After a few weeks I was able to glean from her what the explosions meant. They were: 'What happens in science.' It seemed unlikely that in her very ordinary primary school any really dramatic experiments were being performed. Could it be that she imagined that this was what should happen in science? There are from time to time reports in the press of explosions in school labs; perhaps she perceived them as the norm? But no, it turned out that this was not the case. Emma revealed that the explosions were really in herself. She hated science because 'They tell you frightening things that make you explode inside'. Science, it transpired, was sexual instruction which she didn't want to hear. She put her hands over her ears during the lessons but still exploded inside.

Her mother, when asked about Emma's previous sexual instruction, admitted that she could not talk to her daughter about such things. She was worried because Emma was approaching the menarche and did not know anything about it. She was adamant that she herself could not tell her and begged me to do so instead. When I suggested to Emma in the course of one of our meetings that she might be afraid of hearing in science about babies being born she said no, it was 'the blood vessels breaking' that frightened her – exploding in fact. The blood vessels breaking referred to menstruation which she guessed was going to start soon. She pictured this as a frightening and painful process. She had been told all about it by a boy in her class last year.

It was not sufficient just to tell Emma the facts. Her fear-ridden mother had passed on to her daughter all her own sexual inhibitions. Emma had to be helped to take her hands away from her ears metaphorically as well as literally, before she could take in emotionally what she was hearing. She did this by a slow process in which it was necessary for her to have a sympathetic adult at hand to listen to her and appreciate her anxieties. Finally she was able to talk easily about these matters; she started to work again and passed her 11-plus. She had been so obsessed by her worries, which were being constantly aroused, rather than allayed, by the perfectly sensible sex instruction that she was receiving at school, that she had not had any emotional energy left for schoolwork. Puberty was making both a physiological and a psychological impact on her.

Emma was one of that surprisingly large group of children who have been ill prepared for the approach of puberty. It is not always recognised by adults that the muddled and distorted information that children bandy between themselves about sexual matters can provoke serious anxiety in the more imaginative amongst them. Even when there has not been, as in Emma's case, the additional problem of a neurotic mother to compound matters further, there is often misunderstanding which leads to fear. Worries which cannot be shared soon affect a child's whole outlook on life, and often lead to a loss of interest in work and in other aspects of life.

The worries caused by the imminence or onset of menstruation are usually the first signs of the adolescent syndrome which is specific to girls. In junior or middle schools these signs are often ignored because adolescence seems years away. Teachers feel that although they are dealing with people on the brink of physical maturation, which shows itself in particular through sexual development, the children are still too young to be thought of in terms that in any way imply sexuality.

Clare was another girl whose physiological development at the beginning of puberty had a profound and damaging effect on her education. Clare at age 10 shot up to 5 feet 6 inches in height within eight months. She was, like Emma, a very intelligent girl. She was brought to the clinic because she had started to refuse to go to school. Her problem, it turned out, was not just that she did not want to go to school, she did not even want to leave her own house. This was because she could not cope with a journey during which the bus conductor persistently refused to allow her to travel at half fare, insisting that she must be at least 16 years old.

School was a problem too, however, because no one understood her difficulties. Teachers regularly criticised her for childish behaviour, 'a big girl like you'. Her behaviour actually became more childish as she grew taller and more ill at ease. Her greatest suffering was during assembly which she always tried to avoid. She was constantly being punished for arriving too late to take her place in the hall. On one occasion she threw a faint which was recognised as being a simulation; she was punished for showing off. Her fear of assemblies was subsequently revealed to be due to self-consciousness. She had to stand at the front; an honour accorded to the top form. Clare had been moved to this form before her age warranted it because of her good work. The honour caused her untold misery because she towered above the other children and felt sure that she was being laughed at. Far from being an honour for Clare, this was an unbearable penance. Unfortunately a not too sympathetic headmaster would not listen to such nonsense when he was asked if she could stand at the back: so she absconded.

School, which had once been a delightful place where she had been a success, writing prizewinning stories, running an animal welfare club and supervising the library, had now become a nightmare. Very soon she had become equally unhappy out of school wandering around the neighbourhood. There she was accosted by older boys who had left school. At first she was flattered by their attentions, but soon she became frightened. They treated her like a girl of 16 or more. She had no abnormal fears of sexuality, but she was simply not ready for boyfriends who had little interest in anything else, as few 10-year-olds have. Lolitas do exist, but are the exception; Clare was rapidly beginning to wonder if she should try to become one of them as she found herself derided by the boys and their older girlfriends. They did not know her real age since she had lied to them, saying that she had left school. They assumed that she was of their age-group and behaved accordingly.

Home was also a problem. Her mother, by complaining to the school, had fallen out with the staff, who in return lost patience with Clare as she missed more and more school. Teachers understandably react strongly against bossy belligerent parents, but without such a parent it is to be doubted if Clare would have come through successfully. It was mainly through her mother's efforts that she was found a place in a child guidance clinic, and subsequently in a good secondary school. But her mother's manner antagonised people and Clare got the blame. It is in such cases easy and tempting to visit the sins of the parents on their child, but it is very cruel. Teachers have to learn to tolerate the tiresomeness of anxious parents because anxiety is a natural and often correct response when a child is in trouble. Parents have a right to be concerned about their children and to fight for them. Clare's parents suffered the double indignity of being blamed both by the school and by Clare herself. Her anger was above all turned against her mother and father, the very people who were doing most to help her. She was just reaching that terrible discovery that marks a turning-point in a child's life, the recognition that parents are not after all omnipotent. To her, therefore, they were useless; they could not change the attitudes of bus conductors, headmasters or even boys in the street.

Fortunately for Clare they were not useless. They fought the authorities, the school, the education office, even the education welfare officer, all of whom tended to take a punitive attitude towards her. This was at a time when a concerted effort was being made to counteract truancy; and Clare had got caught up in a wave of official outrage against school refusers.

When her mother eventually got her to a clinic Clare was at first very defensive. By now she was disgusted with the whole world. She was bored with not being at school and angry at being sent to a child guidance clinic. What she needed above all was someone to confide in, but she found it hard at first to trust anyone. In time she was able to make use of the help offered at the clinic, but meanwhile nearly two years of her school life were wasted in official wrangles. She never went back to her junior school and was late starting in a secondary school. Fortunately she finally managed to take her place in a very accommodating comprehensive school where she was allowed to work at her own pace. There, because of her intelligence, she was able to catch up on the work she had missed, but she was late taking all her exams. Although she finally got to university she always had great difficulty in believing in herself, doubting her intellectual ability and feeling afraid of making herself conspicuous. She is no longer physically conspicuous because she has stopped growing. By the time she was 15 she was the same height as most of her class-mates, but at 20 she was still not wholly at ease in her own body.

In Clare's case the simple physiology of adolescence played a part which was damaging only because its significance was not recognised in time. Unlike Emma she attended a school where the attitude was less than sympathetic. Nobody could have prevented Clare's growth spurt, nor could they have minimised its effect on strangers like bus conductors and older boys. But a lot could have been done by an understanding headmaster and staff to minimise the misery that could not be prevented. Bus passes can be arranged in special cases; assemblies are not more important than people's feelings. Teachers, who have closer relationships with children than do headmasters as a rule, can do a lot to modify the dictates of officialdom. Somebody with a little intuitive understanding could have imagined what it must feel like to stick out like a sore thumb every morning of your life.

Teachers with some understanding of the learning processes know that highly intelligent children who take part in all aspects of school and accept responsibility do not suddenly truant for no reason. But there was apparently nobody in Clare's school who was prepared to put him- or herself imaginatively in her place or question the change in her behaviour. She was labelled as a bad girl and punished.

On the whole, of course, teachers working at this age-level do not expect to come across the problems of adolescence. The archetypal adolescent girl, broody, melancholy, unpredictable and obsessed with boyfriends, is not part of the usual primary school scene. More likely there will be little skinny 10-year-olds, far from brooding, leaping around the playground, shouting raucous nonsense and laughing at nothing, apparently just for the fun of being alive. Boyfriends and girlfriends and the whole development of sexuality play only a minimal part in their lives. Mostly, wearing the regulation T-shirt and jeans (school rules permitting), the girls are indistinguishable from the boys, and more often than not they prefer the company of their own sex. They can be seen from time to time gathering into little single-sex groups, whispering and giggling, and the chances are then that the boys will be telling each other smutty stories: the girls more probably will be deciding who is best friends with whom.

Here, nevertheless, are the beginnings of adolescence. These children will in fact be experimenting, extremely cautiously, with ideas that might be called peripherally sexual. They are still resisting the sexual life that is just around the corner, but they are fascinated by it. The advertising agents who bombard them with subtly sexual material know this well. At this age most children make tentative forays into sexual talk then scurry back to the asexual existence that is so much safer. Teachers are more likely to be shown the asexual than the sexual self and, unless they are on the lookout for them, they will miss the developments that are taking place. We tend to see what we expect to see, and on the whole, therefore, we see children behaving as we expect them to behave.

Girls at this age, for example, are expected to be tomboys as often as not. Indeed mostly they need little encouragement to be so. To behave like a boy holds lots of attractions. It is quite likely that they have been given to understand, at least by implication, that being a boy is better than being a girl. Very few children escape this message in some form or other. Boys are allowed, indeed encouraged, to be extrovert, assertive, energetic and noisy. They can shout, fight, play football and come home covered in mud. Girls can too, but they are being boyish when they do so. So it is worth being boyish; it is more fun. Behaving as they have been taught that girls behave, besides being duller, implies a sexual differentiation that they still want to deny. Girls in particular are inclined to postpone full recognition of the implication of mature sexuality. They will reach it early enough, sooner than boys do, and with an even more profound impact on their lives. Physiology will catch up with them, whatever they do in fantasy to postpone it.

In our school playground there are likely to be one or two Emmas: 10-year-olds who already have no possibility of denying their sexuality; and one or two Clares: girls who are as much as 5 feet 6 inches tall, fully developed, mature-looking young ladies. These girls may be dressed like their smaller, slimmer sisters or they may have opted for whatever is the current fashion in dress. It is hard to imagine the Clares rushing round with quite the same abandon as the other children. At times it is hard to remember that they are children at all. They have already made that leap into near-maturity which their school-mates are busily postponing. The others will follow rapidly enough and by the third year of secondary school nearly everyone will have caught them up. Then those few who have retained their boyish figures, who have not yet matured, will be the ones who feel like outsiders. So puberty arrives for some with great speed, for others with too great a delay, and for nearly all with some degree of drama.

The first, most obvious sign of its approach is growth; often the growth spurt, that sudden unpredictable shooting-up that seems to take place overnight, leaving a girl feeling like Gulliver amongst the Lilliputians. Coat sleeves shrink, trouser legs ride above the ankles and everyone around is smaller and thinner. This increase usually happens a year before the onset of puberty. After this a period of slow steady growth is likely to set in. Now, besides being taller, a girl is also beginning to grow stronger and more energetic. All the physiological changes that take place, the rise in red blood corpuscles, increase in heart rate and blood pressure, strengthened skeletal structure, and increase in oestrogen will tend towards improving her health and strength. Although most girls won't become as strong as boys, there will be quite a number who will run and swim as fast as, or faster than, their brothers, and defeat them in sports and gymnastics. All girls should now become more active, not less. They should be able to move more quickly, jump higher, enjoy the demands of sustained physical activities and be generally nimble.

This is not the picture that we usually envisage when we think of adolescent girls. More commonly we imagine the languid lily painting her toenails before encasing them in impossible shoes, or the self-conscious day-dreamer clumsily dropping a tray full of glasses as she trips over the carpet. These are true pictures, but not the only ones. The feelings of lassitude, due to hormonal changes, should be temporary, and can be counteracted by properly regulated exercise. The obsession with appearance and the clumsiness are due to changes in her feelings about her body and she is much in need of adult tolerance on this account. Often different parts of the body grow at different rates, leaving her feeling as though she cannot control her own limbs.

The swings between childish and adult behaviour, between euphoria and depression, co-operation and sullen obtuseness, all owe something to the developing physique and its emotional concomitants, in particular to the increased activity of the endocrine system which is responsible for the sex drive. Adolescence is a time of life when it seems possible to experience opposite feelings almost simultaneously. Girls want to be grown up but they want the security of childhood. They want to be sexually glamorous, but they want to avoid the turbulence of feelings that goes with sexual maturity.

Adolescent girls have little chance of denying their emerging sexual maturity once they have started to menstruate. Until recently the taboo on this subject itself was such that not only are there still women like Emma's mother around who cannot bring themselves to tell their daughters simple physiological facts about their bodies, there are still women, as well as men, around in schools, teaching girls, who deny the significance of menstruation. It seems that for some women this event was greeted with such resentment that its importance has always had to be denied. Fortunately our society's attitude is changing. Research is beginning to make its impact and increasingly the importance of menstruation for a girl is beginning to be taken into account by the more enlightened. There are now more families where the menarche is welcomed as a sign that the girl is ready to join the adult group; some even give parties to celebrate the event; it would be idle to pretend, however, that for all girls the coming of adolescence is a matter for rejoicing.

Because of the society in which she lives, because of her family attitudes and because of the feelings that she herself has, or has not, developed about her own body, a girl can arrive at puberty with already established feelings of anxiety and resentment. If these are not dealt with properly in adolescence, they can remain with her, perhaps doing damage for the rest of her life. Most important are the fears; fears about unknown happenings in the body and less conscious fears about the upsurge of strong feelings about relationships with other people, especially with the parents and with the opposite sex. For a large number the prospect of bearing children seems frightening and the whole process of being a female lacks attraction. Then there are the resentments; resentments about the limiting effects that the body can have and about the implications for life-style of female sexuality. A lot of people resent their bodies when they feel ill. For some insecure adolescents physical development feels like an illness. They are not necessarily aware of all these feelings or able to conceptualise them; they mostly simply react to them, often with behaviour that appears meaningless.

The fears that some girls have are understandable in view of the inadequate instructions about their physiology that they have received. It is harder at first glance to understand why fears should persist in those who have been perfectly adequately prepared, either at home or in primary school, for their coming maturity. The reason for this we have seen in Emma's case: the instruction, though adequate for most, has not been sufficient for these girls because they have not taken it in. Emotionally they have rejected it. Children have a marvellous capacity for shutting out what they do not want to hear, especially what is frightening to them.

Sexual information can be frightening because it arouses strong feelings. In some children it resuscitates old memories of strong feelings which they had forgotten: it often brings back fears caused by the unknown. For some the whole subject of sexuality has been made into a threatening mystery unintentionally by adults, intentionally by their morbid-minded contemporaries, or carelessly by films and television shows that they have seen. A popular television serial in 1977 had a childbirth scene in which a perfectly healthy mother giving birth to a perfectly healthy child screamed incessantly with the same blood-curdling cries that we were familiar with in the romantic films of the forties. 'Childbirth is always dangerous', said her lugubrious husband. This, in the middle of an evening's exciting entertainment, is likely to make much more impact on some impressionable 12-year-olds than years of sensible facts told to them at school. It could make a young girl truly terrified of even looking at the film of childbirth shown in the social education class.

Quite a lot of girls still go through agonies of anxiety about sexual matters because of the secrecy in which they have been cloaked. Children who grow up to believe that all bodily functions are suspect, if not downright indecent, can be forgiven for reacting to the dramatic physical changes of puberty with anxiety. Emma made a common response to unwelcome knowledge in refusing to hear it. One girl, on being given a graphic description of the female sexual processes, from menstruation, through intercourse to childbirth, by a friend, declared that it was untrue. 'My mother couldn't do that, neither could the Queen.' She wept for three days after the arrival of the menarche and for years faced each monthly period with dread.

Even girls with a much more normal attitude to these matters can suffer from quite irrational fears about what is happening to their bodies at puberty. They have nameless fears about conception and childbirth which they feel unable to voice for fear of being mocked. They learn all too early in life that not to know about sex is a matter of shame. They therefore need some wise people around in whom they feel that it is safe to confide their ignorance. If they do not get some adult support their fears are likely to merge into resentment, and teachers are often well placed to give that support.

It is valuable for teachers to remember that children in the age-group 9 to 12 are commonly hard-working, enthusiastic and likely to be at the peak of their form. Any who fall by the wayside, therefore, might well be acting out of character; at this age a falling-off of interest in work can most often be taken as a sign of some inner worry. All of us, adults and children alike, are affected by the state of our bodies; we behave better when we are feeling physically well. We are also affected by worries; we work better when we have not got intrusive anxieties to distract our attention. If teachers can use imaginatively their own experience of emotional unease they will be able to recognise it in the children whom they teach. Emma needed a science teacher who was not so busy trying to put facts across that he failed to notice her refusal to take them in. This might not have solved her problem completely, as some of it lay too deep to be dealt with solely by a change of teaching methods; she also needed help from someone who had time to talk to her on her own and to help her to understand and cope with her fears. If she could have shared her anxieties with someone in school the matter could have been dealt with much earlier and at least a year of her school life could have been made much more fruitful.

The teaching of sexual matters in schools is a subject under constant review. Suffice it here to remind those who work in this field, especially those who are dealing with girls on the brink of puberty, that anxiety is a common response, not an abnormal one. It is all too easy for teachers wishing to inculcate a healthy attitude to those matters to forget that many children have sensitivities and a modesty that are part of their upbringing and are by no means pathological. Sometimes these children are made anxious by open discussion of topics that they have habitually kept hidden. Sometimes they need a small secure group in which to reveal their fears and worries. Girls, in particular, need the opportunity to talk amongst themselves with an understanding adult about what becoming a potential mother actually feels like. It is the feelings not the facts that they need to discuss, and feelings have little place in a science-oriented lesson. Above all girls at this age need teachers who are aware that there are important processes happening in their young bodies which can affect their feelings and even their thinking processes. Awareness of this will lead to a greater sensitivity to signs of any kind of abnormality. In this way difficulties can be recognised earlier and dealt with quickly.

Clare needed someone in school in whom she could confide her miseries about her height. Where the problems created by it were objectively due to the behaviour of others, solutions could be found. All problems however, cannot be swept away. Clare needed someone to help her to see that a lot of what she suffered was of her own creation, largely due to her fantasies about what other people might think. Girls need sane adults around who can give them support whilst they adjust to the realities of a world which can never be perfect for anyone. In school only sympathetic teachers will ever succeed in conveying this to the young; it is not an easily acceptable precept in a society that encourages the belief that happiness is just around the corner for all those who have the right kind of looks and enhance them with the right kind of products. Only teachers who have a genuine interest in, and sensitivity to, the feelings of the young can counteract such propaganda; and with the help of such teachers most of the disturbing impact of the physiology of puberty can be mitigated.

Chapter 4

Dependency

Patricia wept her way through her first morning in secondary school and then through most of the afternoon. She went on weeping at intervals for several weeks and her form teacher in despair called in her mother. 'Pat doesn't like the school', declared Mrs Smith, being a great help as the teacher bitterly commented. Pat had hardly seen the school through the mist of her tears; it was hard to imagine what she did not like. The teacher suggested a visit to her GP to which her mother responded with alacrity, and in no time Pat had her box of pills. She continued, however, to weep for at least two hours of each day.

The form teacher, a kindly man, tried the next professional avenue; he suggested to Pat that she visit the school counsellor, only to elicit another flood of tears. But in time Pat got to the counsellor; there she wept. The difference between this meeting and the rest, though, was that the counsellor did nothing to stop the weeping, in fact he encouraged it, suggesting that Pat must be very very sad.

After a few sessions of weeping to this encouragement, Pat dried her tears enough to look up and agree. She was very sad; she had even con-templated throwing herself out of her bedroom window last night. Her problem was that she felt lost, rudderless, totally unsure of herself. She was terrified in strange places and she had never before had to cope with one on her own. At 12 years of age she had not begun to deal with life for herself. Everyone whom she met was hostile and she did not, and never would, belong.

Some hours of patient work on the counsellor's part helped Pat to get nearer to a true sense of reality. Far from being hostile everyone had put themselves out to be quite inordinately friendly; they were all terrified of her tears for one thing, and would have done anything to stop them. Pat was creating her own hostile world because she expected hostility. This kind of expectation does not come naturally; it is bred in children – especially in girls. They are taught to stay next to their mothers, to keep safe and, incidentally, to keep their mothers from being lonely, and to keep the world at bay. In time Pat learnt how much dependency stemmed from her own expectations of hostility from the world. If we expect people to attack, we find them attacking: if we expect them to reject us, they will reject. Pat had a mother who had warned her all her life to avoid dangerous situations like sitting on swings in parks in case some rough boys pushed her off, and had convinced her that she would never be safe except at home.

She had in fact been taught to feel insecure and to be dependent on adults for her safety. She had loved her primary school because there she had felt safe and cared for; it had been a continuation of home. The warm accepting atmosphere of a small school where you have grown up, often from infancy, is hard to leave behind, especially if you have enjoyed a position of importance in the top class. Bossy little girls love their roles of monitors, organisers, teachers' helps and status figures in the school. They sometimes find the ignominious descent to being the youngest and least important hard to take. If they have been taught to rely on others rather than themselves the shock of change can be overwhelming. Pat had played an important role in her former school – she had felt valued. In her new school where no one noticed her she felt rejected. At least if she cried she got attention.

Whilst for some children the lure of the big school includes the prospect of more and better boyfriends, and for others the promise of more exciting and interesting work, for a large number of overdependent girls it represents nothing so much as a repetition of the first separation from home. Once again the anguish of the first day at infant or nursery school is lived through and the outside world impinges.

Girls are taught to be home-loving and to value the security of the familiar. There are positive aspects to this but when a girl fails to develop an adequate sense of inner security, so that she cannot cope with change, the effect is all negative. Sometimes this inability to cope with change can result from a failure on the part of parents to give sufficient security, so that the child is always unsure in strange situations, but more often with girls it is due to overprotection. The threat of new experiences arouses anxieties that make a girl feel resentful towards the people she sees as responsible for her unhappiness. So the teachers in a new school are blamed for being unsympathetic, not because they are unsympathetic, but because the girl herself is feeling frightened and resentful. She experiences her own angry feelings as being in somebody else instead of in herself.

Having managed to cope with her anger by passing it on to somebody else, instead of recognising that it belongs to herself, she does not see herself as resentful, only as badly done by. If we look around for people who are treating us badly we can usually manage to find them. Pat saw her new school as full of enemies whom, though she did not realise it, she had created herself.

The hopelessness of her life was very real to her. She was in a huge unfriendly society, afraid of everyone, and sure that they were unkind to her. She had no escape. Blinded by her fears and resentments, she could not see how much they were of her own making. Only when she had been given the opportunity to learn about her own feelings, through her talks with the counsellor, was she able to recognise that no one was attacking her but herself.

This pattern of dependency, fear and rejection of a new situation, and projection of the resentments on to others so that they are seen as the enemy, is commonplace. When the fears have any real base, such as the largeness and strangeness of a new school, they must be tackled at that reality level first of all. Children can cope with the largeness if some of the impersonality is removed. A teacher who can treat them as humans in what feels like an inhuman society can be a great help. Fears so excessive that they lead to tranquillers and suicide threats need more. They need someone who can tackle the original insecurity a bit nearer its source. This means often a long period of patient listening and acceptance of the misery to give the child some feeling of security. Only when this has been established can she then be helped to recognise that she is making bogeymen for herself and that the school, though large, is not necessarily hostile.

There will always remain some people, possibly far more than it is convenient for society to admit to, for whom as the late Dr Schumaker told us small is beautiful. Schools are at present for the most part large, often too large for the comfort of a lot of the children in them. Whilst this is the case, if the discomfort is not to ruin their ability to get the most out of school, these children need people around who can help them to find ways of coping with what they perhaps will never wholly like.

In one school where I spoke to all the girls in the fifth year, I found that more than half the girls commented that they preferred their primary school to the comprehensive because it was smaller. These were not by any means all girls who disliked school – some of them had been very successful – but they perceived the primary school as being more friendly. They were known by, and knew, everybody.

It is a reasonable human wish to mix with people whom you know and with whom you can have a real, rather than a merely peripheral, relationship. It can be damaging to the human spirit to have too many impersonal relationships.

Unfortunately, few of the children who will be going through our schools within at least the next few generations will have any choice in this matter. Their schools will be big; they cannot fail to be to some extent impersonal, but the impact of the impersonality ultimately rests with the teachers. Theoretically the school structure dictates the amount of contact that a child has with staff members; in practice it is individual teachers who really make this decision. Some children, especially the more intelligent and those who have been brought up to recognise that the world is a place to be contended with successfully, revel in the opportunities offered in large schools. The size for them can be mitigated by the enjoyment to be gained from taking part in a splendid array of new and challenging experiences. The warm, cosy atmosphere of primary school might be momentarily regretted but it is soon superseded by an equally worthwhile kind of life.

Teachers in primary schools are important to children, and it is for the experience of a kindly, concerned teacher who knows you well and cares about you that girls especially sometimes yearn when they first enter their secondary schools. These children are seen by many a secondary school teacher as tiresomely overdependent on adults.

Anyone who has taught in an inner city, however, can cite at least one girl who has made it abundantly clear from the day she entered secondary school that no adult is of any importance to her, and that nothing that a teacher says will have any noticeable impact on her behaviour — that will depend entirely on her mood and on how her class-mates respond to her. She has had to reject the adult world because it has rejected her.

She is significant just because she claims independence of adult authority. Authority depends on dependency; we demand and expect obedience to authority in the young because we assume that they are dependent on us. We are not, therefore, entitled to condemn their dependence because we see it as an intrusion on our work of teaching. We do better to recognise it as the basis of our communication with our pupils. What they are usually asking for is not that teachers should be totally involved in their welfare, as perhaps they imagined was the case when they were younger, but that adults will give them the sort of recognition that will help them to establish their still shaky identities. When they have been accustomed to receive this in their first school, it is sometimes hard for them to adapt to the lack of it in secondary school.

To be dependent on others and to demand their recognition of us as people, as individuals, is indeed a characteristic of the human species. During their early years children are expected to be dependent on their parents. When they first go to school their teachers expect a modicum of dependence. What infant teacher has never been called Mum? There is, however, a determined effort on the part of teacher and mother and child to increase the child's independence. By the time he or she reaches secondary school there is at least a surface appearance of independent maturity. It is this surface which so often deceives the adults in their lives who sometimes forget that despite their overt demands for freedom adolescents are often more in need of adult support than they were at the age of 10 or 11. Just because they are faced with the real demands of a more adult life, they find it hard at times to feel as grown up and independent as they like to appear.

Jenny, a bright, successful 15-year-old preparing for her O levels and planning to become a lawyer, is a good example of a girl with a surface suggesting maturity. She had a very good relationship with her parents and her teachers, was popular with the other children and seemed to be a relaxed and carefree person. Nevertheless she confessed that she found it terribly difficult to tolerate the departure of any adult from her life. If either of her parents was away for one night she couldn't sleep;

when she arrived at school each day she checked the car park to see if any of the teachers was absent. She worried in case her parents had had an accident or a teacher was ill. She felt that her anxieties would be an impediment in her life so she went to discuss them with the school counsellor.

In the course of a few weeks she began to learn about the basis of her excessive dependency needs. She realised something of the hidden antagonism beneath this oversolicitous concern for the people who she felt should be supporting her. She recognised that she was envious of those who had already made it. Both parents, of whom she was very proud, were successful professional people. Mingled with her admiration, however, was a degree of resentment that they should give time and attention to their work which she would have liked them to give to her. In the same way she admired her teachers but found herself resenting their private lives where she played no part. Rather than admit any of these resentments of which, when she first recognised them, she was deeply ashamed, she had covered them up with overconcern.

This was only a slightly exaggerated version of the normal adolescent need to keep tabs on adults. It usually includes something of this mixture of admiration, envy and attention-seeking. As the adolescent girl moves towards joining the adults' club, she needs to be constantly reassured that she will be accepted by it: this means being noticed. Adults need to be noticed too, but can get by without it: few adolescents can. They need the attention of parents or parental-type figures, and by their behaviour show that they frequently cast teachers into a form of parental role. In fact we all at times unintentionally cast others into the parental role, particularly those who are in a position of authority over us. This is normal and natural behaviour. We learned in our early childhood certain accepted responses to parental figures. We tend to carry on with them until circumstances reveal them to us as inappropriate.

As we reach adulthood most of us become less inclined to accept authority in the way that was expected of us in childhood, even though we might recognise the need for some authority structures. For the most part we react appropriately to authority figures, showing neither excessive resentment of their power nor excessive dependence. In adolescence relationships with authority figures are still in the melting-pot. Most will be struggling to find security in their surroundings for support when confidence in their own ability to sustain themselves falters. Doubts about one's own worth are characteristic of most human beings, although they are usually, in adults, balanced by convictions. In adolescence there are still periods of such doubt that no inner conviction of worth is strong enough to sustain a satisfactory self-image. When this is the case support from someone else is essential. If the teachers, with whom so much time is spent, on whose directions and instructions so much depends, do not seem to know that you exist, how do you fight your own inner feelings of worthlessness?

The adolescent who, in the early years of infancy, learned that the world was a secure place is likely to find ways of coping with the sudden loss of self-confidence that comes with some setback in self-esteem. Her security will not be shaken to its foundations at, say, failure in an exam. Nevertheless the knowledge that there are adults around who know and perhaps even care about you a bit can be a powerful booster of confidence. On such occasions someone whose trust in the security of the world is not well founded is likely to be even more dependent on support from her adult world.

Few teachers will know anything about the early foundations of security or insecurity on which the lives of the adolescents in their charge are based; they can, however, recognise the signs from which a rather shaky foundation can be inferred. An adolescent who really needs too much recognition from teachers is probably suffering from excessive feelings of insecurity. This insecurity is often related to a failure to learn at the right time that people can be reasonably well depended on. There are other causes of insecurity and overdependence, but this is the most common. It stems usually from some kind of failure in the child's early experience. Sometimes parents really have been unreliable, so that a child has learnt at a very young age that there is not much hope of being cared for. The baby who expects food and comfort and receives only abuse and neglect has to learn very early in life that even its basic needs are not going to be met at all times. More commonly the baby from a normal good loving family has needs which cannot be met instantly, because even the best mothers are busy and have other people to attend to as well as their babies.

Normally babies can learn to put up with a lot of frustration. Sometimes, though, they have too much of it too soon, or they are by nature impetuous and need to be responded to with too much immediacy. Some babies are more fragile than others temperamentally as well as physically. These will suffer what they experience as neglect; they will be the crying babies and the difficult feeders; often they find, as they grow older, more than average difficulty in trusting that things will come right eventually. The result of this will not be a precocious development of independence. The baby who does not find that her needs are being met is more likely to become a demanding baby than a passive one. Only the totally rejected become passive with a kind of despair. Most babies will make even more desperate attempts to obtain the security that has been missed. Children whose infancy did not provide a sufficient source of security might then tend to be over-dependent later in life. This is not their own fault and we should not take a punitive attitude towards them. It is much better that we take a sufficiently sympathetic attitude to at least recognise that their needs are genuine.

There is a lot of evidence around at present to support the view that dependence and overdependence in girls are not innate, as some would contend, but a learned response, a habit of behaviour which has been produced by a learning process. Insecurity could be said to be a learned response to an insecure situation. A more straightforward and learned response, however, is one in which the learned behaviour comes about because there is a reward available for that behaviour. There are parents who make their children dependent because they like them that way. A good many parents in our society seem to like their girl children to be dependent. In fact there are grounds for believing that not only parents, but other adults, including husbands, like girls to be dependent. The literature of the various women's movements is full of examples of how girls are rewarded by society for being dependent rather than independent.

The most popular experiments to demonstrate this are those in which a baby is dressed alternately as a boy or as a girl and given to a woman to play with for about ten minutes. Women consistently encourage the baby dressed as a boy to engage in extrovert activities, to play with toys designated masculine and to be adventurous and independence-seeking. The baby dressed as a girl is cooed at and cuddled, kept firmly on the knee and praised for being pretty and sweet: not the kind of treatment designed to foster too much independence of spirit.

All men and boys do not, of course, show total independence, and by no means do all boys cope adequately in adjusting to new environments, but we give them a few more props than we give to girls. It is important for teachers to recognise overdependence in girls because it can create problems for them in adjusting to life later. The Schools Council Sixth Form Survey found that girls experienced far more difficulty than boys in adjusting to the freer, less-controlled form of working required for sixth form studies. They found more difficulty than boys did in organising their own work.

Certainly little boys are rewarded for being adventurous at a very early age. Little girls are helped more than boys. Researchers have shown that the books that children see before they even get to school are full of stories where the little boy takes all the action and the little girl sits by passively or at most acts as his help-mate. Little girls are rewarded for smiling, and indeed women, all women, not just mothers, tend to smile more at little girls than they do at little boys. It is not surprising, therefore, if many little girls respond by smiling back; some continue to do so perhaps for the rest of their lives, in the hope of eliciting a smiling and therefore approving response from others.

Adolescent girls do not, of course, by any means all smile all the time, but by the time they reach their teens many girls have already acquired a deeply ingrained conviction that to succeed they must please; and this means being dependent. They therefore suffer from disapproval and react to it in a different way from boys. Adolescent girls often take as a personal rejection the ordinary criticisms that are an accepted part of everyday school life. Their whole inner being can sometimes feel wounded by a simple correction of a faulty piece of work. Their ways of showing their hurt can vary widely of course, from bursting into tears to indulging in rampant disruptiveness.

Boys are not expected to react in this way. Sometimes they may well feel like doing so but their upbringing has shown them that not only is such a response unacceptable, it is also unnecessary. They have learnt not to depend on personal relationships and the overt approval of others as a main source of reward. A boy does not demand quite such constant recognition of his person. 'If I forget your silly birthday would you fuss?' asks Professor Higgins of Pickering in *My Fair Lady*. 'Why', he asks, 'can't a woman be more like a man?', that is, more self-sufficient, less demanding, less dependent.

However, the need for satisfactory interpersonal relationships need not always be labelled pejoratively as excessive dependency. It can also be seen as a healthy and valuable attitude towards other people which should be encouraged rather than distrusted. The impersonal relationships between teacher and taught which some schools encourage can actually be damaging. A society in which the young are taught that important human relationships can be remote and that important human beings can be treated almost as strangers could be a dangerous one. We could be doing a greater service to our young if we actually encouraged them to take personally remarks which are directed at them since they are made by persons. The more people you can treat as distant, the more insensitive will be your response to people in general. If you can treat a teacher, who is an important part of your life, as though he were not really human, you can do that to other people, perhaps in increasing numbers, for the rest of your life. If teachers treat the young in an impersonal way it is likely that they will respond in like manner.

It is certainly possible to teach without having a close personal relationship with those whom you teach. There are teachers whose interest in their subject is greater than their interest in the children they teach. They often do well with intelligent and well-behaved children whose needs for recognition are being met elsewhere. Some children learn a great deal from teachers whom they hardly know. Their interest in learning is great enough to enable them to gain even from the most uninvolved teacher or indeed from the worst form of teaching.

These are fortunate children who come from homes where the importance of education is axiomatic and where they feel sufficiently secure in their personal relationships. Their dependency needs are satisfied outside school. Others have perhaps, *faut de mieux*, developed in themselves an impersonal attitude to life so that they allow nothing to impinge on them, having learnt that adults are not dependable. But they are potentially dangerous, unfeeling people who are likely to find interpersonal relationships with the opposite sex difficult for the rest of their lives and who if chance pushes them in the wrong direction may become successful criminals.

We find teachers who get excellent results whilst working in a private school, where the received attitude is cool, who come into the state system and are lost. They are astonished to find that their pupils apparently will not listen, in spite of the fact that they are actually choosing to be at school. Sometimes they do want to hear what is being said but their feelings are getting in the way of their learning. In this case they might be amongst those who feel that they are being rejected because they have not been overtly accepted. The cool academic manner comes over to them as indifference bordering on dislike.

There is no doubt that the need for recognition as an individual is harder to meet in our large and highly structured schools than in the smaller, more personal ones. Eric Midwinter spoke recently of the 'factorylike structure of education buildings'. Certainly a great many of our secondary schools seem designed to impede rather than to further communication. Their position, size, architecture and even the curriculum play a part in this. The girl who feels lost and unnoticed even in a small school can feel really frightened by the remote and machine-like atmosphere of a large modern establishment. 'I wanted to run away but I couldn't even find the way out', said one girl describing her first day in a new school. It took her two terms to settle down at all and despite being highly intelligent she never really enjoyed this school, although at her former school she had been extremely successful and always happy according to her own account.

Nevertheless, the nature of the establishment is never as important as the people who are in it. Individual teachers can therefore compensate for a great many of the errors which have been made largely by administrators who are remote from children. Teachers who feel intruded on by what they consider to be excessive dependence can bear in mind that the best way to cure somebody of behaviour due to something that is lacking is to give them what they lack. The best way to cure over-dependence, therefore, is to provide a secure and responsive environment. Teachers can provide this without exerting themselves unduly, first by being dependable in their relationships, and secondly by making sure that they recognise the existence of everyone with whom they have dealings.

Being dependable includes such mundane matters as marking and returning work which has been set. It is easy for teachers to forget the agony and arduous work that can be put into homework by conscientious students. Girls notoriously take more care and time over their work than boys; often they put far more effort in than is recognised. Not to receive even a tick or a comment suggests indifference bordering on rejection. If you have not got time to mark the homework, do not set it. Similarly, if a student asks questions in class they should be attended to: 'I didn't understand what we had to do and I didn't dare ask a second time' is a constant complaint. Some students ask questions partly to get information and partly to get attention: that kind of attention-seeking is always better responded to than ignored, for it is due to a real need for attention and can be responded to by a teacher who recognises it for what it is and finds time to talk to the attention-seeker on her own. Any adolescent, however, is capable of recognising when she is making too many demands and can learn to reduce them with sympathetic guidance.

Being dependable also involves treating all pupils as far as possible in the same way, keeping one's own prejudices and preferences to oneself. It requires the controlling of one's own impulses and moods so that a hangover or a staffroom wrangle doesn't impinge too much on the classroom atmosphere. Above all it requires the recognition of everyone's existence by mentioning them by name from time to time. These might seem trivial matters, but they are sufficient to meet the dependency needs of the average pupil and will do wonders for classroom harmony.

Since, as we have seen, insecurity, feelings of inadequacy and the consequent need for recognition are the norm in adolescence, if they are not attended to at this stage in life they can become endemic. So whether the adolescent girls in a school are normally dependent because they are human beings, or abnormally dependent because they are rather insecure human beings, they need teachers who will reassure them by showing them that they are recognised, by acknowledging that they are important because they are human.

Chapter 5

The Physical Education of the Adolescent

Elizabeth was a small, even undersized girl who moved to a new comprehensive school in her second year of secondary education. After one term she was placed in a remedial class because her work was so poor. Here she found herself in a relatively small group of children with one teacher for most of her classes. This teacher soon noticed that Elizabeth's absences from school were on the increase and that when she was in school she made very little contact with other children. The report from her previous school showed that Elizabeth's attendance there had been 100 per cent and that she had not been seen as a child in need of any special help, just an average pupil.

It soon became evident to her teacher that Elizabeth's behaviour was deteriorating. Whereas at first she would stay away on one or two days of the week, now she was absent three or more times. Elizabeth was initially unwilling to talk about her absences but, because of the sympathetic attitude of the teacher, she was eventually able to reveal that she had originally stayed away from school on days when there were PE classes, but more recently had lost interest in coming at all. She was very unhappy, and PE made her more so.

The reason for her unhappiness, she said, was her feeling of inferiority because of her small stature. She thought there was something wrong with her because all the other girls of 13 had nice figures, and she was thin and flat. She was ashamed to go into the showers so she stayed away on PE days. She hated PE anyhow because she always felt tired and she was too clumsy to be able to play any games well. Matters were made worse by the fact that her PE kit from her previous school did not match that of her new school. When she did get to a PE lesson the teacher invariably commented that she was different from the others and must get the right kit.

These circumstances on their own could not account for all Elizabeth's behaviour; they are common enough, and cause a lot of misery to girls, but rarely drive them to truancy. Elizabeth's teacher therefore suggested going to have a talk with the school counsellor in the hope that the real root of her problems might be discovered. The counsellor soon discovered that there were troubles at home as well as at school. Her parents had moved to the new district in the hopes of finding work after the father had been made redundant. He was still unemployed and the mother, who had also worked before, was now jobless too. They had no money to buy new uniforms, let alone PE kits, and little time or energy to notice Elizabeth's misery, caught up as they were in troubles of their own. Elizabeth should perhaps have been a solace to them, instead of which she was increasing their difficulties by her refusal to go to school.

Her problems seemed slight to her parents, compared with their own of no work, inadequate housing, no acquaintances in the neighbourhood and a sudden drastic drop in their living standards. Elizabeth at least had somewhere to go during the day, her mother had said to her bitterly. It did not occur to her parents that she too was suffering from the home situation, and indeed it did not really occur to Elizabeth either at first. In the throes of adolescence her personal obsessions took precedence, in particular her worries about her appearance. Her thin figure, the result of a perfectly normal physical structure, coupled with a rather late development, was only significant because she experienced it as such. She equated it with a lack of femininity, and she felt she was a freak.

Elizabeth talked to the counsellor about her present feelings and began also to discover how long they had been fomenting. In time she agreed to the counsellor's meeting her parents, and together they discussed her difficulties. As a child she had always had a rather strained relationship with her mother who, uninterested in girls, had hoped that her only child would be a boy. Elizabeth, therefore, when she was younger, had played at being a boy. Her mother had always dressed her in shorts or jeans 'to save trouble', and had given her the impression that feminine clothes were rather silly. She was a cool, rather detached woman who was able to talk about her daughter as though she were the child of someone else. She described how Elizabeth had never wanted to be cuddled, had never wanted dolls and had been a tomboy until she was 11. She agreed that Elizabeth's energy had diminished since their move, but had put this down to the change of air. She was not indifferent to her daughter's needs, just uncomprehending and preoccupied. About the truancy she was very angry, though she did in time come to see something of Elizabeth's point of view.

The PE mistress, unfortunately, was not so willing to see anyone else's point of view. She was young and inexperienced, and at first she was inclined to feel that Elizabeth's refusal to make any effort even when she got to a PE class was an implied criticism of her teaching: to Elizabeth she described it as laziness. Neither of these interpretations of Elizabeth's behaviour was valid. There was no rejection of the teacher, only of the whole PE syndrome, and the laziness was caused by a kind of depressed resistance to life that had its roots in a lifetime's feeling of inadequacy engendered largely by her mother's attitudes. The coming of adolescence along with a distressing change in home circumstances brought on the crisis. Already full of self-doubt and somewhat ambivalent about her mother, whom she wanted to please by being as boy-like as possible, but whom she also wanted to punish for being unsympathetic, Elizabeth withdrew from the conflict. She was on the way to rejecting femininity altogether; not that she felt it was unacceptable, rather that she could not attain it so she would give up trying. She both wanted to grow up and be accepted as a developing young woman and at the same time, resisting the idea, she wanted to stay as the little tomboy though knowing that the role no longer suited her. She had lost her enthusiasm for energetic boyish pursuits, but did not feel any happier in the role of a growing young woman, although at times in fantasy she became one. She imagined that if she had what she thought of as the perfect figure boys would be attracted to her; at other times she shunned the idea of boyfriends and felt frightened at the prospect of growing up. Her feelings of being unacceptable were increased when she was constantly reminded by the PE teacher that she was different. This she experienced as being reminded that she was physically different; therefore, in her own eyes, deformed.

It was necessary for Elizabeth to do PE, as it is for all adolescents, but it was neither necessary nor desirable that PE should be fraught with such problems that she truanted on account of them. Elizabeth's problems were those of a high proportion of perfectly normal adolescents; clumsiness, lassitude and anxiety about physique. Battles about PE kit can be found in any group of 13-year-olds; individually they do not constitute tragedy, collectively and further exacerbated as in Elizabeth's case by external circumstances they can cause a lot of trouble. PE teachers, who have the major responsibility for physical development, need to realise how easily small matters can get out of proportion for adolescents, and need to have an understanding attitude. Once out of proportion, little problems become big ones for the unstable young.

In their efforts to involve girls in PE teachers sometimes forget that the main purpose of the subject is not the success of the good students but the physical good health of all. Perhaps because of the attitudes of their college lecturers some of them have never realised this. Of course PE teachers, like any other teachers, need to aim at success and need to encourage their students to do likewise. But even more than most teachers they need to bear in mind that schools are for children and that the needs of the young have to come before those of the adults. All the young have to be catered for, not just those who are fortunate enough to be gifted or who have the capacity to enjoy physical activities whether they are good at them or not. It takes a stretch of the imagination for those of us who enjoy games to put ourselves into the position of those who are filled with horror at the thought of organised activity, yet it is these people more than any others for whom PE lessons should really cater. They need compulsory activities because they will not exercise themselves by choice.

Exercise is essential for the growing young. Without it many of them sink only too easily into the lassitude that Elizabeth was displaying. This is characteristic of the 14 to 15 year age-group of adolescent girls in particular, but it can strike at any age and at any type of girl; thin girls and fat girls, hard-working and lazy, happy and sad. Its origins may be psychological but its effects are physical as well as psychological and can be disastrous. It can be the end of any interest in school, in work, in thinking even, an all-too-common response to education on the part of adolescent girls, and one which can persist into the rest of their lives, leaving them as underfunctioning and inadequate adults.

Schools subscribe too easily to the body/mind split fallacy, allocating time to physical activities but seeing them as inferior to the more important exam-oriented intellectual work. PE teachers, feeling themselves labelled as lesser beings where the intellect predominates, too often overcompensate by setting too high a premium on achievement as such. Not all adolescents can achieve a lot physically, but they all need exercise. They need it because through it they can learn to be in touch with their bodies, and because they have muscles to develop and energy to expend. They need it because exercise breeds energy and counteracts the tendency towards withdrawal and inactivity of body and mind which characterises those who find the struggles to grow up hard to cope with. They need it in school in particular because they spend so much of their time sitting around and so much of their energy in specifically cerebral processes. They also need it because psychologically the early adolescent years can produce tensions which can be given an outlet by physical means.

None of these reasons will be very convincing to adolescent girls who hate PE. For most of them musculature can stay undeveloped as far as they are concerned and the alternative to sitting about in school is, of course, staying away from school. Tensions, they find, can be pleasantly diminished by smoking and drinking and, maybe, through sexual adventures, though these more commonly increase than diminish tensions. The lassitude that creeps over so many of them at the very thought of exercise is most often a psychological resistance to having their quiet life intruded on by others. So something has to be done to brighten up the prospect of physical exercise if these girls are going to benefit from it.

As it is hard for those who have always enjoyed games and PE to understand what a torture these things are for some people, for PE teachers it must be particularly difficult. They can do so, however, if they will cast their minds back to those occasions when they themselves found that making that extra effort seemed almost too difficult. The difference between those who are good at PE and those who are not is that the former make that extra effort because they know that the rewards will be great; the latter know that there is little reward at the end of a phenomenal effort, when, for example, even moving a limb feels like being asked to run a mile. Without some awareness, therefore, of what the point of all this is, these people will never learn to enjoy exercise; they can hardly be expected to endure it. They will always manage to lose their kit, loiter in the cloakrooms during games, or go off sick, even if they do not overtly truant.

This seems a terrible indictment of the adult attitude to games which were presumably designed for fun. Most girls on the brink of adulthood will accept the need for keeping their bodies healthy. They will appreciate adults who really want to help them to get and keep a good figure; the prospect of being able to feel comfortable in a bikini is no mean attraction. But they will not be convinced of the value of PE to this end if they do not perceive that the adults also share these values. Used as a con trick to get them to take part in disagreeable activities against their will, such ideas will not carry much force.

The fact that they are laying down the foundations for a healthy or unhealthy old age, with a view to keeping their faculties as long as possible, is not likely to be alluring to the young, but the idea of preparing to bear children with ease and comfort, even enjoyment, will have much more appeal if it is put forward with conviction. A girl who is in touch with her body can really enjoy pregnancy and childbirth, and PE should put her in touch. This is the most important part of any physical instruction of young girls, that they should gain a sense of the value of their own bodies. If PE is taught with this in mind, girls can appreciate its importance, they can develop a healthy relationship with their bodies that has been so lacking in our culture. Physical activities which emphasise their failings, games in which they continually fail, showers which make them feel humiliated and teachers who criticise their physical performances will have exactly the opposite effect.

Equally discouraging to girls is the attitude that persists in most schools, in spite of the Sex Discrimination Act, that certain games are suitable only for boys. Nina, unlike Elizabeth, had a passion for games, but her main interest was football. At school she was only allowed to play netball and hockey, and when she tried to start up a football team she was severely reprimanded. Outside school she organised a girls' football club which began to attract the attention of the local paper. The headmistress of the girls' grammar school which she attended was outraged to see the name of one of her girls mentioned in the press in such a vulgar and unladylike connection. The fantasy that girls cannot take part in physically demanding sports should surely have been dealt its death blow by Virginia Wade in her Jubilee Year win at Wimbledon or by East European girls at the Olympic Games. But it is not the physical demands of masculine games that underly the prejudice against girls taking part in them, it is the effect on the imaginations of the spectators that is feared. Judith Okely (New Society, 7 December 1978) points out that the Greater London Council has 'for years banned public displays of female wrestling'; it has not, however, prevented female wrestling from taking place. Whatever the bases of these prejudices, the young do not subscribe to them; they feel therefore put upon by adults who refuse to let them play football claiming that it is dangerous. There are plenty of arguments against, as well as for, boys taking part in sports like boxing, because it really is dangerous and is primarily concerned with attacking people. The arguments against girls doing so, however, have a different and less rationally defensible base.

Our attitudes to how girls use their bodies need rethinking in the light of an honest appraisal of their source. Until this happens girls will continue to resent being asked to take part exclusively in sports which have been designated female and by implication inferior. Hockey played by girls is, whether on ice or grass, fast and sometimes as dangerous a game as that played by boys, yet when it was depicted as the pastime of Angela of the Fifth it was considered a gentle feminine game, unfit to be classed with cricket which was somehow more masculine. Netball, the one exclusively feminine game, can be played by men when it is changed to basket ball which is faster and more exciting. Tennis was allowed to girls only late in its history, and then at first only in a modified form. I can recall seeing underarm serving at the Wimbledon Championships of 1947, a relic of the belief that female muscles were not powerful enough to cope with the serve invented by men.

A new generation of adolescents who have been reared in a climate of anti-discrimination Acts will not stand for these kinds of prejudices. PE teachers need to take note of this. Girls, like boys, gain a sense of attunement to their own bodies if they are allowed to use them freely. In our society we are only just beginning to risk letting girls use their bodies freely, and we are still a long way from being able to accept this as the norm. Surely only when we do so will the insulting custom of using female bodies as sex symbols, and as objects for advertising material goods, be abolished. PE teachers who have already learnt to value their own bodies have the privilege of passing on this achievement to the young if they choose to do so.

No one passed it on to Elizabeth. Her mother overtly failed to value her daughter's femininity, making her pretend to be male as the only alternative to undertaking an undervalued feminine role. Her PE teacher, presumably not having given the matter any thought at all, helped to perpetuate her rejection of femininity. Elizabeth, already seeing herself as deformed and ugly, could get no reassurance from the team-games in which she took part and which she loathed. Unlike Nina who demanded to play football, she demanded to be left alone. Both girls suffered from unimaginative teaching. Team-games, whilst being forbidden to girls if they are designated masculine, are still inexplicably compulsory in some schools where they are considered feminine: hockey, netball and lacrosse (perhaps the most lethal of all games) come into this category. Yet these games might well be specially designed to confirm the Elizabeths in their hatred of bodily activity. Hundreds of young people who dislike them are still being tortured mindlessly by wasted hours spent shivering on the periphery of various playing-fields dreading the approach of some ball which they will inevitably deal with incompetently, if not disastrously. It is hard to imagine the philosophy behind the perpetuation of this cruelty to children. The probability is that there is none, only indifference.

PE teachers need a philosophy; theirs is an important role. They have the responsibility of helping not just the enthusiastic athletes to be more successful but also the unwilling, the clumsy, the inept and the frightened to find some satisfaction in their own bodies. Only a sensitive and concerned adult can help self-conscious adolescents to get over the shame that so many of them feel about their real or imagined physical failings.

Real failings do of course exist, not just in appearance but in skills also. Actual physical deformity, however, usually elicits more sympathy from adults than does the anxiety caused by imagined ugliness or simple ineptness. The clumsiness that is commonplace in early adolescence rarely arouses sympathy and yet it can be a cause of great misery to those who suffer from it. This can be as much due to congenital conditions as many a more obvious handicap, but it is equally likely to have psychological origins.

Where innate clumsiness due to prenatal causes or early injury is present, teachers must be ready to help the children concerned to face up to and accept their disability. Girls, subjected to so much propaganda about the importance of female beauty, suffer greatly from any real physical malformation or malfunctioning. A teacher with their interests at heart can help them by bringing the problem into the open. If a teacher is willing to discuss the facts of a handicap and to examine such means of overcoming it as are available, a girl can face up to it with more confidence. She can recognise that, contrary to popular belief, there is nothing shameful in deformity, it is simply a handicap like many others. She can be advised as to how to organise the sort of physical exercise programme that is most suited to her needs and be helped to see that her disability is not nearly so obvious to others as it is to herself and need not therefore be of any great significance in her life if she can overcome her worries about it.

Others who have no physical defects can, and often do, suffer from clumsiness when they are developing physically at an uneven rate, especially when they have had a sudden growth spurt in their early teens. Although dexterity should be at its peak in these years, there are time when it is at its lowest. A good many people will have had the experience of feeling that they would fall over their own feet whilst chasing a hockey ball or drop ignominiously the cricket ball they were trying to catch, in spite of years of previous experience of being good at games. This is very discouraging, but a straightforward explanation of the causes can do a lot to alleviate the shame and anxiety engendered by the experiences. A reminder that this is just a temporary phase in body growth leading to much more agility can help to dispel fears of total failure. Meanwhile, devising exercise which is not competitive for these people is essential. If a girl can feel that she is increasing her dexterity by such exercise she will be greatly heartened and more likely to be co-operative, especially if she can be reassured tht the clumsiness will go once she has adjusted to her changing body.

Sometimes psychological conditions such as heightened anxiety, self-consciousness, or inordinate fear of failure can produce the same kinds of physical defects. Sometimes the kinds of depression from which adolescents suffer as they tackle, or fail to tackle, their resentments and disgruntlements, can make for a tendency to clumsiness which looks more like an attack on the world. In all these cases clumsiness is a handicap not to be despised but to be regarded with sympathy. Always what is needed is an adult who can help them to face up to their failure and find means of coping with it through some experiences of success. This needs PE teachers who can find the time and the patience to organise some form of exercise where success is inevitable. The most obvious kind is the non-competitive variety such as yoga or dancing. Many young people take up yoga voluntarily, and few, if any, adolescents fail to enjoy dancing, so long as the type of dancing is the currently fashionable one. There can really be no justification for teaching only the dances of bygone eras when all dancing involves valuable and enjoyable exercise.

Besides clumsiness, lethargy such as Elizabeth suffered from is the most frequently found hindrance to the enjoyment of PE by adolescents. As it is possibly due to depression it should be attended to as such and taken seriously, in case it is due to a more complex syndrome. The girl who feels unwilling to make an effort is often using up all her energy in fantasising because she cannot cope adequately with life as she finds it in reality. Whilst this is a useful compensatory mechanism for people who feel inadequate, and used judiciously it has its value, when over-used it can be destructive. Elizabeth, like a large number of adolescents, did not use the mechanism judiciously. Her life seemed to her so hopeless and her own inner world so barren that she spent most of her time imagining herself in a totally different world. In this way she not only became more isolated from reality, when reality actually impinged on her in a physical way in a PE lesson she could only withdraw into resentment. If she had been offered some really enjoyable activities she could have been brought back into reality fruitfully; as it was she was driven farther inwards.

Nina, an intelligent competent girl, able to organise others and set up a team on her own at the age of 14, was also driven to live her own life with interests centred outside school. Unlike Elizabeth she was successful in intellectual as well as athletic activities, but this success was not enough to counteract the disapproval of her behaviour by most of the school staff. In spite of her abilities and enthusiasm she was not liked; as a result she became increasingly rebellious in petty matters. Ultimately, although she obtained good grades in her O levels, she was discouraged from staying on in the sixth form as she was not perceived as having the right kind of school spirit.

Nina's enjoyment of life and of physical activities was natural and healthy, yet she found no encouragement. Elizabeth's rejection of her body was neither natural nor healthy, yet it was not much greater than that of many a normal healthy adolescent; but because it received no sympathy it overburdened her in an abnormal way. Adolescent girls are very body-conscious; they have little choice to be otherwise. Living in a world that depicts the female body as being only acceptable if it attains to an ideal shape, and constantly informed from every side that their main role is to be acceptable, girls would be blind indeed if they did not notice that bodies matter. Apart from this, the physical changes of adolescence bring a girl face to face with the realities of, and importance of, her own body in a way that can change her attitude to herself immeasurably. A girl's body represents her whole being and if she feels inadequate physically she will also feel inadequate psychologically.

Ideally only someone who is herself truly reconciled to her own body should be in charge of the physical development of others. Unfortunately we find sometimes people working in PE departments who seem to be lacking in this necessary maturity. It is this lack which is often responsible for all the disagreements about trivia such as showers and PE kit, and which therefore destroys for an unnecessary number of girls all enjoyment of the subject. The obsession of some teachers, for example, with the importance of communal showering as a sign of mental health is likely to be a sign of immaturity in the adult's relationship with her own body. For a variety of reasons a lot of young girls are sensitive about appearing naked before others. Sometimes girls have been brought up to feel that nakedness is immodest. Ruthlessly pushing them in the opposite direction will not cure this, it will merely make them unhappy. More often nowadays girls know that they should not be ashamed of nakedness and yet unaccountably find themselves to be so. Usually they are suffering from some mild form of fairly commonplace sexual inhibition which would succumb better to an understanding attitude than to ruthless disregard of feelings.

Often girls feel sexually inadequate because their physical development is at a different stage from that of their friends: their breasts are too large or too small, their hips too fat or thin. Some, however, are ashamed to change in front of others because of the poor quality of their underwear, for an adolescent a matter of bitter shame. It is worth at least considering whether all this misery can be justified by arguments about the important hygienic outcome of showering. Cleanliness no doubt comes somewhere near to godliness, but human kindness presumably comes nearer still, and this is what these young girls need. Of course they must learn to use showers, but learning is never satisfactorily achieved when bullying is involved. Girls who hate showering feel bullied by those who force them into it. If they find a teacher with a sympathetic attitude, they can learn from her, gradually, to overcome their self-denigratory ideas and oversensitivity; they can come to grips with reality and recognise that few, if any, of the others in the showers are really interested in what they look like; mostly they are equally self-absorbed and egocentric. There will, of course, always be some girls who will tease and taunt, but girls who are frightened of such teasing can be helped to overcome their fear if they realise that adults sympathise.

It is less easy to help the girl who is ill-clad or, worse still, wearing dirty underwear, but a sympathetic teacher, tutor or counsellor can do a lot to alleviate the problem. Clearly her first task is to alert the girl as kindly as possible to her own responsibility in these matters. It is not beyond the scope of most present-day adolescents to see to it that they are at least cleanly clad, but those from inadequate homes sometimes need a lot of help. As they can cause suffering to others as well as to themselves if they are not clean, it is important for someone in the school to monitor cleanliness. Parents who refuse to co-operate need just as much help as their children, but should not be allowed to get away with this sort of neglect.

This might well not be the PE teacher's province, but she is usually the person who must initiate action and follow it up. A direct assault on the girl herself in this sensitive area could be disastrous, so ingenuity and tact are needed. Meantime it is possible to find ways round the necessity for changing in public and nothing is to be gained by ignoring the suffering of these girls. They cannot alter their feelings just because they are being forced to comply. They are more likely just to refuse to comply.

The commonest way of refusing to comply with the dictates of a PE teacher is to lose the PE kit, so that attendance is impossible. Some PE teachers do not realise that a lot of girls also lose their kit, or leave it at home, because they hate wearing it. Some girls suffer a great deal from adults who do not understand that their bodies are private and precious to them. To have to clothe this body in an unbecoming PE kit which exposes parts of them that they prefer to keep covered is for them a matter of real suffering. These are often the girls who are sufficiently self-aware to know that these clothes are neither graceful nor becoming and whose means of retaining their self-respect depends on a degree of dignity which they feel is impinged on by this forced uniform. We need to respect the dignity of the young if we want them to have self-respect. Some girls look hideous in shorts because their figures are unsuited to them.

PE kit is a vexed problem that seems too often to assume a ludicrously high level of importance in the minds of adults who should really have more serious matters to think about. To punish a pupil who enjoys PE, but forgets her kit, by preventing her from playing the games that she enjoys can never be justified in educational terms.

There is no doubt that the majority of PE teachers are not just responsive to children's needs, but are likely to be more responsive and more popular than any other teachers. The rest will always observe that they have more opportunity than others to get to know their pupils well and that this is one of the most rewarding aspects of their job. The popularity of the games teacher has been part of a well-founded legend since games were first taught. It is sad, therefore, that there should be any who, as a result of mistaken ideas, fail to establish themselves in this role. For many girls PE and games have been the salvation of their school careers; for all they could be amongst the most enjoyable and useful subjects.

To ensure that they are fulfilling their real role, PE teachers need to be constantly on the alert. The best of them will find ways of being sensitive to the anxious and shy, adaptable to the inept, imaginative in organising non-competitive and innately rewarding activities for the less committed, sensible and non-punitive about kit, and above all sympathetic to those who do not enjoy exercising their bodies. They will find in practice that none of this will militate in any way against their leading their teams to victory. So long as the desire for victory is the result of a commitment towards always aiming for the highest achievement, as well as for personal satisfaction in success, this is a commendable objective. It is not however the main purpose of PE classes, any more than the relatively few brilliant higher examination successes should be the main purpose of a school.

Chapter 6

Keeping Up Appearances

Marie was a loner, or so she liked to pretend; she lived a solitary life in school and rejected offers of friendship. In fact she was lonely, but afraid to try to make friends because she believed that no one would like her. She suffered from serious acne which was somewhat disfiguring. She always tried to sit in a corner and usually managed to find herself a place where no one could sit next to her. She took little part in class discussions and never ventured a comment without first being asked a question. As she caused no trouble and produced average, if not brilliant, work she got through three years at school without attracting anyone's notice.

During the fourth year, however, more attention was paid to individuals in her school as careers discussions began in earnest. Marie's careers teacher recognised early in his first inverview with her that all was not well. He saw from her records that she had been considered intelligent when she first came to the school and suspected that she was now under-achieving. He spent a lot of time with her and she gradually gained enough confidence to talk to him freely.

Marie revealed that she was acutely self-concious: so obsessed was she with her appearance that she thought about it day and night. She was quite certain that she was hideous, that everyone thought so and that they shunned her for this reason. Her parents had moved to England from Canada when Marie was 10; shortly after this her younger sister had been born. Within a year Marie had developed her skin complaint which had got progressively worse as she moved into her teens. Her parents dismissed it as adolescent acne and made no arrangements for any medical treatment.

The careers teacher believed that Marie should have more help than she had received. He enlisted the education psychologist, on the grounds that she was under-achieving. Her parents agreed to this and were pleased when it was confirmed that her intelligence was well above average. When, however, it was suggested that her skin complaint might have some psychological origin and a visit to a psychiatrist was suggested, they refused, so nothing further was done.

At school the careers teacher enlisted her year tutor to do what she could to help Marie. Between them they managed to enable her to some extent to recognise that she was being oversensitive about her appearance. Involving other children in making some effort to incorporate her in their activities, they saw to it that Marie became a little more forthcoming. She began to recognise that she must trust in others if she wanted them to accept her at all, and she started to try rather harder to be friendly.

It is not unnatural for a girl who has a physical disability to be worried about the possibility of being rejected by others; the importance of physical appearances to adolescent girls and boys is axiomatic: they are often vain to the point of narcissism. Every girl's (and boy's) self-image is bound up with her perception of herself as an acceptable or unacceptable human being, and adolescents in particular need constant reassurance about their appearance. Physical changes have made them much more body-conscious than they were a year or two before, and physical beauty assumes a quite disproportionate importance. To a good many adults beauty rarely seems lacking in the young. Some of us even think that, whatever their spots or their puppy fat, adolescents have as a rule such a natural charm and grace that though they may distort or disguise themselves under layers of make-up, the freshness and enchantment that is inherent in all young things still shines through. It does not shine in the view of the young themselves, though, as they gaze into the looking-glass. They see only the spots and the puppy fat.

A bad complexion can be a disaster because it is one of the most difficult blemishes to hide and, being on the face, is felt to be most conspicuous. The idea that acne is associated with sexual inhibitions in some people's view is no comfort to the Maries of this world. Most of us have some sexual inhibitions; it is as well that we have. Most adolescent girls have some sexual anxieties; these are in no way improved if the poor girl is led to believe that somehow these anxieties are manifesting themselves on her face like a mark of Cain. What she needs is not this pseudo-scientific jeremiad but reassuring facts and medication.

There are plenty of good antidotes to a great many adolescent skin complaints. Girls should be encouraged to go to their GPs and ask for them. They should also be encouraged to refuse to be fobbed off with 'it's just your age' or 'your nerves'. Maybe it is both, but it is also susceptible to amelioration. Not all skin problems are easily solved but a lot of adolescent ones can be dealt with adequately if the right treatment is given early enough.

Some girls are afraid to see a doctor because they believe either that a complaint like spots is too trivial, or that it is something too shameful, or that it can never be cured and they cannot bear to face that fact. Some are so guilt-ridden that they actually feel that they deserve their spots; others hope that if no one's attention is drawn to them they will go away. An intelligent and sympathetic adult with a bit of knowledge and some common sense can do a lot to alleviate real misery and help them to see the value of proper treatment.

In some cases more expert help is needed. Marie's skin complaint might well have been a reaction to the birth of a sister just after she had moved to a foreign country and just as she was entering her teens. The beginnings of sexuality in the young often produce a great need on their part to deny its existence in their elders. The birth of a sister prevented Marie from doing this: her parents were obviously fully sexual. She resented this but kept quiet about her resentment and convinced herself that she was being punished by her spots.

It was a true tragedy for her at this time of life because a bad complexion is so difficult to conceal. 'No boy will ever want to kiss me', she said bitterly and not without some justification in her experience of life. Frederick, the hero of *The Pirates of Penzance*, asks if there is not 'one maiden here whose homely face and bad complexion have caused all hope to disappear of ever gaining man's affection?'. Gilbert might well nowadays be classified as a male chauvinist but his sentiments were acceptable to his audience in the nineteenth century; they are still the foundation of most advertising aimed at women in the twentieth, and the adolescent girl who can resist it is rare. And what do such sentiments tell her? That if she is not pretty not only is she sexually undesirable but as a person she is unacceptable. She has no hope of gaining man's affection; she is doomed to a life of solitude or spinsterhood.

Many young girls nowadays may deny vehemently that they agree with such sentiments. Those are the views of the oldies, the unreconstructed who do not know what it is all about; their behaviour, however, belies their claims. They need, like every generation of girls, to be loved and wanted, and their appearance must therefore seem to them to be acceptable. The modes of presenting that appearance may vary from generation to generation but the importance of the world's regard remains the same.

Since we still live in a society which lays emphasis on the importance of feminine beauty, even to the extent of exploiting it as a significant aspect of the economy, it would be dishonest to dismiss as unimportant nonsense the physical preoccupations of teenage girls. Teachers, therefore, who have so much influence if they are prepared to use it, should remain aware of the feelings of the young. Whilst PE teachers have most responsibility for physical well-being, others too can do a lot to alleviate unnecessary misery. Casual and joking references to physical disability should always be avoided. Hermia in *A Midsummer Night's Dream* reminds us of the horrors of being either 'so dwarfish and so low' or 'a painted maypole' in her tirade against Helena. Yet many a tall girl is still laughingly called a beanpole, and has to laugh back; and many a small one endures the epithet 'titch'. A girl's body represents to her the physical manifestation of her inner world. It is a manifestation that is there for all to see; if she dislikes her body she may well feel that she herself is not likeable.

It is never funny to be called tubby; to be fat is a nightmare for a

15-year-old girl. She has the evils of overweight presented to her from every direction. She can feel like a criminal if she increases her girth by an inch or her weight by a pound. It is of course folly, sometimes dangerous folly, for a young girl to allow herself to become excessively fat either through lack of exercise or through over-eating. Obesity in the young is something that is not to be taken lightly. But the anxiety that is caused by the plumpness which is one of the characteristics, even one of the charms, of this age is sadly misplaced. Unfortunately advertisers present girls with such a wildly improbable picture of the ideal feminine shape that the poor little fat girls feel like freaks and even the normally chubby think they are abnormally ugly.

Plumpness can easily grow into obesity in some girls if eating habits are not controlled. 'Comfort eating', that is, the taking-in of food to compensate for an inner feeling of emptiness, is a common adolescent tendency. A girl who will eat hardly any protein and an excess of carbohydrates and sweets needs guidance. Most of all, however, she needs comfort. She almost certainly needs this from her own mother because the relationship that a girl has with her mother at this stage is a very profound one and of great importance to her. A daughter who is comfort eating is a daughter who feels, rightly or wrongly, that she is not loved enough. Mothers have to try to respond to this by demonstrating their love. They might think they are doing so enough already, but the evidence suggests that their love is not getting through to the daughter. They might even be demonstrating it in the wrong way, by too much indulgence, for example, rather than too little. Counsellors or sympathetic teachers can help here when the relationship between the mother and the daughter is not going well. Sometimes they can offer the support that a girl needs – by listening to her woes and helping her to discover what it is in herself that is preventing her from having the good relationship with her mother that she needs. Certainly, whatever the source of her unhappiness, unhappiness there is if a girl over-eats knowing that she is doing physical damage to herself. Instructing her in diet is only a small part of the battle: understanding and concern are often a much larger part.

Some good home economics teachers see the recognition of these sorts of problems as part of their role. Others, unfortunately, get caught up in spite of themselves in the academic demands of their subjects and lose sight of the practical value that is inherent in them. It is only too easy for school lessons on important human subjects like biology and home economics, which are closely related to the actual lives that girls are living, to be accepted by children as just another necessary bit of tedium. It is not sufficient to learn and write notes about a 'balanced diet' in home economics lessons. As these are, only too often, exam-oriented, the less intelligent girl can see them solely as an academic exercise and not as in any way related to her personal experiences.

One little 12-year-old I saw recently was sitting in a home economics department surrounded by glistening pans and shiny kitchen utensils. She was preparing her project for assessment, copying from a textbook detailed instructions about how many rinses she should give her hair after she had shampooed it and how much more advantageous it was to brush your teeth down than across. Her hair was filthy and matted, her clothes were ill-fitting and grubby, her very beautiful face was pale and not recently washed. It is highly unlikely that she used a toothbrush from one year's end to another. She lived, I discovered, in a house where there was no water or electricity laid on. Her family were squatters. There were about seven of them being brought up by a very feckless but amiable mother. The child was quite often ill at school because she had not had any breakfast, not because of real poverty, although undoubtedly that was there, but because of the carelessness and indifference and a general lack of attention to the basic needs. What was the point of this girl writing about two rinses after her shampoo? Yet she, more than any other girl in the class, needed lessons in home economics and hygiene.

Obviously all lessons cannot be geared to one or two children, but some imagination and attention paid to the real needs of real children in the class could have made that a very valuable exercise instead of a boring and meaningless chore for this girl and probably a number of other girls in the group. A more valuable use of the time devoted to this subject might have been for all the pupils to investigate those aspects of hygiene that more especially related to puberty. Special emphasis could have been laid, by the teacher, on the areas in which particular need was shown by individual girls. Done tactfully this would not require that any one person was singled out as having special needs, but no one's problems would be overlooked. Bad feeding habits, obesity, forgetfulness about cleanliness, spots, these can all be made subjects of discussion and an opening for sound advice to be given in an acceptable form.

It might not seem to be the concern of teachers whether or not a girl considers herself sexually desirable, whether she is fat, thin, short or tall, or indeed whether she is happy or not with herself. It is their concern, however, to get across to these girls what has to be learnt. Girls who are too obsessed with matters other than work are not as a rule interested in learning, as every teacher knows. The most meaningful way that has been found of re-establishing interest in learning is for the teacher to take an interest in the pupils.

Marie certainly was not cured of her disabilities and never reached her full potential intellectually but she did change her attitude to other people for the better. As important a lesson as any other is the recognition that we need to trust people if we want them to accept us. Although there is no doubt that the world values beauty in young girls, everyone who lacks it does not have to become a recluse.

Miranda's problem was created by her beauty; on the face of it, not a great cross to bear. She had discovered by the age of 14 that she could command attention wherever she went and was well launched into a delightful social life. But besides being beautiful she was also very bright. Wanting to do well in her work, she found it difficult to reconcile the two aspects of her life. It was not, she explained, that she had not got time for study as well as for discos and parties, it was that they conflicted philosophically.

The philosophical conflict was a genuine one: she had recognised the dangers inherent in success. Success breeds rejection, not just by girl-friends – that, anyhow, is easily coped with – but by boyfriends, which is another matter altogether. It is easy to cite envy as the basis of such rejection and no doubt this, one of the commonest of emotions, has a lot to do with it, but there is more involved. Whilst a girl who is success-ful with boys may be seen as a threat by some less fortunate girls, on the whole she will be popular with quite enough of them to keep her contented. It is the threat that she poses to boys when she is cleverer than they are that constitutes the real problem. Miranda feared that she was liable to make herself unpopular with boys in her school if she was too successful. Furthermore, she herself was prepared to subscribe to this state of affairs, in that she genuinely disliked the competition: 'I don't want to do better than Michael, but if I don't work it's silly.'

Not wanting to do better than Michael is such a commonplace occurrence that we tend not even to notice its existence. It was brought most starkly into the limelight by Martina Horner when she set up a piece of research to demonstrate how successfully intelligent girls reject their achievements. Asking male and female students to complete a story that starts with a girl coming top of the list in her first year of medical school, she found that a high proportion of the female responses suggested in one way or another that she had no right to be at the top. The most telling were the ones which had this girl giving up medicine, taking up some less prestigious profession such as social work, or marrying a brilliant and successful doctor.

There are, of course, societies such as the American Indians studied by Erikson in which the element of competition does not appear to exist. Whether the reason for this is related to child-rearing processes or to man's natural tendencies does not affect the issue as far as teachers in our schools are concerned. For them competition is an innate part of the educational system. From the day they enter kindergarten girls are told to be competitive, to win. At the same time they are given contradictory messages by home, school and society. Mothers tell their daughters that school is important, whilst in almost the same breath some of them say that girls do not need all that much education. Schools tell them to be competitive and yet expect them to be conforming and submissive. Society says: 'Get yourself a man and you will be acceptable.' Even the most highly emancipated young suffer from these strictures. If girls have not male partners the doors of paradise will be closed to them.

Discos are not perhaps paradise to us but they certainly are to any 14-year-old girl who dares not go to one without a boyfriend. They may look like places that do not require escorts, but the young know better. A few visits can be made alone or with girlfriends, but ultimately they are discontinued as it becomes obvious that discos are part of the mating game too. Later in life society is centred on couples; single women make the numbers uneven in a way which, oddly enough, men do not. We, in our wisdom, know that this is not all that life or marriage is about; the young do not.

Girls have no illusions about what the world is telling them and it bears more weight than most of what is told to them in school. They see the same message stridently presented in every advertisement and every journal that they come across. Nevertheless, in school they are told that life is about passing exams. They must study, and postpone competition in the marriage market until after they have made a career.

The brighter girls like Miranda suffer quite as much as do their less intelligent sisters: they are the ones who are even more confused. They really want to make their careers the centre of their lives, but they are torn between what the schools tell them and what the rest of the world is saying, for example, 'men don't make passes at girls who wear glasses', and 'wearing glasses' is exemplified above all by being brighter than your boyfriend.

Psychological theories as to why girls find it so hard to compete with boys have tended in the past to be rooted in an assumption of instinctive passive submissiveness on the part of the female. Today there is more recognition of how much of this masochistic attitude in life is socially conditioned. Karen Horney, since way back in the 1930s, has been pointing this out, but until recently she has not been given much of a hearing. Now it is beginning to be more generally accepted that society makes women into passive dependants and that society can therefore unmake the role. No society is better geared to doing this than a school which, at least in principle, subscribes to the view that girls have as much of a right to be intellectually successful as boys.

Teachers, if they are going to change attitudes in their pupils, need to examine their own standpoint first. They need also to recognise that the fear of competitiveness does not necessarily spring from simple humility or a kindly loving nature. Girls often feel resentment against an upbringing that represses their natural inclinations. This resentment has usually had to be suppressed but it makes itself evident in ways of which the girls themselves are sometimes unconscious.

The ferocity with which some of the girls in Martina Horner's study attacked the imaginary successful girl does not suggest a meek feminine submissiveness, much more a resentment against someone who has had the temerity to break the rule implying thereby that the rule was not necessary.

'Anne is an acne-faced bookworm ... As usual she starts showing off.' 'All the Friday and Saturday nights without dates or any fun – I'll be the best woman doctor alive. And yet a twinge of sadness comes through – she wonders what she really has ...' 'The male medical students don't seem to think very highly of a female who has beaten them in their field.' (Note 'their' field!) 'Anne is pretty proud of herself, but everyone hates and envies her.' One girl even gives Anne a nervous breakdown.

Freud labelled this kind of attitude 'identification with the aggressor'. More colloquially it is known as 'if you can't beat them join them'. These American college girls were already determined to maintain a society which, despite its economic dependence on being the most competitive in the world, insists that women do not use their talents to the full because men do not like it if they do. The aggressor with whom they were identifying was not men but society which had browbeaten them for the whole of their short lives into a belief that, as Martina Horner puts it, 'It isn't really ladylike to be too intellectual'. It takes great courage to resist being ladylike when you are constantly reminded that to do so will condemn you to a life of solitude. It takes even more when, like Miranda, you receive strong reinforcements for opting for being beautiful instead of clever, the two being considered mutually exclusive.

Teachers are in a position to help to alter viewpoints. They can do so by initiating discussions on relevant topics and helping girls to become aware of how much they themselves are subscribing to their own predicament. Some girls will already recognise how damaging these attitudes are: many more will initially suppress such awareness. They need to be helped to understand why they hold to such beliefs, and only convinced adults can help them. As good a place as any for starting a discussion is with the magazines that girls read; from *Honey* to *Cosmopolitan* they preach the same message, in however disguised a form: look beautiful and attract men. It is not the looking beautiful that is to be deprecated but the degrading quality of the rest of the message as a sole purpose in life. It is this that has led some of the more thoughtful adolescents within the last few years to make protests in a manner which tends to deny feminine beauty or at least diminish it as far as possible. The recent fashions, in which girls have hidden their more obvious charms under crumpled cheesecloth and worn-out jeans, were at a conscious level an attempt to break the feminine image that has for so long been exploited by advertisers. At an unconscious level it might well also have represented a flight from awareness of a fear of femininity. There is good reason to fear the feminine role but to admit to such fear is hard; it is easier simply to see oneself as rejecting the bad aspects of the world's fantasy of what it means to be female. Girls need to be helped to realise that they are also in danger of rejecting the good aspects if they throw the whole of femininity away.

This is what happened to a good many of the lesser breed of bluestockings after the nineteenth century in female education. Girls' schools were frequently staffed by teachers who had had to battle through prejudices to gain a decent education, many of them fully qualified graduates on whom no degrees could be conferred because they were female. These women, after their hard-won battle, were not for letting anyone accuse them of being soft on their pupils. Ronald Searle's band of hockey and lacrosse stick waving fiends were probably the last of a, fortunately, dying breed of schoolgirls who needed to demonstrate this particular kind of toughness. No longer do teachers address one another by their surnames without prefix in staffrooms, as they did when I started to teach; no longer do they speak of their pupils solely by their surnames either. This uncouth habit still persists amongst some schoolmasters, being thought to denote masculinity, and some boys still suffer from it. Girls, however, are now spared this bit of pseudo-masculinity, but in some schools they are still not spared the relics of boys' school uniforms. Ties have nearly been abolished – an incomprehensible garment in anybody's wardrobe – but some form of figure disguising habit that is a residue of the old cult is still insisted on in some schools.

More common, however, these days is a much-disguised sexism which seeks to limit girls' own attempts to establish equality of opportunity. In terms of girls' appearance this manifests itself in the great trouser debate. A substantial proportion of the teaching profession still objects to girls wearing trousers in school, and it is hard to discover any rational basis for these objections.

At an irrational level the reasons are all too easy to surmise. At my convent boarding school, with a solid tradition of French puritanism behind it, we were forbidden to wear trousers even in plays: they had to be imitated by tubular pieces of cloth fastened above the knees and worn under tunics. The several implications of this were not lost on any of us, despite our sheltered lives. Nearly forty years on from then the feeling that girls in trousers are not quite nice still rests on fears of female sexuality being made explicit.

It is possible that this fear also underlies the deep passions that are aroused whenever the topic of uniform is raised, most of which attaches itself to the discussion of girls' uniform. Other fears are there as well, however, and it is extremely important that teachers should examine these and try to put their views into some kind of rational order.

Our clothes, besides being a decoration, are also a protection against the world, almost another skin. Adolescents need decoration and protection that accords with their emerging self-image. Often in doubt about their identity and insecure in their developing bodies, they need to take this extra skin particularly seriously.

Not all adolescent girls, by any means, mind wearing uniform. For a great many of them the protection afforded by the anonymity which it engenders is a great relief. At a more simple practical level it saves a girl having to worry about what to put on. It rarely nowadays protects a girl who is poor from revealing the fact to her neighbours; shabby uniforms are just as misery-making as any other unsatisfactory clothes.

A rather sophisticated 15-year-old boy quoted by Edward Blishen in *The School That I'd Like*, pointing to the naivety of adults in these matters, said: 'It is still seriously thought that if we all wear the same types of clothes we'll all go round thinking our parents earn the same amount of money.' It is noticeable that the schools in which uniforms were abolished first were the private schools where a great disparity of wealth is not so common as in state schools. However, for girls the need to compete with others in wearing attractive clothes is always there, being bolstered up by just about everything that they see and hear. For this reason alone, some limitation on choice of clothes can be valuable. Where there is a danger of some pupils feeling really inadequate because of their clothes, uniforms serve a useful purpose. They also fulfil an important role for those adolescents who value the sense of identity that a uniform provides and who like to have it known that they belong. Adolescents need groups to which they can owe allegiance and uniforms typify this allegiance. Often enough their own choice of clothes is sufficiently constrained to amount to a uniform. The need to be as like as possible to your own group, which underlies all fashion promotion, limits the choice of an adolescent's clothes at any time.

A uniform that you impose on yourself, however, is very different from one imposed from above. The simplest solution to any problem about uniform, therefore, is to consult the pupils themselves about it. Attitudes will be found to vary from district to district, from school to school. Millions of girls have been educated throughout the world in countries where school uniforms are unheard of, so it should not surprise teachers that quite a number of their pupils would rather wear their own clothes.

The intensity with which some members of staff insist on the application of rigid rules about uniform tends to bear little relation to any consideration of the real needs of their pupils. Passions are inappropriate where the only matter under dispute is the colour of a pair of socks or the cut of a skirt. Yet sane and otherwise balanced teachers will go into paroxysms of rage at seeing a girl wearing yellow stripes where brown spots are the rule.

Clothes in fact touch us all deeply at a level over which we do not have complete control. No amount of rationalising that tights are unhealthy, high heels are damaging to the feet, jewelry can cause accidents and jeans do not get washed enough, can do away with the less rational aspects of the disputes. All these statements are true, but they are not the true reasons for adults' complaints about tights, shoes, jewelry or jeans – or any other of the multifarious complaints. Black stockings were a misery that my generation had to endure at school; when in the 1950s black stockings came into fashion again, teachers, who at school had worn black stockings through no choice of their own, raged against girls who chose to wear them.

There is nothing new in this battle. In one of P. G. Wodehouse's earliest school stories the wearing of puce-coloured Turkish slippers in class is seen as a successful and symbolic act of defiance by a hero. The young know of the need that the adults have to control them and they recognise that clothes represent one of the most important arenas in the battle for supremacy. Teachers need to recognise this too and to understand why they choose such an arena. There is silent defiance in physical display, in every breach of the uniform rule. To make such a breach gives power to the young person. It must be recognised that adults have always been fearful of giving the young too much power, not always without justification.

The control of the young and the retaining of the reins in the adults' hands is one of the major problems of any teacher – the more inexperienced or insecure the teacher, the more difficult this problem. It might seem odd, therefore, that teachers would actually choose an area of disagreement by insisting on the wearing of certain clothes when so many battlefields already exist. Before we blame them, however, for intransigence in this matter, we should look at that other group of adults who have to deal with the young: their parents. We find, confirmed by the recent report from the National Children's Bureau, that clothes are the most frequent basis of disagreement between parents, not just teachers, and teenage children. Whilst most 16- and 17-year olds claimed to have a good relationship with their parents, large numbers nevertheless admitted to arguing with them about clothes. Adults find the adolescents' choice of clothes a problem because it represents their approaching adulthood and their burgeoning sexuality which adults throughout history have tried to check in the young. Any new adolescent fashion or any defiance of adult rules about clothing is one more reminder that the young are joining the adult sexual club.

Since girls suffer especially in their painful journey into this club when they feel that their appearance is not acceptable, the cruelty of trying to make the transition for them even more difficult should be faced honestly by adults. Teachers who are prepared to recognise what is going on may still decide that the advantages of wearing a uniform outweigh that of not doing so. This can be a reasonable attitude;

it is only made unreasonable when failure to conform to the rule is perceived as a heinous crime.

If teachers can remember how desperately a young girl needs to feel that her own body is acceptable and how important her appearance is to her, they will learn to curb their own natural tendency to try to impose too many restraints on what the young look like. If they also recall that appearances for the young have a lot to do with their feelings of being sexually viable, teachers might be less clumsy in their strictures on clothes. If they can bear in mind the struggle that many girls like Miranda are coping with, being torn between emphasising the importance of their physical appearance and concentrating on their intellectual life, they might be less eager to make dogmatic rules which can make life even harder for the adolescents. Beauty may be only skin deep, but skins are very important. If it can be remembered that clothes are a second skin, the seriousness with which the young treat them can be more easily tolerated. Only someone who has never suffered from anxiety about clothes or appearances can pretend that such matters are never of importance. It takes maturity to put them into perspective and that is the prerogative of the adult, not the adolescent.

Chapter 7

Classroom Control and the Normal Adolescent

Even the most satisfactory of pupils can cause havoc if their teachers are unprepared for the battle that so many young people feel they must fight. If teachers respond by fighting back they will ultimately fail to make contact. If they take personally all the criticisms which are made of adults in general they will be unnecessarily hurt, and not much use to their pupils. If they feel rejected because the young appear to be rejecting them they will suffer.

There is a crudity that characterises adolescence that stems from an inability to empathise with others and that is simply a product of immaturity, not malice. The vanity and apparent self-satisfaction revealed in so much of the chatter of adolescents is a thin veneer over their insecurity. When we meet such behaviour in older people we recognise it for what it is. In the old it is harder to tolerate because we feel that they should know better. In the young it is always worth accepting at more than its face value. Exhibitionism is at its worst during the teens and a lot of adolescent behaviour is nothing more than an attempt to make some impression in a world where there is no certainty of being accepted. As a teacher you have to be able to bear with a great deal of this testing out of the world without taking it personally.

Even the best pupils can be a trial at times. Camilla, for example, whose mother is a journalist, has just handed in nine pages of closely reasoned argument to support her view that Hamlet is not mad but a misunderstood genius (a bit like herself). Linda, on the other hand, says who cares? Nutcase or not, he's a bore. And so you start another class with your best Lower Sixth, knowing that if you don't enjoy this one you'll be ill-prepared for the battle of the week: 3R6 after break. There, dominated by Dolores, they will be at the ready, awaiting her witticisms at your expense. You mention Hamlet? 'What's that then, a cigar? A new group?' Shrieks of mirth. Not damaged or destructive people, just ordinary run-of-the-mill teenage girls, each one of whom will use you unconsciously, if she can, as a receptacle for all her confusions, irritations and disappointments with life. Each one will see in you roles that you cannot possibly fulful, or even know about, and each will, being the centre of her own world, see you as acting primarily in relation to herself and responsible for satisfying her needs and demands.

Teaching can be an enjoyable, exciting, tiring, boring and even frightening occupation. The adjective that is applicable depends on the teacher, the taught and the establishment they work in. Above all it depends on what attitudes and feelings teachers can muster to bring to this work.

Most people go into teaching expecting to get some pleasure out of sharing their knowledge with people younger and less knowledgeable than themselves. Indeed, if they do not have some such expectations they have chosen the wrong profession. Unfortunately some teachers who start off with the greatest expectations and the best intentions become sadly disillusioned. Others become bored.

It is really exciting to discover how much thinking a 16- or 17-year-old can do; how mature some of their ideas are and how sensitive they can be when faced with great literature. At the sixth time around, however, sometimes the predictable theories about Hamlet can begin to pall. Occasionally the argumentativeness that results from what Piaget calls the adolescents' newly discovered ability to hypothesise can lose its charm. The lack of experience of real life and the banalities of some of the brilliant discoveries may be more evident than any desire to learn from another's experience or explore other people's ideas.

Similarly, for some people mathematics hold an almost unending interest. The delights of opening up the minds of the young to the possibilities inherent in numbers can be perennial, so long as the pupils share the enthusiasm. Not quite so exciting is the ploughing through of a mandatory syllabus, designed by a head of department with a different approach from your own, with unwilling 15-year-old girls who are marking time before they can leave school.

Teaching is a demanding, difficult and sometimes almost impossible task because of the conditions under which teachers and pupils have to work. It requires constant effort, occasionally at heroic levels. If from time to time there are some who fail to live up to the demands of their role we should not be surprised. There are few professions in which failure is so much on show to the public and in which it is so rarely forgiven. It is extremely difficult to be at the top of your form, alert, responsive and enthusiastic during every hour of every day. Yet that is what people expect of teachers. Teachers even expect it of themselves. Such a level of aspiration is bound to produce failure. Failure produces discouragement and in turn provokes the teacher to look around for a scapegoat. If he is not to blame himself he must blame the pupils or the school.

It is not my intention to cite scapegoats; they are available for all to see and have been tabulated endlessly. It is interesting that ancient buildings should usually be the first on the list because they are probably of the lowest priority for teachers, compared with the size of classes and the morale of a school. Some of the most inspired teaching in the world is done in buildings that have been around for centuries with little if any alteration. Class size is another matter. A lot of effort (and a little research) has been involved in demonstrating that class size does not affect teaching significantly. No good experienced teachers will be deluded by this into denying their own experience that teaching large numbers is neither as effective nor as rewarding as teaching small numbers. However, whilst it is convenient for those who hold the purse-strings to listen to what they like to hear, we will have large classes with us for a long time to come in state schools. As with buildings, the solution to these problems is not within the scope of the ordinary class teacher. Indeed the whole structure of our educational system is constantly, and probably justly, dismissed as inadequate from almost every viewpoint; like all human institutions, it bears scars of human fallibility. Nevertheless, it also incorporates a lot of worthy human aspirations, and meanwhile children still have to be educated and teachers, until the required reforms or revolutions arrive, still have to teach children whatever the constraints.

Working in establishments with an inbuilt structure, teachers sometimes suffer from the inflexibility of frameworks which they have not designed themselves. They do not therefore always have freedom to adjust rules to individuals. This is an aspect of their role that can work to their advantage or disadvantage, depending both on the school and on the attitudes of the teachers. If they can see the ready-made structure as a set of reasonable boundaries that can give security to the young for whom it is designed, they can make use of it and work well within it. If, however, they see it as an unnecessarily restrictive imposition that curbs their freedom to work in a fruitful way, they have more of a problem.

If they examine their own attitudes carefully they can come to recognise when, for example, the rules they want to make are valuable both to themselves and to the young, and when they are really only bolstering an adult's position without relation to the young's needs. They must examine the ready-made structure of the school in the same light. It could be that the structure is really likely to prevent their pupils from fulfilling their potential. In such schools, teachers have to face up to their obligations and do what they can to change matters. Sometimes changes have not been made simply because no one has given the matter enough thought. It could on the other hand be that the structure is not as damaging as some teachers imagine. It is important therefore, for teachers to look into their own motives before they blame the school entirely for what may be their personal inability to work within its framework. Ultimately, the teacher's individual response as a person to those being taught is often more important than any structure.

Arguments about formality versus informality in education will not be easily solved and there are many young teachers who find themselves desperately frustrated when they attempt to enter into them. Schools, being institutions, are of their nature cumbersome and slow to change. Since most schools are too large for truly satisfactory relationships to be established between teachers and all their students, many respond to this problem by an excess of formality. Those teachers who are brave enough to refuse this easy way out frequently come in for a great deal of censure, especially from those insecure members of society who are frightened by change.

There are, however, unfortunately teachers who reject the given structures without substituting any other workable organisation. These do no good to themselves or to their students. However worthy their aims, the result can be chaos if they work in complete contradiction to the standards demanded by the rest of the staff. Such teachers, eager to criticise the status quo, do not take into consideration the unfortunate realities that schools are bound to be less than ideal since they are with very rare exceptions inadequately staffed and starved of funds. In spite of these facts, either a relatively structured or a relatively free form of classroom government can work if the teacher has goodwill.

Whether the form of classroom government is free or not, there will always be someone around to criticise it. Whether teachers are strict or comparatively easy-going, they will make mistakes and have these mistakes pointed out to them by someone. It might be helpful for teachers to realise that the controversy between tough-minded and tender-minded (to borrow William James's terms) approaches to child-rearing is probably as perennial as child-bearing. Certainly almost since books were first printed tracts on this subject have been available. As early as the seventeenth century a spate of them had already been published in English; from the innumerable exhortations in them to avoid indulging children we can infer that to do so was pretty commonplace. In fact what is nowadays called permissiveness, and in those days was cockering, has been with us a long time.

Roger North, writing around the early 1600s, tells us that 'Fondness makes parents Indulg all things to children'; though he clearly shared the view of many of his contemporaries that this really should not be the case, he accepted the undeniable fact and suggested ways of making good use of it, ways which nowadays would be called behaviour modification.

In the eighteenth century Miss Austen expected her readers to dislike her favourite heroine, Emma, who responds to an over-indulged childhood with wilful behaviour. Her hero Mr Knightley, however, after a lifetime of observing these indulgences, ultimately confesses that he is losing all his 'bitterness against spoiled children', commenting that they might well correct themselves as they grow older.

Perhaps Charles Dickens set the final seal on the assumption that child-rearing required only sternness to succeed, with his poignant pictures of children not just physically ill-treated but, equally seriously, emotionally starved. Few readers, even in a century which allowed children to work themselves to death before they ever reached adolescence, failed to be moved by his heart-rending stories. Little Dombey, abandoned at the age of 6 to the mercies of yet one more horrendous educational establishment, 'sat as if he had taken life unfurnished and the upholsterer was never coming'. He epitomises all of that child neglect that finally shocked society into a new and caring approach to education.

A Methodist minister, the Rev. Charles Shaw, at the beginning of this century, contrasting the education that he received around 1840 with that available to the young of 1900, spoke with genuine conviction of the board schools 'all glorious within like palaces'. To us today they might seem more like prisons, but they represented a revolution in publicly admitted attitudes towards child-rearing that is manifesting itself still, in particular in the behaviour of our adolescents.

The blame for the difficulties that we are finding in coping with young people today is frequently laid at the door of Sigmund Freud whose revelations about the relationship between upbringing and subsequent behaviour are seen to have sparked off a positive riot of over-indulgence by tender-minded parents. Though himself the most strait-laced of nineteenth-century parents, there is no doubting his influence on such radical thinkers in the sphere of child education as Susan Isaacs and A. S. Neill. Yet, paradoxically, the followers of one of Freud's most devoted disciples, Melanie Klein, sound very much like their seventeenth-century forebears as they postulate 'postponement of gratification' as one of the cornerstones of good mental health.

Clearly throughout the ages thoughtful parents and teachers, whilst inevitably swayed by the climate of opinion of the times in which they lived, have tempered their responses to fashionable doctrines with their own good sense. Others, less thoughtful, have sometimes followed fashion without enough good sense. This seems to be one of the characteristics of present-day child-rearing habits which perhaps distinguishes them most from any recorded in previous centuries. Theories abound as to why so many parents feel unable to cope with their young nowadays, when in the past there appear to have been so few difficulties. Whilst attributing a fair share of this thinking to a false reading of history and a tendency to yearn for what Peter Laslett has called 'the world we have lost' with a singular myopia about the disadvantages that we have now only too thankfully lost, there is some truth in the belief that it is harder to be a parent today than it ever was. It is certainly harder to be a teacher of adolescents; this is a fact undisputed even by those who would still somehow find it possible to lay the blame for it on the teachers.

Sociologists tend to see the cause as the disintegration of the extended family, though historians like Laslett have produced some considerable evidence that the nuclear unit is not such an innovation in English life-style as is commonly maintained. Psychologists such as Bruno Bettelhein have pointed to the unique position of present-day mothers in that they are bringing up their children in a way which is qualitatively different from that in which they themselves were brought up. Having rarely taken part in child-rearing themselves, they are following no model except those which they can glean from the theories they read about. Politicians of all parties can point truthfully to the influence of new and not very satisfactory social systems in changing the relation-ships between parents and children.

These and a host of other factors have no doubt contributed to the present dilemma. Solutions cannot therefore be simple or all-embracing. There are nevertheless overriding principles which trans-cend fashion and there are some fairly fundamental procedures which can be relied upon with some degree of consistency to facilitate the good resolution of difficulties between adolescents and adults.

That there is no foolproof blueprint for dealing with the problems presented by adolescents is axiomatic. Neither mice nor men can hope for such perfection. Nevertheless, despair is not an appropriate response to even the most frenetic behaviour. If the adolescent rebellion has already started advice about being prepared in advance rings pretty hollow, and even the most meticulous preparations can still be flawed. But, bearing in mind that whilst each adolescent has, of course, a unique experience of being a human being, there are some general principles to be observed which can be helpful.

Some teachers, especially those who are young enough to feel close to their own adolescence, can find themselves feeling so much in sympathy with rebelliousness that they forget their own responsibilities. In reality they are not much help to the young if they give rein to these feelings. To a teenager anyone over the age of 20 is already old and is responded to as an adult. This means that she is expected to demonstrate some form of adult sense of responsibility, enough to make the young feel that they could turn to her in a crisis, for example. This is sometimes hard to accept when one is barely feeling like an adult oneself and when one's perceptions of older people are much like those of the adolescents. Nevertheless, a teacher has taken on an adult role and must accept it for the sake of the pupils.

For the most part it does not require any special skills or high intelligence to be a good parent to an adolescent, though undoubtedly those do best who are possessed of some common sense and stead-fastness of purpose. Without these it is too easy to be swayed by immediate circumstances. To be a good teacher of other people's adolescent children, however, requires more than this. We are now talking about a professional role in which a response has to be made to large numbers of pupils who have reached adolescence at more or less the same time, any number of whom might be going through difficult phases and all of whom are needing, and usually demanding, some form of attention.

Teachers who really do not enjoy the company of adolescents and who continue to work with them always run the risks of ruining their own as well as their pupils' peace of mind. And even those who enjoy their company can find themselves tripped up by their own lack of preparedness. Since none of us is so perfectly mature that we have grown up completely in every aspect of our behaviour, our infantile side can be sparked off by the behaviour of the young. Only too easily adults can find themselves actually quarrelling with adolescents as though they themselves were still in their teens. Yet since what the adolescents need more than anything else is firm adults to test themselves against, somehow adults have to find the means to remain adult, however strong the pull towards acting like an adolescent.

They will find these means if they themselves can feel secure. Teaching will never be done very well if morale is low. Low morale is caused in particular by too much unrestrained adolescent revolt. Adolescents settle their score with the world at school as often as at home. No matter that neither institution is actually responsible for the discoveries that are made by all teenagers that the world is neither perfect nor perfectible. Teachers are a useful target for the dissatisfaction. Society should therefore be geared to recognising that those who are undergoing the strain of the adolescent onslaught need support. Understanding and sympathetic inspectors, advisers, heads and senior staff are important to the well-being of teachers and therefore of pupils in schools. They are of far greater significance than any number of new buildings, new curricula, new teaching methods or reorganisations of structure. Schools are run by people for people and it is the people in them in the last analysis who make or break them.

Undoubtedly there are some schools where no one should be asked to teach. If the ethos of a school is so alien to real education that everyone, young and old alike, is disgruntled and the teachers are beginning to feel despairing, only the most gifted and dedicated should stay. The ordinary newly qualified teachers who have little choice of school should not feel personally responsible for failure in such surroundings. They should change schools as soon as possible before their courage and idealism slip away. Idealism, a much derided quality amongst those who involve themselves in education only for their own personal aggrandisement, is still an essential characteristic of any worthwhile teacher. Far from being an irrational trait it is the only rational basis from which to undertake the awesome task of educating the next generation and making or breaking the learning experiences of other people's children. Idealism is realism if it is supported by sound knowledge. Sound knowledge will not cause teachers to ignore glaring faults in the system, but it will raise their morale, and help them to enjoy their work.

Teachers of adolescent girls frequently find themselves becoming jaded and discouraged. How is it, then, that there are still some around who manage to maintain their freshness and enthusiasm year after year? If you turn to the books written by successful teachers about their work you are likely to find inspiring but discouraging accounts of boundless energy, total commitment, passion and, in some cases, sheer genius. These are hard to emulate. How much more valuable, therefore, to turn first to oneself and assess one's own potential and then to look to the pupils and discover their positive attributes. This way, whilst still keeping their sights on reality, teachers can find a continual source of renewal of inspiration within themselves and within their students.

Perhaps the most valuable asset of all that a teacher has is self-esteem: one that is most hard to maintain in the face of hostile propaganda and unsupportive authority figures. Hang on to it, however, and as a teacher you will find that in the end it is all that matters. The young will always have something to learn from the old, and they will learn most from those whom they respect. All adolescents are looking for a secure world in which they can rely on adults who know where they are. If they do not find teachers to be such adults they will look elsewhere for their models and will reject what schools have to offer.

It is my belief that teachers under-estimate themselves. This is not surprising because nearly everyone else under-estimates them, especially those who have no connection with the profession. So often the real reason for failure is that the teachers undervalue themselves, forget that they know far more than the pupils in front of them, forget that their knowledge could be as exciting and interesting to their pupils as it once was to themselves and forget that the young, too, are human and happy to be given something – even knowledge – so long as it is given in a friendly spirit. Most of all these teachers, who take the dangerous road of thinking of their classes as enemies, fail to see the support that is sitting there in front of them. They do not recognise that they have in most schools at least 50 per cent of pupils who are longing for them to succeed. I refer of course to the girls. This is not to say that boys too do not want successful teachers, but girls in our society, if not in every society, are well embedded in the role of helper. Unlike boys they are positively encouraged to show their nurturing side, their sensitivity and the dependence on others that comes from caring about them. There are of course a great many boys too who develop these characteristics, but unlike girls they often do so in defiance of society's demands rather than in response to them. Girls are allowed to care.

Given sufficient encouragement and a very moderate degree of security and affection, it has been found that even the most destructive girl is happier in a protective role. All girls do not, of course, have sufficient of the necessary good experiences of life to make them concerned for others. Sometimes it is possible for a school to make good this omission by giving special attention and filling in the gaps. By far the greater number of girls in our schools, however, are not in need of any very special treatment. They simply need teachers who have the sense to tap their goodwill.

The evidence that there is goodwill there to tap is available for those who choose to look for it. That it is sometimes heavily disguised cannot be denied. Teachers, therefore, must learn to see beyond the disguises. Most commonly indifference is used as a cloak for all other feelings. Only when it is recognised why this mask has to be worn will it be possible for an adult to get through to any other feelings. It is important for teachers to get through to a girl's feelings, for their own sake, as well as for that of the girl. For the girl the concern of the teacher is important because on this concern may rest her power to learn. Most girls need human beings to respond to them so that they in return can respond at a human and caring level, and most girls in school are dependent on their teachers at a level far beyond what the average teacher imagines. I do not suggest that teachers should concern themselves with the feelings of their pupils at the expense of the subject being taught. On the contrary, although an interest in pupils as people can itself revitalise the subject for the teacher, without a solid content no teaching can be successful.

Any lasting effects of education, however, must have its roots in real interest on the part of the student. There are some who will be interested in a subject however it is taught. They will succeed in spite of bad teaching. There are others who will become interested because of the enthusiasm of the teacher, sometimes in spite of that teacher's total lack of interest in his pupils as people. A real passion for a subject can be infectious, and there are undoubtedly a few teachers who possess this passion but who lack the ability to understand their pupils. They make a relationship in spite of themselves because the momentum of their enthusiasm carries their pupils on with them. These teachers are few; there are far more who are interested only in their subject and unaware of the total lack of interest on the part of their cowed and angry pupils. Others are interested in their subject and their pupils and find it hard to communicate their interest.

For the vast majority of girls there is no doubt that most learning takes place when there is a good relationship between the teacher and the taught. Great teachers have enthusiastic pupils whatever they teach, but ordinary, good, concerned people who make no claim to greatness can do far more than they realise. They can engender enough enthusiasm in even the most unpromising pupil if they enjoy their own subject and can make a satisfactory relationship with those whom they teach. Anyone who doubts the importance of teachers to their girl pupils should consider the following comments made by girls in the fifth and sixth forms in a wide variety of schools from all parts of the country:

> If I get on with a teacher I usually get on well with the subject: the opposite is true too. (a 17-year-old)

> A teacher should be understanding, easy to talk to, treat you like a human being, and some of them don't; [they should] take an interest in *you* as well as your work. (ditto)

They were not alone in their viewpoints. The vast majority of girls in discussion and in answer to a questionnaire revealed that they were influenced by their teachers' attitude towards them to a degree far beyond what teachers usually imagine to be the case. Nearly two-thirds of them, for example, said that the motivating factor in selecting a subject as a 'favourite' was at least in part 'the teacher who taught it'. A surprising 15 per cent said they made their choice solely because of the teacher and had had no prior interest in the subject: 'It was just magic. The whole attitude towards it made me love music.' This was from a 17-year-old girl who had shown no prior interest in the subject.

The same girl gave a good example of what happens when a pupil feels let down by a teacher. She talked about her love of English derived from home where 'the house was filled with books', and her first secondary school where she had been encouraged to write. At her second school she had 'a terrible teacher who took all joy out of it. I went home and read', she said. But she didn't take English as an exam subject in the sixth form, although she was planning to be a junior school teacher and would have liked to have done so. 'It would have been awful', she said. 'You can't enjoy a subject unless the teacher's OK' was a typical comment from a 17-year-old in the sixth form; 'The personality of a teacher matters and makes it more interesting'; 'An interesting subject with a boring teacher can turn you off the subject'; 'Mutual respect on both sides is essential', from an 18-year-old; 'They should have time to be interested in you', from a 15-year-old. One girl who was not in any way influenced by her teachers in choice of favourite subject nevertheless said that 'an ability of the teacher to *talk* to the pupils about outside subjects which may be of importance' was the quality she most valued. 'You begin to feel you matter then'.

'Teachers should recognise you as a human being', said a 15-year-old; asked to enlarge, she said: 'Although this is a friendly school – you don't shake when you meet the Headmaster – I don't think they know me here – I don't think anyone cares much who *I* am.' She was about to leave school and felt she had been approved of in that 'No one has disapproved', but felt that she 'hadn't really begun; it's all so impersonal, perhaps if I go to work they'll get to know me more but they should do so at school'. Her complaint seemed to rest on the fact that no one communicated with her directly. 'It all goes on behind your back and you're just a pawn to take exams.' She was a bright 15-year-old going on to sixth form college but her expectations of enjoying it were not high. 'I expect it'll just be a bit like school. I'll be a nonentity again.' She was no nonentity but, like many others, felt unrecognised and undervalued.

So as to assess the measure to which girls generally felt they were valued by the school they were attending, or had just left, we asked the question 'Do you think that at school you were approved of, disapproved of, or just accepted?' Here are some of the answers from the girls who did not think that they were approved of:

No way of knowing . . . Five years is a long time to be in a school and feel that they don't know much about you. (16-year-old just left high school)

I don't think they really noticed . . . They noticed if I didn't do my essays and when I was successful in sport . . . They didn't see me. (18-year-old now at university)

I would have liked more communication between pupils and teachers. Staff didn't seem concerned at all. (17-year-old just left comprehensive school)

I don't know. Good ones go unnoticed. But at the end of five years it's a bit of a let down to think they might not approve. (bright 15-year-old leaving comprehensive school to go to sixth form college)

I don't think they noticed me. Perhaps because I'm shy. (16-year-old about to leave comprehensive school)

As I was unmusical and not sporty I wasn't ideal. It would have been nice to be approved. (18-year-old now at university)

A successful person is someone who doesn't get in the teacher's way. (15-year-old in first year sixth of a comprehensive)

Apart from these replies, large numbers of those who felt accepted reiterated the same theme: 'I would have got so much more out of school if I'd been able to talk to someone.' 'It would have been nice to have an adult around who could really listen.' 'I don't think the teachers really know what you're about. They're not like us so they don't care what we think' (from an intelligent 16-year-old who was leaving school against her parents' wishes because 'There's nothing for me here').

None of the girls quoted above made a blanket condemnation of her school. They were not grumblers. But to 'go through all those years' and not at the end to know if anyone even noticed you would give most people a feeling of painful insignificance. Certainly that girl had little encouragement to value herself. There was no pastoral system in her school and no one whose job it was to notice her: 'only a class teacher but she doesn't hold tutorials. We suffer the lack of it. I like the idea of a tutor for about six pupils so that we could discuss academic and personal problems.'

Some teachers inevitably would consider that the fact that there are girls who feel unnoticed is no concern of theirs. Some girls do not want to be noticed: 'I have no idea what the staff feel about me and it doesn't worry me. I get on with most of my fellow students.' This was a 15-year-old in a comprehensive school. She was actually the only one of a sample of around 200 to state categorically that she did not care what people thought, but that does not invalidate her viewpoint.

Education is after all about learning and we might well ask whether the oversensitive egocentricity of teenage girls should be taken so seriously? Perhaps they are asking too much of their teachers if they expect approval. But it is not really approval that they are asking for, it is mostly just recognition of their existence. One girl stated categorically that she was not expecting approval from the staff. She particularly valued the honesty of one teacher who 'keeps me up to mark by never overpraising. It makes me feel that my work's worthwhile.'

It is always as well to err on the side of over-estimating the amount that girls in their teens depend for the security and self-picture on the views expressed by their teachers, just because their dependence can be so much greater than any teachers realise. One highly intelligent 19-year-old at university still could not forgive her teachers for their apparent indifference to her as a person: 'All those women, they'll just be going on teaching now and not thinking how important they were to me. They won't remember I existed.' As she had attended a relatively small private school it is highly improbable that she had gone unnoticed. For her, however, still in the throes of the struggle to establish her own identity, it seemed as though she had been rejected because she had not been overtly recognised. She was an insecure girl whose work was not up to standard because of her anxieties. She needed more attention than she had previously received to help her to stabilise. She had wasted time at school trying unsuccessfully to cope with her depression, but at university, with some help and attention, she was at last able to catch up.

Many a busy teacher trying to get through an examination syllabus with classes of thirty or more and acres of paper to mark will find these unrealistic demands irritating. The irritation is best tackled by acceptance. These demands are not unrealistic for those who make them. The young do feel overwhelmed by their needs for adult support. If we can accept that they begin to seem less tiresome.

Of course, every one of everybody's feelings cannot be responded to all the time. It is indeed reasonable for teachers to question whether girls who are asking for so much recognition are not just too dependent. In some cases undoubtedly they are, but this overdependence itself is something that has to be reckoned with. In most cases they are simply expressing the normal insecurity that characterises their age-group, which is often greater than was the case a few years earlier. In their younger years they found security in making use of the adult world for their own ends. Teachers, like parents, were still fairly remote powerful figures and their approval was more or less taken for granted. Only the very deprived child lacks the protection of this fantasy that the world is a safe and accepting place, full of adults who can be relied upon. Most young children assume that they are approved of and rarely actually speculate on the matter.

Adolescents, on the other hand, speculate a good deal of the time on whether or not they are being appreciated, not, of course, just by adults, but by anyone they meet or even indeed just pass by in the street. Shop windows seem specially designed to reassure them that they look all right, and boy- and girlfriends are necessary to confirm that they are personally acceptable.

What teachers need to understand and appreciate is that in the early and middle teens the opinions of adults are of absorbing importance. Some adults believe that in adolescence only one's own age-group is listened to and respected. This shows a great misunderstanding of the nature of adolescence. Certainly friends are important, but the family and the school are more so. Dependence on friendship takes over completely only when family and school, that is, adult, support has broken down. The fact that adolescents often make life difficult for adults does not in any way detract from the truth of this. Most of their bad behaviour stems from feelings over which they have not yet learned to gain full control. This is due in part to the nature of youth in general and in part to their own nature in particular. That the young have always been frivolous and troublesome is axiomatic. Every burst of indignation at the behaviour of the younger generation is matched with reminders of the diatribes against the young of Athens or the apprentices of mediaeval England. As the youth of Oxford in the first Elizabeth's day, according to the Earl of Leicester, made it impossible for the old to 'carry a winepot through the streets' with safety, so the pupils of the second Elizabeth's day make it pretty hard for the old to carry themselves through the corridors of a school with safety. Where we hope to find a difference is in the attitudes of the adults concerned. The Earl of Leicester is reported by Milton Waldman to have written stern notes warning the academics to look to the behaviour of the undergraduates, many of whom were not much older than our present-day schoolchildren. The academics responded with punitive measures that would shock our most rigid disciplinarians. Teachers today receive similar warnings from the press, television and politicians. Some still respond punitively, not apparently having learnt the 400-year-old lesson that this does not work too well. Others respond, to their own advantage, by looking for the best in their pupils and encouraging it to grow.

The least satisfying of reactions is the one in which a teacher simply provides information and leaves it to the recipients to do what they like with it. There will soon be few recipients left. It is possible to see your pupils as exam-passing machines whose role in your life is to enhance your career through their successes in the subjects which you teach. Fortunately there have always been teachers who have believed that their responsibility goes farther, who have believed in developing the creative abilities of their students. Of recent years these teachers have been encouraged, and we see the results in magnificent feats of inventiveness and discovery by children of all ages.

Despite all the criticism directed at the teaching profession, a perennial target for the disaffected, there have been, in fact, marvellous advances in education. They show themselves not only in a general improvement in literacy, but in particular instances of scientific invention and artistic production. Children design and make telescopes, write and produce plays, sing, dance and play musical instruments at a level unattainable by their parents. They read copiously, borrowing more books than ever before in the history of public libraries. They write poetry and prose, paint and sculpt, often superbly and nearly always with freshness and unself-conscious enjoyment.

All this comes from the skill of the teachers in fostering the innate abilities of their pupils. Where then does it go? Why in so many of our young is it dissipated? And why, in particular, do so few girls maintain this creative attitude to learning? If we attribute the success of children in school to good teaching, and we are entitled to do so, we must look also at the failures in terms of teaching failure.

We must therefore continually examine the kind of environment that we provide for girls in their adolescence and the kind of response that we make to them as teachers. We must question whether we give them all that is needed or whether, with the best of intentions, we succumb to pressure and stifle their intuitive selves in our attempts to make them conform to the requirements of our system. We avoid such pitfalls when we are prepared to give at least a sympathetic hearing to those who find difficulty in conforming, before we condemn them completely, and a high proportion of adolescents will be non-conformists for at least part of their school lives. If we accept this reality we will not find it too difficult to maintain a reasonable level of discipline.

Chapter 8

Classroom Control and the Difficult Girl

Sophie was a classic discipline problem; she wasted not only her own time but that of her teachers and most of the children in her class as well. She was an attractive, lively girl so her influence was quite considerable. She was not lacking in intelligence but was totally without commitment to work. Since she had arrived in her comprehensive school three years ago, she had shown little interest in study, hardly any ability to concentrate and absolutely no intention of doing anything that anyone else told her to do.

Her problem was solidly founded in excessive parental indulgence. Since she had been born, a beautiful blue-eyed blonde, as her mother fondly described her, every wish had been granted, indeed anticipated. She had swanned her way through her primary school, smiling winningly, and when necessary bribing her friends to do her will with lavish presents.

As she reached adolescence, however, the lighthearted scatterbrained behaviour that had seemed part of her charm in her childhood was beginning to look a little desperate. Sophie found herself like many another over-indulged child, pushing the boat out farther and farther, making more and more demands, in an unconscious effort to discover where the boundaries were: who was going to stop her? The feeling that you have the power to do anything that you want, whilst at a conscious level attractive, can at a less conscious level produce anxiety. Sophie had always had unlimited material possessions and, being an only child, had always been able to command attention when she felt she needed it. There was no malice in her, simply an obdurate determination to get her own way. The first really powerful resistance to her charms which she encountered was in her secondary school where a teacher's insistence that she do as she was told completely took her by surprise. She decided to have a screaming fit rather than obey and was eventually hauled out of class by a distraught head of year.

Her screaming did not end there, she continued it when she got home and an irate mother was on the doorstep when the headmistress arrived next morning. Throughout the following three years this head was to have many a further interview with Sophie's mother, whilst just about every teacher in the school found, at one time or another, a battlefield being created in or out of the classroom by Sophie.

The visits from Sophie's mother quickly changed from tirades against the school to desperate pleas for help. She was now beginning, rather late in Sophie's life, to see something of the error of her ways. Whilst Sophie's demands had been for the normal delights of childhood it had been easy enough to pander to her every whim. Now, however, as she rushed headlong into a turbulent adolescence, a different Sophie was emerging. Her current demands included the right to stay out all night, to bring her boyfriends in at midnight for drinks, even to drive her father's car and already, at the age of 13, to go on the pill. Her father, who lived in a world of greyhound racing and working men's clubs, was inclined to treat his daughter as though she were the 18-year-old that she could easily make herself look like. He would take her to clubs and buy her drinks with total indifference to the law. Her mother, a more level-headed person as a rule, had taken fright at Sophie's sexual proclivities and made desperate efforts to retrieve the situation by a complete reversal of policy. She tried clamping down on her freedom and forbidding her to go anywhere. Sophie, already a deeply insecure child under her ebullient exterior, acquiesced at first, behaving meekly and submissively at home, only to vent her fury on anyone around when she got to school. Alternately she would defy her mother and come to school as smiling and exuberant as ever.

Meanwhile Sophie found her way to the school counsellor. Here she thought at first that she had discovered a home from home: some one who would make her the centre of attention once again. It was not long before she was disillusioned, discovering that it was by no means possible to choose to visit the counsellor whenever it suited her to miss a class, nor to hoodwink him into believing that all her bad behaviour was a response to other people's cruelty. In time, with the counsellor's help, she began to learn to recognise something of the insecurity that she had always experienced as a result of not knowing where the boundaries to her behaviour lay.

As she emerged from the first bouts of rebellion she made genuine efforts to change, but she found herself constantly on shifting sands, not knowing what to expect from her parents. Her father, when in a good mood, continued to over-indulge her; when, however, he saw how far Sophie was prepared to go, he would suddenly become enraged. Her mother made a consistent effort to be firm, but went to extremes. She forbade her to go out, to invite her friends in, even to take part in a drama club on Saturday mornings. She met her at the school gate whenever she could and organised weekend trips which prevented Sophie from making any life of her own.

Naturally enough Sophie rebelled at this, and her mother would then relent for a while so as to establish some peace in the house. What Sophie needed was a framework for her behaviour but not a strait-jacket. Unfortunately the framework that the adults in her life were providing was either so shaky that it gave no support at all, or so rigid that no self-respecting adolescent could accept it. She needed the security of knowing what was expected of her as much as she needed to experiment with life. But when she found adults, like her teachers, who told her in no uncertain terms what was expected, she could not accept their rules; yet she needed rules more than anything else.

To appreciate that, whatever their protest, adolescents, like younger children, still need adults to tell them with conviction what they are expected to do, we have to remember that the insecurity of not knowing where they stand is more than most adults can bear. Freedom poses a painful threat. A good many people who have reached middle age recently are still floundering just because the rules have been changed so much and so suddenly. How much harder then for an adolescent, with so little experience on which to base judgement, to know what to do in a world without clear direction! How much more difficult for a young child. Sophie had had so little direction in her early life that now, with the best intentions, she could not find her own way; and despite all her nuisance value, her intentions were by no means all bad. She needed, as do so many adolescents, something fixed and certain in her life but something that related to her own particular circumstances: rigidity was not the answer. Unfortunately, as her behaviour got worse she found that at school, as well as at home, she was the subject of other people's whims.

The school, an inner city one, had so many problem children that many teachers took the easiest way out and ignored, as far as possible, bad behaviour. Some, however, ruled with iron rigidity and simply excluded the Sophies from their classes. What Sophie and most of the other difficult children needed was neither of these approaches but a clear and consistent pattern of discipline that they could understand and learn to respect.

Of course, this is as difficult for teachers as it is for parents because there are so few absolutes now. To ask people to be both flexible and firm can sound like nonsense to a distraught parent faced with an enraged daughter or a desperate teacher faced with a class full of recalcitrant young girls. Flexibility is only possible for people who are feeling secure themselves. This means that adults who want to give the young in their charge a reasonable degree of freedom can only do so when they know what they themselves can tolerate. It is a sound axiom for a newly qualified teacher to recognise the difficulties that can be caused by being too lax; and it is always important to feel in charge. Young men sometimes have advantages, especially when dealing with the Sophies, in their powerful voices, greater physical strength and the charm of their masculinity; although simply to overpower is not enough – to appear serene and calm is essential. Serenity comes from knowing the score.

Volumes have been written about classroom management, a popular area of research, but teachers very often find that, faced with a Sophie, the more complex techniques desert them. It is not unfortunately always possible, for example, to obey the golden rule of ignoring the trouble-maker because she gets her rewards through attracting your notice. The rest of the class, after all, do not ignore her. They are actually more likely to pay attention to her than to the teacher. A headmaster once complained to me that the advice from a psychologist, asked how to deal in school with a boy he had in treatment, was 'Just treat him like everybody else'. 'How', asked this headmaster reasonably, 'do you treat someone like everybody else when he's hanging from the picture rail and everybody else is in his desk watching him?'

The principle of not rewarding attention-seekers by giving them too much attention is a sound one for everyday practice but it is not enough. The need to be an attention-seeker must eventually be met because it stems from some unsatisfied urge. The level of attention-seeking escalates at first when it is not met and only sometimes diminishes; when it does not diminish there is likely to be serious trouble. Sophie's teachers had ignored her behaviour at first from astonishment rather than strategy; they had just never met a child like her. By the time she was lying on the floor drumming her heels the one teacher who had stood up to her was also baffled. This stage could perhaps have been pre-empted if a concerted effort had been made earlier.

For a start, a school should always be prepared for a Sophie. Too often teachers expect children to behave as they themselves behaved when they were at school – totally differently from Sophie. Mostly they were good, law-abiding, hard-working pupils. Even those of us who were nothing of the sort were successful and intellectually able. It is important for teachers to remember all the time that the vast majority of pupils are quite different in their interests, their intellects, their experience of life and their expectations of school from their teachers. It is always hard for teachers to remember, for example, that by definition they are of above-average intelligence and that most of their pupils are not. These pupils will therefore find it less easy to learn and less rewarding to do so than their teachers did. It is equally hard for some teachers to realise that this fact is only of minor importance to many of their pupils, whose expectations of success in learning are realistically limited. If teachers can adapt their thinking to encompass the really different approach to life that a Sophie has, they will be less shocked by her behaviour and therefore less likely to feel her to be a threat. A teacher who is not threatened is more likely to have a relaxed and responsive class. Sophies behave better in such classes.

If you want to enjoy your work, begin each class by creating a pleasant atmosphere; this way you are already halfway to establishing peace and order. Forget about Sophie, think of the other nice girls and how friendly they are likely to be. Beam around at everyone without catching any particular eyes and say the equivalent of 'Nice to see you all'. Try to mean it and you'll find that very often you can. Tell them, briefly, what you are going to do as though you really recognised that you were about to give them a valuable experience: that of learning something new and interesting. This will nudge you into making sure that you really will teach them something new and that it really will be interesting. (If you can't guarantee that, what are you teaching them it for?) Above all make it sound possible for them to achieve what they are aiming at.

For any group of 14-year-olds or younger, especially for the duller ones, a promise of a reward for good work at a given interval works wonders, 'Concentrate for twenty minutes' (the outside time limit for many a 13-year-old) 'and then we'll stop for five minutes, and . . . listen to an interesting tape-recording; watch a snatch of film; see some slides; hear a story told by one of the pupils or the teacher; play with computers; have a quiz'; and so on. Only the highly intelligent, dedicated pupil in the early teens concentrates unrewarded for long on the more tedious tasks. The less tedious work is rewarding in itself and needs no carrots.

Reinforcement of good behaviour rather than bad is an excellent maxim, easier to carry out in a primary than a secondary school. Adolescent girls will not respond to Smarties as a reward for behaving in an acceptable manner. The Sophies have had a surfeit of those anyhow. Teacher attention as a reward is likely to be more successful. But praise for the Prodigal Son or Daughter for at last doing what the rest of the class has been doing all the time has to be tempered with recognition of the need for praise that everyone has. So find time for a lot of praise all round a lot of the time.

Avoiding head-on collisions is a difficult but not impossible task. A clear picture in the teacher's mind of what level of order and conformity is really essential helps to keep the atmosphere relaxed. Young teachers often aim at a too-controlled class in their fear of complete chaos, just as often as they go in for the dreaded permissiveness. Once the level has been established in the teacher's mind, then the start of any deviation from it can be noted immediately and if possible nipped in the bud. This is better done by quiet words in the ear and a request for a meeting after the class than by a loud reprimand. If you try to retain a respectful attitude to pupils, even the badly behaved, you can demand one back, and if you do not demand an impossibly high standard from them you will usually reach a possible one. If you show, and demand, no respect, of course you will get none. On the other hand, for their sense of security and your own, you have to be very fierce indeed if they once overstep the mark that you have decided upon as reasonable; you must make sure first, however, that they have understood it and accepted its reasonableness. This is when, and only when, employing sanctions, sending out of the room or raising the voice is justified. It should be a rare and startling experience for your pupils when you go to these lengths; its rarity value will impress on them the seriousness of your rules and enable them to respect them.

If a confrontation is inevitable, try to arrange for it to happen after the class, not during it; then recognise that a badly behaved child feels badly done by whatever the realities. A teacher can dissipate this feeling by not attacking but inviting the pupil to state her grievances: 'What is it? Something must be wrong for you to feel like this,' and stating the teacher's position reasonably, without passion. 'We're both here to do a job. Do let's get on with it then we can have a nicer time.' Avoid threats; make a positive appeal. Sanctions, however, rather than threats should be clearly understood by the whole class and should always be applied when rules are broken. If they can be applied with regret rather than rancour, but never with hesitation, they have more chance of being accepted and perhaps taking effect.

Teachers should see the battles with these children not as fights to keep their own ends up but as a necessary process as a preliminary to helping the children to learn. This way they will not put themselves into uncompromising positions from which there is no escape; they will not, for example, demand immediate total compliance but will leave the dissident pupil time to simmer down, do things at her own pace and not lose too much face. So long as it is clear to everyone why a teacher is behaving the way he does, there is little room for argument; the teacher's behaviour needs always to be based on a true commitment to the task of teaching and a true concern for those taught. Such behaviour does not require dogmatic attitudes or fear of losing: there is nothing to lose if you are not trying to win, only to help.

One Sophie of my acquaintance declared one day to our astonishment that she would like to be a teacher. She had met a teacher who had cheerfully admitted that she was in the wrong on some relatively minor matter. This Sophie was overcome with gratitude and relief; she wanted immediately to identify with this paragon of maturity who knew her own limitations and was not worried by them. Most teachers could easily become such paragons.

Ultimately to succeed in establishing a successful relationship with the pupils, teachers, all teachers but particularly new ones, need support from other teachers, especially when they have a difficult pupil to deal with. There are far too many schools where young teachers are intimidated by older and more experienced members of staff and by the fear of bad reports so that they dare not admit to having trouble with a class. This is contagious; a staffroom in which one teacher, feeling that it is taboo to mention discipline problems, pretends that all is well when it clearly is not, soon becomes one in which everyone has this anxiety.

Such problems are much more easily solved if they are brought out into the open.

On those occasions when it is only a teacher's behaviour that is responsible for the lack of discipline, other teachers, instead of condemning, will in a well-run school give help. It is the senior staff who have to set this pattern of supporting instead of discouraging the less efficient, and usually less experienced members. If younger teachers can be humble enough to ask for this help they will generally get it. Sophies cause everyone bother but the most skilled teachers can find ways of mitigating that bother. In the right atmosphere in a staffroom they will share these skills rather than simply stay silent and secretly contemptuous of those who lack them.

It is up to the young teachers, however, to have the courage to insist on being helped. They are no longer in college needing, perhaps, to impress a tutor rather than admit to failures that they imagine might reduce their final teaching grade; they are out there responsible to the children they teach, and this includes the responsibility of not letting Sophie prevent others from learning. If everyone who teaches Sophie and finds her a bore gets together for even five minutes to discuss her, an amazing amount of work can be done by the more experienced staff in working out a scheme which can be followed by everyone, and which can therefore be more likely to succeed.

Teachers are always more powerful than their pupils if they can learn not to be afraid of them. The most useful lesson that older staff can teach younger is that there is no need to be afraid of most pupils because most people really do want to please and to be pleased; even the Sophies do. Teachers who are not afraid can be firm without arousing antagonism because they can make the majority feel secure; once this happens they will find that majority on their side. So long as they remember their duty as teachers to make learning possible for everyone, the slow as well as the quick, and this means making it interesting, they will always have the majority on their side and the majority will soon be bored by Sophie.

Chapter 9

The Bully and the Bullied

'Head Cracks Down on Bully Girls' runs a headline in a daily paper; below it is a dramatic account of girls running a protection racket and, reputedly, causing terror in their comprehensive school. Beside this piece of news, and taking up twice the space of the newsprint, is a picture of a girl's legs, thigh high, accompanied by the caption 'What are these legs trying to tell you?'. Over the page we are left in no doubt about what the almost-naked model clutching her fur toy is trying to tell us: and we are promised another Glamour Kitten on the same page tomorrow.

Newspapers are in the business of making money. No doubt journalists are so accustomed to the treatment of women as passive sexual objects that they are quite unaware that they themselves contribute to the making of bully girls: or perhaps they are not unaware, merely uncaring.

There are still women who are not insulted by being used simply as things for satisfying male sexual desires. Girls themselves choose, one must presume, to expose their genitals and wave their bottoms to form part of the daily newspaper fare, but these are in a minority. Most young girls arrive at their teens still protective and sensitive about their own bodies; few of them fail to react with shock at their first exposure to the blatant pornography that is prevalent nowadays in parts of our press.

A young girl cannot conceptualise, let alone articulate, such complex ideas as that contempt for women underlies this journalism, but she can feel intuitively that she is attacked by it. A sufficiency of propaganda unfortunately will soon habituate her, and she will begin to take it all as a matter of course. Sensitivities are not difficult to bludgeon into insensibility; but the damage that is done through this bludgeoning remains for a lifetime. Accustomed throughout much of their lives to seeing themselves as subservient in relation to men, and often brought up by mothers who apparently accepted this role, we find in many girls ground already well tilled for the seeds of sexual exploitation. Nevertheless, the experience of the insult is still there, though mostly it becomes deeply buried.

There are two standard reactions to insults which are felt but not admitted to: one is a denial that the insult happened; the other is rage. The denial can show itself in a passive, depressed acceptance of things as they are: the commonplace withdrawal from commitment and descent into triviality which characterises so much of the behaviour of the less articulate adolescent girl: or it can be manifested in the noisy insistence that they enjoy things as they are that characterises some of the girls who choose to make their living from exposing their sexuality in public. There are now, however, increasing numbers of young girls whose resentment at the treatment that they receive from life, as girls, is beginning to show itself in overt although inarticulate rage.

Violent behaviour has become so much part of our everyday life that we hardly pay it conscious attention when it involves men; we still manage to be frightened, however, when girls are the perpetrators. Yet young girls are exposed to violence in the same way as boys are, in the press and on television. They are also exposed to that violence that is reserved exclusively for girls, the violent assaults on their inner sexual being by a society that is prepared to denigrate femininity for the sake of titillation. This kind of violence is in itself bullying.

Bullying is notoriously the province of those who feel themselves to be despised and persecuted. Most bullies have themselves been bullied. If they feel bullied in an atmosphere which encourages the expression of violent feelings by violent acts they will bully in this way, and this is the atmosphere in which many young girls live. No longer is it sufficient to shout insults; shouts must now be accompanied by blows. The feeling of being despised increases as the sense of personal inadequacy grows, and the anger grows in proportion.

The girls who run protection rackets and pull out one another's hair in chunks might not claim that they are persecuted; nevertheless they feel it. They respond to the climate of the times. And that, today, means fighting back when you are made to feel inferior, and for the most part fighting with no holds barred.

We live in a bullying society. Unions and bosses bully one another. Police and villains do likewise, and in doing so contribute the story-lines of some of the most popular television series. Education systems bully children who fail by constantly reminding them of the competitive nature of their world, by grading and by failing them; in competition only a few can win, the majority lose. Some teachers even bully those children who irritate them or remind them of their own failures. Any use of superiority, be it of physical or intellectual strength, to cow another into submission is bullying.

Adults, in particular teachers, get driven into bullying the young just because they themselves feel bullied. They are bullied by a system that depersonalises them. Teachers coping daily with large groups of people who cannot be responded to personally as individuals and complete human beings always run the risk of becoming bullies just so as to survive. The lack of individual personal communication makes so often for a failure to experience others as persons, the perfect climate for bullying.

Totalitarian states based on a philosophy of bullying begin by deper-sonalising their citizens; they are characterised by massive rallies and huge state-dominated youth organisations. All such states manage to produce vast numbers of bullies as well as the well-behaved subservient citizens who accept being ruled by a firm hand, and who too often condone the disciplining of such dissidents as want to alter the smooth-running system. Schools can unintentionally do the same. If individual teachers are not constantly alert to the dangers of developing a bullying society, for the sake of peace and quiet, they can condone a system which of its nature can breed bullies.

Schools do not on their own create bullies; they can nevertheless encourage them. If we look into the lives of most school bullies we will find two dominant factors, intellectual failure and a disrupted and frequently violent home. Professor L. F. Lowenstein, in a recent study of over 5,000 schoolchildren considered to be bullies by their teachers and by other children, found that a highly significant number of these bullies showed similar characteristics. They had parents with relationship problems, and they had homes which lacked values and standards, such as respect and consideration for others; as a corollory to this they were disruptive and unsuccessful in school. They showed, in fact, a pattern characteristic of those we call delinquent.

Perhaps the most worrying bullying of all is that done by young children to their immature parents who have inadequate ideas about the needs of the young. Even very young babies can bully mothers who are not strong enough in their convictions about what they are doing. These mothers respond with the kind of emotional neglect that passes for permissiveness but is really a cover for insecurity, and is felt as indiffer-ence. The freedom that is given to such young girls and boys alike to express all their rages and show no concern for others creates bullies. We see these in increasing numbers in nurseries and infant schools as well as in secondary schools.

When girls reach their secondary schools, therefore, a small but significant minority of them will have already had a sizeable career as bullies. Not only will such girls have spent their young lives in a world which demands that they accept the subservient sexual role: they will also have spent a disproportionate percentage of time either taking part in bullying of one sort or another, or at least watching it in their own homes, between their parents or on television. So many aspects of their lives will have gone towards increasing their bullying tendencies that the task of reforming them is a formidable one.

Mandy was such a girl, the kind who, though still only a fraction of the school population as a whole, makes more impact than a hundred ordinary good students. Like the bully-girls who reached the headlines, she terrorised younger children. Mandy was nearly 6 feet tall and she dressed and acted so much like a boy that she was often mistaken for one. She went to football matches so that she could enjoy the fights and there she terrorised those smaller than herself. She saw herself, and invited everyone else to see her, as one of the boys. She was especially aggressive to women members of staff whom she would threaten with assault if they crossed her in any way, and she upset many of them by her swearing. Anything that sounded remotely like criticism could cause her to explode into foul language and temper. Even the teachers whom she did not abuse found her disruptive and unco-operative and apparently indifferent to them.

Mandy's suicide attempt surprised her form tutor. Perhaps this was all that it was intended to do; it was not too serious, in that having taken a lot of aspirin she told a friend what she had done. It came after she had been excluded from her youth club for two weeks. The youth leader was an important person in Mandy's life because he was in a position to accept her for what she was; he did his best not to criticise or try to coerce her. He had tolerated a lot of difficult behaviour, being able to relate it to its source in Mandy's unhappy life, and as a result had won her affection. But in the end she pushed him too far by stealing from the club's funds.

Mandy came to trust the youth leader because he was not disturbed by her language or frightened by her threats. She was able to reveal to him a side of her character little in evidence in the classroom. He knew that she came from a home filled with violence and depression. Her father, who had made it quite clear to her that he had never wanted a daughter, had been reported to the NSPCC because of his attacks on her. He subsequently left home, and from the age of 13 Mandy lived alone with her mother. This was no great improvement because although the attention she had had from her father was usually brutal it was at least sufficient to indicate to her that he was aware of her existence. Her mother paid her no attention at all. She was a woman whose only defence against her deep depression was heavy drinking. She neglected Mandy totally, staying out late at night, sometimes all night, and often not seeing her for six or seven days on end. Mandy was left to fend for herself which she did, inevitably, inadequately.

Mandy's reaction to such a life was, not surprisingly, bitter. She resented both her father and her mother: her father for his brutality to herself and to her mother, and her mother for allowing it to happen without putting up any resistance. She resented most of all his justification of his brutality on the grounds that females were inferior beings. He made Mandy conscious of her lack of obvious feminine charms by constantly harping on her height, yet at the same time he depicted all things female as contemptible. Mandy, seeing what feminine submissiveness had done for her mother, was not attracted to that role, so she took an opposite one. Nevertheless, she still longed to establish herself in her father's eyes as the sort of girl whom he could admire; like most girls, she needed her father's approval however much she disapproved of him. Her inability to be acceptably feminine was therefore an added bitterness. Unable to express all these conflicting feelings in her chaotic home, Mandy played out her anger in school against teachers and children.

She attacked women teachers and girls because they represented her mother and the self that she would have liked to be. In particular she attacked those girls who showed what she felt to be excessive femininity; she resented above all the Sex Kitten image of women. Her anger being two-fold, against aggressive men and passive women who allowed themselves to be demeaned, she took the two-fold course of brutality coupled with pseudo-masculinity.

All over England this is happening; indeed the increase in female violence is causing anxiety throughout the world. Girls who become terrorists, who help their boyfriends to mug and who themselves attack physically when thwarted, cause consternation everywhere. They also provide exciting headlines and maintain adult anxiety at a titillating fever pitch. They are declared to be more dangerous than delinquent boys.

Girls are no longer reacting to brutality with cowed acceptance. Battered wives are not a new phenomenon, but until recently they were at most treated as a joke. What Erin Pizzey uncovered was not unknown, it was just tacitly ignored. New-found courage has grown out of her bravery which has helped other women to stand up for themselves a little more. Mandy could not, however, stand up to her brute of a father; she could only take out her rage on people outside the family.

Like many other terrorised and therefore terrorising females, Mandy dealt with her misery in places where it was safer and more rewarding to do so than at home where it originated. And also like many other terrorists, Mandy had more than one side to her character. The aggressive, fight-loving, excessively masculine picture which the school had of her was certainly valid, but there were others.

Despite the strong masculine character that she portrayed, Mandy was actually a frightened child. She was terrified of the prospect of leaving school. Far from feeling indifferent to her teachers, she felt totally dependent on them for virtually the only security and support that her life contained. Like so many aggressive adolescents, her attacks were attempts to find the limits of her own destructiveness, to see if the world could survive her anger; like the small child in the temper tantrum who goes on until a timely parental intervention, a smack in fact, relieves him of the responsibility of deciding when to stop. When we have been hurt ourselves we want to hurt others, but we want to stop hurting them too.

Unfortunately, none of the teachers in her school, other than the youth leader, had made much attempt to stop Mandy. Frightened by her aggression, most of them had simply excluded her from their classes and done little to look further into the causes of her behaviour. Those few who were too powerful for Mandy to attack kept her in submission and for this at least she was actually grateful.

What the youth leader knew that was positive about Mandy was that her aim in life was to work with handicapped children. This was a true ambition based not on fantasy but on reality. Whilst still at school she was already spending every Saturday morning and the whole of her holidays working in a local playgroup for the handicapped. She made an immediate intuitive response to handicapped people young and old; they in return loved her. Because of his knowledge of this side of her life, the youth leader was able to believe in Mandy. Because he knew the good as well as the bad he was able to see her as a damaged human being rather than as an ogre. He could therefore respond sympathetically towards her and she in her turn could begin to trust him. In time he was able to help her to stop bullying younger children.

It is always worthwhile for teachers to try to find out more about a student who is causing trouble, especially if they can find out more of the good things. A few bits of positive information about someone works wonders with our attitude towards her. The positive side to Mandy's character was in all probability as much an outcome of her tragic experience as was her negative side. People who have been damaged by life can make positive use of this damage if given a chance. They can see the need to be cared for, they can feel other people's damage and want to repair it, vicariously, as it were, repairing their own. This does not of course always happen; feelings have to be channelled in a constructive direction. Stalin's way of implementing his response to a tragic life experience was not one that would meet with universal approval; neither was all of Mandy's.

The correct response to Mandy was not to be overwhelmed by concern for her unhappiness but to bear it in mind when appropriate. Mandy needed the limits that teachers set on her behaviour, she needed to know that her bullying and aggression could not be tolerated. But she also needed to know that the people who set those limits cared about her as a person. It is the teachers' attitude rather than their actual method of discipline which ultimately affects how the pupils behave. This is why her youth tutor could help her.

Mandy could accept far more restraints and even punishments from him that she could from any of her other teachers because she knew that she could rely on him for tolerance and real concern. Under her rejecting aggressive exterior was a sensitive caring girl who needed adults to respond to her emotional handicaps in the way that she could respond to other people's physical handicaps. Because there were not enough people around who recognised the dependence under the

independence Mandy continued to act out her needs like a baby screaming for attention.

Mandy kept her caring side hidden because she felt that she needed
her own private life; she had a resistance to letting anyone know about
her kindness or her concern for other people, until she felt sure of their
concern for her. She was playing the tough role and she wanted no one
to question that this was the right role for her to play. She had been
presented with the choice between playing the bully girl of the
newspaper article and the sex kitten of its pictures; she opted for the
bully. Femininity, softness and slavery were all one in Mandy's eyes.
She had seen her mother beaten and she had been beaten herself by her
powerful, domineering and aggressive father. She was going to give no
one the opportunity of bullying her.

The role of helping, nurturing and showing concern for others, so
long taken to be the feminine prerogative, had turned sour in Mandy's
opinion. It fitted too closely to the sex kitten picture. She had to hide all
such tendencies from any but the very few adults who could be trusted;
in fact she was hardly able to admit to this even in herself.

She was not alone in this. Toughness in boys, not only accepted but
admired and positively encouraged, looks attractive to girls who are
tired of being asked to be submissive. Because this male toughness
implies a hiding of a gentler, more caring, feeling the Mandys feel
constrained to hide theirs too. In doing so they present to society an
exclusively aggressive front, giving no evidence of any kinder, more
gentle personalities.

Teachers faced with a good number of such girls can be forgiven for
finding it hard to believe that they have any attributes other than those
made explicit by their aggressive behaviour. Even those girls who only
assert themselves in perfectly legitimate ways are looked on with
suspicion; whilst those who behave like boys by being physically violent
are liable to strike terror into the hearts of adults. When girls take up
male delinquency roles and bring their behaviour into schools in the
form of bullying teachers cannot ignore it.

Delinquent behaviour as such amongst girls used to be a rarity;
Borstals were designed for boys. This picture is changing but it is as well
to remember that girls still account for only a small proportion of the
delinquency figures. Girls, despite their new-found belligerence,
remain on the whole far more conforming than boys. Those who do
break the law continue to cause more consternation than their male
counterparts because in doing so they shock society out of the
complacent stereotype of a gentle and compliant female population.

Although this is no longer applicable, to the younger generation at
any rate, there is still good reason for believing that girls on the whole
will obey and uphold the law most of the time given the least encouragement. When they do break it, apart from the few highly disturbed girls

who become completely out of control, they still tend not to be as openly defiant of society's rules as their brothers are. Where the boys set up the football fracas the girls, for the most part, will merely cheer them on, though the more extrovert like Mandy will join in if they can.

Delinquents on the whole, however, are not very progressive in their outlook and there is a tendency for these more aggressive males to be rigidly sexist. The girls are simply not allowed to take part, they may only encourage and support. Gangs and marauding groups make it quite clear that they see themselves as doing something specifically male. In the same way as those who take part in some of the current forms of dancing maintain that it's too strenuous for girls (they are not likely to have heard of Margot Fonteyn), so the exciting activities like taking and driving other people's cars and motorbikes, breaking up football matches and vandalising the district are essentially a male prerogative. Girls may throw a few bottles on to a pitch and do a bit of screaming and tearing out of one another's hair, but the real manly stuff that gets the police involved is still the boys' preserve.

As Mandy has shown, all girls do not accept this. Those girls who do try to carry their battles for the right to be as delinquent as boys into the male arena tend to find themselves up against the boys as much as against the police. They also tend to become so extreme in their behaviour that there seem to be no limits to what they will do. It is as though, having joined a new club, not having any traditions to fall back on, they have yet to devise satisfactory rules. Male delinquents usually have some form of gang law to which they subscribe, if only for self-protection. Girls who move into this area have to make up their own rules.

Few of the adults with whom such girls come into contact have thought seriously about why so many of them are behaving in this way. They have merely deplored it. The link between sexuality and aggression, well known amongst boys and responsible for the thousands of rapes that take place each year, are not recognised in girls.

The real problem is not that the girls are following in the boys' bad footsteps but that we are no longer providing them with a clear enough picture of what footsteps they should be following. We offer them few alternatives to accepting either the role of bait to the predatory male with all its concomitant sexual exhibitionism or that of belligerent, aggressive imitation male. We encourage sexual awareness by publicly discussing and displaying sexuality at every turn, then condemn it when we come across it in young girls.

The strange charge of being in moral danger, for example, which is apparently a crime judging by the treatment meted out to those deemed to be in such a state, is never to my knowledge made against an adolescent boy. I doubt if many boys of 14 or 15 have been whisked off to community homes because they have been found to be indulging in sexual practices, yet girls are still suffering this indignity in a world that hardly allows them to forget their sexuality from the moment that they are tall enough to see a television screen. The real moral dangers in which they live, those of being reduced to insensitive automata, of having their sensitivity to others crushed by the indifference of the world to their needs, of having their sexuality treated as a commercial property and their bodies presented to them as objects for the titillation of the lascivious, are condoned by an acquiescent public.

Morality apparently is, as in the words of a former South African Cabinet minister, 'like objectivity, in the eye of the beholder'. When we make so little effort to save young girls from this, can we be sure that we are entitled to say who are delinquents?

Schools can do little to alter the state of the outside world but they can do something to support those girls who have a genuine complaint against a society that shows so little sense of responsibility in its attitudes to girls. These girls cannot be blamed themselves for having had inadequate parents, for having been neglected or over-indulged, for having been exposed to an excess of television or to having been encouraged to be extrovert in a world that still demands submission from them. Nor can they be blamed for their dawning awakening to the fact that unless they resist the slavery of passive dependence that reduced so many of their mothers to drudges they will go the same way too.

It is not the assertiveness that the present generation of adolescent girls are showing that is the danger, it is the lack of knowledge about what to assert. If we gave them better standards to live by their new-found confidence could be a great boon to society. The girl who has a sound ethical foundation and can be assertive is a power for good. Those without such a foundation need to be helped to establish one by all the adults with whom they come into contact.

Teachers therefore will be well advised to examine their own beliefs about what a girl's behaviour should be like and temper them, where necessary, with reality. Certainly girls are bullying more, being more aggressive, more defiant, less compliant and less malleable. Boys have always been like this and society has managed to continue to function. Girls also, however, can retain a great deal of positive aspects of femininity even when hidden under a more aggressive exterior. These aspects can only be reached by teachers who feel secure in their acceptance of the more outgoing and aggressive type of girl who is emerging as a result of the changes in thinking about the female role. Anyone who still expects girls to behave as his grandmother did is on a losing wicket. If he is prepared to accept that they might occasionally behave as his grandfather did he will find that they actually only do so occasionally and that mainly to make a point.

The point they are making is as often as not that they are unhappy and feel unloved. They are aware of the great promise that the world is supposed to be offering to them and are equally aware that it is by no means coming their way. When in addition they feel that those who teach them have little sympathy or understanding of the protest that they are trying to make, they are likely to attempt to throw off femininity altogether and in doing so take on the worst kind of delinquent role.

The girl who decides that she prefers masculinity to femininity is usually reacting to a society that says that masculinity is superior. She is entitled to her preference and harms no one by her choice. If, however, she sees masculinity as being equated with aggression and bullying she damages not only herself but all those other girls who are trying to establish a viable role for themselves in the face of opposition to any female emancipation. What teachers can do is to work hard against the prevailing atmosphere that creates these bullies. They can first of all try as far as possible within the limited time and scope at their disposal to understand the feelings that the girls are expressing. They can in the process help girls to recognise the merits of a feminine approach to life and to recognise the threat to their femininity that is contained in so many of society's attitudes. They can encourage the Mandys to see that masculinity does not need to mean aggression.

Where it becomes not only aggression but bullying it has to be dealt with immediately it appears, before it gets out of hand. This can be done first by working with the individual bully, but it also requires attention to the other people who are involved. This includes in particular those who are being bullied.

There are some victims who unwittingly bring bullying on themselves, besides those who just have the misfortune to be around when there's a bully about. Often victims are people who are in some way slightly different from the accepted standard. The difference can be as slight as living in a part of town that is considered unacceptable or in a village from which no one else in the school comes. Quite often it is a physical disability, smallness or weakness of some sort, which brings on the bullying, and sometimes it is a withdrawn attitude that is interpreted as unfriendliness. There are a few highly neurotic children who manage to get themselves bullied because their sense of guilt is so great that they actually get their relief from it only by being punished. These are rare; far more common are the perfectly normal children who get caught up in a round of bullying in which each member of a group in turn becomes the victim and each in turn joins the bullies, in a desperate attempt to stave off the role of victim from herself.

Bullies will usually find a considerable amount of support for their activities from their fellows. Other girls will band together with the bully girl for self-protection. Quite often the victim is too frightened to appeal to authority for help; if she does she is likely to suffer more.

Telling tales is still seen by the young as a major disloyalty and the victim who does so is likely to be subject to further, though perhaps more covert, bullying that is harder for the adult to detect.

To tackle bullying successfully, therefore, both the bully and the victim need to be considered and ultimately the whole group has to be involved. Once the bully feels herself to have adult concern and recognition she will be more able to admit to her bullying and less dependent on the support of her group, less in need of the temporary sense of superiority that bullying brings.

When the victim is also making some contribution to her plight she too needs to be helped individually. She needs to find ways of becoming more acceptable to the group, especially if her feelings of isolation have led her to accentuate the situation by behaving in unacceptable or unfriendly ways. Professor Lowenstein suggests that training in social skills can often be of value. This includes taking a more consciously positive attitude, developing a real interest in other people and seeing their point of view as well as one's own. Actual practice in making friendly overtures and responding cheerfully to others can do wonders for some children who have been unaware of their own behaviour. The painfully shy and oversensitive, who are often victims, need more than training, however, because their problem lies deeper; they need constant support and continued encouragement from sympathetic adults.

It is indeed always advisable for the bully to see that the victim receives attention from adults. There are those who believe that this in itself is sufficient deterrent to those who bully primarily to attract attention to themselves. It is hoped that when they learn that the victim rather than themselves receives attention, and they are ignored, the attention-seeking bullying will cease. This rather naive application of a simple principle has long been found to be inadequate, however, by experienced teachers. Unfortunately attention-seekers are usually people who really need attention, and if they do not get it one way they will look for it in another. It is therefore worthwhile trying to find out why they are in such need of attention.

Jane, for example, got bullied seemingly because she was gentle and caring, but in reality because she too was an attention-seeker and her method of seeking attention was in itself a subtle form of bullying. As a bully who was herself bullied she needed adult protection but, also, some more sophisticated understanding of what she was doing. She made other girls feel inadequate by being excessively gentle, meek and concerned about people; but her very caring was a way of dominating, from which people found it hard to escape. There was a kind of subservience in her attitude that inevitably attracted the bully in others. She had no real friends in school but tried to make transitory relationships with all the more disturbed and depressed girls. With these she would start by being protective and generous, demanding in exchange their total loyalty to herself, and invariably losing it. Any new girl who arrived was sure to be taken up by Jane, and equally surely would begin to avoid her after a week or two. Jane became the butt of her classmates; they would tease her and call her names. One or two girls were particularly aggressive towards her and used to take delight in pushing her around until she reacted suddenly with screaming rage. She would end up sobbing, the centre of the attention, both scared and excited, of the rest of the class.

Jane's background was a particularly bad one in that she was not just neglected, she was positively ill-treated by her mother. Her parents were divorced and although her father came occasionally to see his children he was only too anxious not to notice anything that was wrong.

Jane gave to other children the maternal protection for which she herself longed. She gave it mostly to those whom she recognised intuitively to be as rejected and lost as herself, or to those who were new and insecure in the school. She attracted bullying because she demanded attention from others without being able to give any really reciprocal attention, and because she did so by trying to emulate the very behaviour that they rejected. Her protective behaviour was overdone, and experienced by its recipients as false. Her need for love and attention was so great that she grabbed at it greedily and, inevitably, it slipped away.

Jane refused to come to school because she was afraid of a pack of girls who threatened to beat her up. The form teacher took the matter up with her class. It transpired that Jane had become friendly with someone else's boyfriend; with her usual intensity she had taken this boy over and tried to make him give allegiance only to her. The teacher asked the girls to talk about what they thought should be done.

The class at first treated the incident with contempt, feeling no sympathy for either party.

Squabbling over a man, honestly!

Crumbs, if they're going to quarrel over a flipping man they make themselves sound like glorified whores.

They'll make him feel he's God's gift to women.

Once they had got through this ritual however, they began to get down to a more serious discussion; but first there were battle-lines drawn up for and against Jane, with a lot of outspoken criticism of her fickleness in friendships. In time, however, they were able to see how destructive their attitudes were; as they began to be more sympathetic towards her they were also able to make admissions all round of how terrified they themselves were, of being attacked physically or insulted verbally, in fact of being bullied.

Their biggest fear was that of being excluded from the group. Everyone was so afraid of being lonely that she joined a group, any group, so as to feel accepted. To prove themselves to be part of the group these girls would eagerly assist in bullying those who were not. Jane, having already made herself an outsider, had transgressed further by taking a boyfriend from a group to which she did not belong. In adolescence belonging is of tremendous significance. It is better to belong as a bully than not to do so at all, even though inevitably the bully will herself one day be bullied.

Only when a feeling of security has been established by the teacher will the bullies and the bullied feel safe enough to talk about what is going on and admit to any complicity. Once this has happened the reasons for bullying can be looked at and plans to avert it in future can be laid. Children do not like bullies and will be more than willing to try to find ways of curbing their activities.

This is one area in which teachers can feel sure that, if they behave tactfully and sensitively, they will eventually find that they have everyone on their side. Girls are still aware that to be bullying and destructive has novelty value; they are also aware that this is not the only way that they want to be. The girl like Mandy who is more ferociously aggressive than the boys knows that she is acting out of the character that society expects to find in her. She is therefore consciously being defiant – as well as rejecting the laws of society she is rejecting any place in it for herself. The girl who, like Jane, is trying to buy her way into friendship can learn that she is going about it in the wrong way at the same time as her tormentors learn how to cease their tormenting.

Mandy used physical violence on others and Jane brought it down on herself. If they had both been boys not so much stir would have been caused. Unfortunately the aggression of boys is taken for granted but, it is to be hoped, we will always live in a world in which girls are expected to be non-violent. This will only be possible if we recognise that whilst the present-day world is pushing girls into more aggressive modes of expressing themselves it is at the same time putting excessive pressures on many of them. Teachers therefore have to allow them some freedom for the legitimate expression of strong feelings if they are to be prevented from degenerating into violence.

Girls do not want to be violent, they want to be accepted and to be allowed to assert themselves. When this assertion is recognised as normal behaviour the need to push it further into delinquency and bullying will diminish. Once the novelty of their aggressive behaviour has worn off, so has some of the reinforcement for such activity. Girls whose teachers show no more alarm at their noisy defiance than they do at similar acts by boys will drop their defiance much more quickly than will those who sense that they are still managing to shock. Girls whose teachers recognise that problems can be created by societies, and not just by individuals, will have more chance of being understood by these teachers. Understanding should bring the necessary impetus to help these aggressive and unhappy girls towards a more positive attitude to their femininity, despite the encouragement to reject it engendered by so much that goes on in the world around them.

Chapter 10
School Refusal

Mavis wanted to leave school, but she was only 14. She was bitter about the law (passed during her school life) that trapped her into yet another two years of senseless boredom. 'You've got a good job ain't you, Miss? You didn't have to stay on after you was 14 did you? What they want me to stay for? I could get a good job if they'd let me go.' I confessed that I had stayed until I was 17, but omitted to mention the further ten years that I had spent studying after I had left school; to Mavis such masochism would have been incomprehensible. She had just given me a very graphic reminder of the dreadful imposition that what we call education can be on the spirit of some children. When the process has become meaningless, to stay on at school is not just a bore, it is an imprisonment.

Of course there would have been no good job awaiting Mavis if she had left. It is unlikely that, with the little education that she had managed to glean during her scant attendances at school, she could have got any job at all. But her time could hardly have been any less fruitfully occupied than it was currently. With no encouragement from home to take any interest in schoolwork, Mavis could see little point in any of it. Her mother, who certainly set no value on education, was an amateur and not very successful prostitute, living in a couple of rooms in a rundown part of an inner city. Mavis herself at 14 had already taken to prostitution in a rather haphazard way, not, it would seem, either for profit or for enjoyment, but out of a mindless desperation. This was the only way in which she could experience any semblance of a relationship and give her life a fragment of meaning.

I came across her whilst I was visiting a school. Mavis drifted in on the off-chance of seeing the counsellor during one of her rare forays into the building. Mostly she truanted but, being quite intelligent, she managed to accrue just enough marks on the attendance register to avoid investigation by an already overworked education welfare officer. She would attend at registration time, then drift off; she usually sought out the counsellor at some time during her visit, knowing, as she put it, that 'The counsellor thinks I'm OK. No one else does.'

She was a girl who during her primary school years quite enjoyed learning. Secondary school with its acres of corridors, different teachers for each subject and hosts of new people to adapt to was all too much for her. 'It's too big, Miss; they don't know who you are.' Mavis hardly knew who she was herself; she was therefore especially in need of other human beings who would help her to reach a sense of her own existence. But it would be pretty hard for most of her teachers to know who Mavis was; they saw so little of her and she made so slight an impact.

She was a pale wraith of a girl, without colour or vitality, talking to me she came to life only when the conversation turned to cigarettes. She was 'dying for a smoke, Miss', and disappointed to learn that I had none to offer. I recognised her feelings of deprivation and sympathised. Tobacco is addictive and real withdrawal symptoms can be experienced even by quite young children if they are deprived of a drug on which they have come to depend. Mavis revealed that she had started smoking at 8, but only become really seriously dependent at around 11. She saw her history of waning interest in education in terms of her increasing need to 'get out and have a fag'. Although clearly her truanting had its roots deeper than just the need for tobacco, there was some truth in her perception of her dilemma.

Truanting for Mavis was linked with smoking because cigarettes were initially a means of alleviating unbearable tension exacerbated by boredom. The tension was a result of a lifetime spent in unloving and unrewarding circumstances. The boredom was due to forced involvement in studies that were becoming increasingly meaningless to her in an alien and impersonal environment. As her absences increased lessons became even less comprehensible because of the growing gaps in her knowledge. This increased the temptation to truant even more. At first she was missed from her classes, but as time went on, teachers, catching only an occasional fleeting glimpse of a faint shadow called Mavis, hardly registered her absence. So with no one at home to supervise her and apparently no one at school to care she was well set on a road of total rejection of what school stood for.

However, by the time that she was in her second year a counsellor had been appointed to the school. As the months went on Mavis allowed herself to be inveigled into her office. Having discovered that there was somebody in the world who seemed to be interested in her she began to make the counsellor's room her first port of call whenever she decided to drop in on school; she took to making frequent visits, but not of course with any regularity. Order, punctuality and regularity played no part in Mavis's chaotic life.

On her own the counsellor had little chance of fighting against Mavis's background, her indifference to learning and indeed, as it seemed, to life itself. The teachers in the school were by no means unconcerned for the children in their charge, but they too were working against fairly overwhelming odds. In a school where almost every pupil qualifies by reason of home circumstances for the attention of one or other of the social services, such an unsatisfactory student as Mavis can easily be overlooked.

Mavis nevertheless is a human being, a member of our society, bound by the same laws and therefore entitled to the same consideration as any other member. She is forced to go to school as part of an education system that is supposedly designed for all children. Indeed the law that makes school attendance obligatory was designed expressly for the Mavises. Children of parents who value education need no legal pressures to get them to school. Mavis has equal rights to the attention of her teachers with, say, the high flier on her way to Cambridge, or the hard worker whose reports are full of 'tries hard'. Rights are one thing, however, the means to put them into practice quite another; but it is only by admitting to these rights that teachers will find any way of responding to them.

It is hard for some to recognise the rights of students who make no claim to interest in education and who seem to reject everything that teachers and schools stand for. It is hard for teachers to remember that their own experiences of education have often been completely different from those of some of their students, and that different home backgrounds produce different attitudes. Rifts of incomprehension can open up between children and the adults who teach them because it has never occurred to the teachers to look seriously at the different sets of values that exist in the world. Perhaps the hardest task of all for teachers who belong to, aspire to or have just joined the middle class is to recognise the validity of the life-style and viewpoint of those of their students who do not so belong and who have no wish to do so. It is particularly hard for teachers to recognise and admit that these children have no idea what middle-class values are and do not want to know. It is equally hard for some of us to adapt to the idea that intellectual matters are of no consequence to a large *majority* of mankind. Most teachers reached their positions as a result of a commitment, or at least an acceptance of, the idea that intellectual matters are of paramount interest.

Most teachers, indeed, have reached their position in life as a result of subscribing to this viewpoint. It is often very hard to face the reality that their values are not the only values, and that the importance that schools attach to learning is not always shared by their students. It requires an even greater leap of the imagination to remember how little these values are shared by the families of a great number of their students. If you work in an inner city area where the main concern of the adult population is to stay alive and keep their families fed and clothed, and moderately entertained, you have to face up to this reality, however much your own personal view is that life is about something higher and nobler than bread and circuses. However much you have considered the lilies of the field and how they sew not and neither do they spin, most of the parents of your pupils will be occupied primarily with the twentieth-century equivalent of sewing and spinning and will have little energy to spare for the finer aspects of life. Nevertheless their children are able and willing to broaden their thinking when they find encouragement and responsiveness from their teachers. Their enthusiasm is directly related to the quality of their relationships with their teachers.

Mavis had shown, from her response to her primary school education, that she could make relationships with her teachers and enjoy her work. Primary teachers find it easier to get to know their pupils individually than do secondary teachers. They see them every day and in most cases for the greater part of the day. Children like Mavis, whose earliest essential relationships are so tenuous, need real relationships just because they find the greatest difficulty in making contact with adults at anything other than a superficial level. Mavis, with no father, and a mother who had almost no concern for her and who herself made nightly superficial relationships with men almost before Mavis's eyes, was not likely to have learnt much about the value of warm human contact. Good teaching in her early years had nevertheless made its impact. Mavis had enjoyed school, had liked her teachers, made friends and begun to learn.

Now in secondary school where the atmosphere was relatively impersonal, where there were so many people, teachers and pupils to relate to, and where no one made any special effort about her, Mavis soon sank into the shadows again.

Teachers whose job it is to purvey knowledge and guide students through an examination syllabus can easily find themselves obsessed with getting results, whilst forgetting what education is supposed to be for. It is hard for those who have themselves enjoyed learning to adapt to a Mavis. They have to make an effort to recognise that as intellectual processes do not mean much to these children their feeling self must be harnessed if they are to learn anything. In some teachers their own feeling self has sometimes been neglected as a result of a university education that emphasised thinking as a process opposed to feeling. Those who find it difficult to escape from this trap also find difficulty in sympathising with those whose thinking processes have atrophied through no fault of their own. Sometimes a conscious effort to adapt is needed before such teachers can make contact with these pupils.

Some teachers suffer because they have so much to give and it is not accepted by their pupils. Some children suffer because they are so used to being spoon-fed by television that they do not see the need for work – they just do not understand why they should endure the pain of studying – and some teachers have a convenient amnesia about the pain that studying used to cause them. Nevertheless some teachers find themselves feeling offended, almost insulted, when their carefully prepared and enthusiastically presented knowledge is received in stony silence, or worse, with noisy resentment. The hard but important lesson that they have to learn is that other people are not to blame for the fact that they do not share our rather esoteric interests.

It is not a crime not to be an intellectually oriented person. It is, however, a pity not to be able to enjoy any use of your intellect at all. Everyone can in fact think, and teachers who keep this reality firmly in the forefront of their minds will eventually find ways of stimulating the thought processes of the most reluctant students. They will only do this, however, if they continue to respond to these students as people with true intellectual needs. Trying to force unwilling students into modes of thinking which are alien to them is a sure way of creating truants. Discovering their natural mode of thinking and helping them to stretch their own intellectual muscles is not an impossible task; it is not even a difficult one compared with the self-defeating activity of ignoring the true needs of children and trying to force-feed them intellectually.

The alternative approach of some teachers of pandering to the supposed lack of ability of their students by making no demands on them at all is equally invalid. This is an easier way out than that of making too many of the wrong kinds of demands, but its ultimate outcome is similar. Mavis had been subjected to this kind of neglect and had responded with the boredom that is the inevitable outcome of understimulation.

Some teachers see boredom as an inescapable aspect of school life. Sometimes, having been under-extended, they were themselves bored at school, in which case they do not imagine that it is possible to make lessons interesting all the time. Sometimes teachers have had the unfortunate experience of losing interest in their own work before the end of their courses of study. These people, who have already begun to treat intellectual work as a necessary chore to be got through for the sake of obtaining a qualification, only too easily pass this attitude on to their students. Ideally we would hope that they might have a special sympathy for the less intelligent; unfortunately the opposite is often the case. Because they have not yet faced up to their resentment about the poor teaching that they received they will sometimes unwittingly inflict knowledge, rather than give it, in a manner that makes studying as much of a penance for their students as it was for themselves. Inevitably they bore their students.

There are more children suffering from boredom in school than there are suffering from excessive pressure to learn. This is the true danger to real intellectual work. Whatever their ability, pupils who are bored will soon start to lose interest, often they will indulge in bad behaviour and usually they will look for something else to do. They truant in the hope of finding more interesting occupations.

Girls, unlike boys, find on the whole that they can interest themselves more outside school than in it. Boys tend to hang around the least salubrious parts of the town. Girls sometimes join them, but, if they can manage to stay at home, they can find ways of occupying themselves. Boys and girls shoplift very largely to alleviate boredom rather than to acquire goods.

Mavis truanted because she had lost interest in school. Her boredom increased her need to do something about her perennial state of heightened tension and anxiety. What she did was to smoke. Attendance at school decreased in attraction as the need for tobacco increased. No one had taken much interest in her, although the school was organised in a way which theoretically catered for the needs of all the children. In practice, as is sadly often the case, a good many children probably slipped through the net. A year head with no specific training in pastoral care, a heavy teaching load and an excessive supply of children with special needs has a difficult task. Even the most caring tutors cannot make sure that a child's needs are met when the subject teachers are more committed to their subject than to their pupils.

Mavis's way of life was not a search for alternative pleasures to those provided in school; it was more of a rather desolate search for substitutes for the love that she never received at home and the notice that she rarely received at school. Nothing could be done to alter her home life. With a little thought perhaps something more could have been done to improve her school experience. By the time the counsellor arrived Mavis was already on her way out, counting the months until she could leave. The strength of the attachment that she made to the counsellor was indicative of her need for human contact.

Carol was a truant of a different sort. Far from being bored with school, she claimed that she loved it. She was hard-working, conscientious and given to producing reams of beautifully written work, most of which, unfortunately, only reached her teachers through the post. Carol, much as she loved school, could not get herself to go there. Every time she arrived at the school gates something made her turn back. She would burst into tears, complain of tummy-ache, sickness or cramps of one kind or another; occasionally she fainted. Her love of school, it seemed, was in her mind but not in her body.

Carol was what has been rather inaptly termed a school phobic. The term is inadequate because the phobia does not as a rule relate to going to school but to leaving home. It has more to do with inability to cope with separations, with excessive dependency and with parent—child relationships than with school as such. Carol might well have loved school if only it could have taken place at home. As it was she found herself, day after day, becoming more and more frantic, as the time for leaving home to go to school approached.

She was referred to a child guidance clinic where every effort was made to help her to resolve some of her anxieties: to no avail at first, as she soon began to be taken ill on her approach to the clinic. She was visited at home where she was found in bed refusing to get up. It was on this visit that Carol finally had to admit that she was herself perhaps contributing something towards the difficult position in which she found herself. She recognised that by not getting up she was preventing anything happening, any change taking place. She was also keeping everybody, particularly her mother, on a string running around attending to her.

Carol, the good, hard-working, conforming little girl, who just suffered from feeling ill, had turned a corner. She was now set on the difficult path towards discovering that she was actually gaining something by her illnesses and that, if she was going to recover, these gains would have to be given up. What Carol was doing was not deliberately and consciously attempting to keep everybody at her beck and call; there is no doubt, however, that this was what she had achieved. She found that she needed to achieve it so that she could have as much of the world as possible under her own control. She was frightened that if she were not in control the world would get out of hand. What she was most frightened of, though, was that if she did not stay at home watching over things her mother might get ill, might even die.

This is a commonly expressed anxiety amongst those who have been diagnosed as school phobic. The fear that the mother will suffer for the child's absence is much stronger than any fear of school itself. Paradoxically, it soon becomes clear when these children begin to talk about their feelings that underneath this fear is often a suppressed animosity to the mother that is perhaps too strong to be admitted to. This kind of suppressed anger often masquerades as excessive concern.

Carol's animosity revealed itself in time to be largely due to her inability to separate herself from her mother. She felt frustrated at her own lack of independence yet fearful of trying to exercise any. Her mother was a very controlling woman who, although wanting her daughter to go to school, could not help undermining any efforts that Carol made to get there. 'You'd better not try today dear, remember how ill you felt last week.' Like so many mothers of these children she was very possessive and found it hard to let her daughter develop any independence. Carol's anger at this was deeply suppressed and came out only in her own obliquely controlling behaviour. Consciously she feared that ill might befall her mother; unconsciously she sometimes wished it would.

As with many phobics, Carol's problems began at a change of school. She had managed reasonably well whilst at her primary school, having a great many illnesses, especially at the beginning of term, but getting to school reasonably well in between times. The school was in the same road as her house, and Carol's mother had attended it herself. It was the change to the more remote geographically and larger, more impersonal school that aroused in Carol all her anxieties about being separated from her mother. These anxieties were exacerbated by a home life which was very inturned and unchanging. Carol's family, consisting of father, mother and herself, rarely went out and then only to see her grandmother who lived in the next street. Carol's mother was in fact almost as phobic as Carol herself. She too had a kind of love/hate relationship with her own battleaxe of a mother who really dominated the whole family. The only man in this set-up, Carol's father, was gentle, timid and retiring; he managed to sink into the background at every opportunity.

It is not unusual for this pattern of dependent and controlling behaviour to run in families. In a society in which few people move from their own patch, few problems are created; but as the pressures which are put on families to move around the world, and on children to go far from home to reach school, increase, this kind of behaviour shows itself. Carol's problem was only an extreme version of that experienced by a much larger section of the population than is generally recognised. The less extreme school rejector, who quite likes school-work but hates school, can usually be helped to discover for herself what she hates about school. This is likely to be a sense of insecurity that is generated by her overdependence on home and that is increased at every major change in her life. Moving to a new district and a new school is a common precipitating factor. Once the habit of staying away has been established it is very hard to break.

Carol did not get back into school for nearly two years, and then only gradually established a satisfactory attendance pattern. Unless they are recognised in time these children will soon become too frightened to break their habit. A fear of what the other children will say is a major contribution to the difficulty of returning after an absence.

Those schools succeed best in getting these children back which offer specialised facilities. Because of their anxieties these children find it hard to face large numbers and find the impersonality of institutions a great threat. What is needed is a unit that is small enough for a child to feel secure in and a teacher who has patience and understanding. The change from school to home has to be made in graduated steps with, in many cases, attendance only being demanded for half a day a week at first. Once the child has recognised the rewards to be gained by attendance, the hours spent at school can increase. Similarly gradual introduction into normal classes for a small part of each day can lead to increased attendance as time goes on. Where teachers are understanding and sympathetic, criticism of the child's former absences, or even unnecessary references to them, can be avoided.

The process of returning a school phobic to a school is always a slow one. Each step that is taken has to be recognised as a satisfying experience before the next can be ventured. Only by co-operation between all the staff concerned can it be a success. Co-operation by the parents too is necessary and often extremely difficult to come by, as the parents are so rarely able to see what they are doing unintentionally to prevent their child attending school.

Another type of truant whose parents collude with the absence from school is the girl who is kept at home to work. Barbara was this kind of truant, though she had not been seen by her school in this light. She and her mother had been taken to court because of her absences and her mother claimed that she wanted Barbara to attend. She had actually pleaded with the court for help in getting her daughter back into school. It was only when Barbara went to see the school counsellor that the true picture emerged.

Her visit to him was precipitated by a family row. Barbara arrived at school weeping and her form tutor, being able to get no sense out of her, suggested that she might like to talk to the counsellor. This she did and once her tears had subsided she revealed to him what the row had been about. Her mother had wanted her to stay at home to look after the children and Barbara, for the first time in her life, had refused. She spoke bitterly about the court proceedings, saying that her mother had lied because nearly all Barbara's absences were at least connived at by her and more often than not deliberately engineered by her. Barbara was expected to stay at home to look after both her mother and the younger children.

The counsellor was able to check up on this and verify what Barbara had told him. In court she had been too frightened to confront her mother with the truth, but now that she had found someone who would listen to her she poured out her story of misery and frustration. Not only had her mother blamed Barbara for her absences and lied to the court, she had also taken from her money that she had earned on her paper round and from working in a local shop. Barbara did not resent giving up some money as she was fond of her mother and sorry for her. She recognised how difficult life was for a woman with a husband out of work and seven children, but she felt that she was being used.

Barbara was the oldest and inevitably she had to bear the burden of responsibility. As she calmed down she was able to admit that she understood why her mother had been too ashamed, and scared, to take the blame for breaking the law and keeping Barbara at home. She recognised that her mother needed the money that she earned, but felt bitter that she had to earn it working during hours when she should have been at school. Barbara was not particularly fond of school, but she quite liked schoolwork and was ambitious to get a decent job when she left. She was determined not to follow in the footsteps of her father whose unemployment was said to be due to a 'bad back'. Barbara doubted the reality of the back because she saw that he was fit enough to go drinking, playing bowls and darts, and helping friends with odd jobs like moving furniture, making garden sheds and repairing cars. She saw him as a shiftless idler who would draw the dole for as long as he could. She wanted something better for herself. Unfortunately her father thought it was a waste of time to educate girls. Although her mother did not agree with him, she was always defeated by him when she tried to argue and in the end gave way, putting convenience before Barbara's needs.

During the course of the next term Barbara's life as she relayed it to the counsellor grew rapidly worse. Her father's behaviour deteriorated further, he brought another woman into the house, her mother took an overdose and was hospitalised for a time. The parents rowed incessantly and Barbara herself went into a deep depression. She became scruffy and unkempt in appearance and difficult and touchy in her behaviour. Her teachers were ready to write her off as an academic failure who had no real interest in her work. The counsellor had to work hard to persuade them that they were seeing only one side of Barbara and that her behaviour was the result of unbearable pressures at home. She had in fact great interest in her work and as her absences were now much less frequent she was beginning to show herself to be an intelligent girl. Her form tutor, who had faith in her, encouraged her to aim at taking some CSEs or even O levels. Together with the counsellor he worked out a scheme for her to make up for lost work. But the family situation was becoming impossible and towards the end of her third year Barbara declared that she could stand it no longer.

By good fortune the counsellor was able to enlist the help of the social worker who had dealt with Barbara's mother after the suicide attempt. She knew the family well and recognised that if Barbara continued to live at home she would never be able to achieve anything in school; the pressures were too great. Relatives were found living nearby who agreed to take Barbara in on condition that she attended school regularly.

The change in her behaviour was dramatic. Not only did she begin to attend regularly, she tidied herself up and started to work hard. She gained nine CSEs, five of them at grade 1. With such a history of previous school failure this was a remarkable achievement, indicating that Barbara had real intellectual potential that she had not been able to make use of. She returned home after her exams and found work in a local factory. She planned to enter a nursing training when she was 18, but meanwhile she told the counsellor that she needed to help her mother out financially. Now she felt much more self-assured and self-respecting and thought that, being more secure, she could cope better with her own home.

It is not always possible for teachers to recognise that non-attendance is due to circumstances outside the child's control. Family affairs cannot be revealed to all and sundry and had there not been a school counsellor available for Barbara to talk to she might well have left school without any qualifications and with an undeserved reputation for truancy. Teachers can usually discern something of the truth if they can find time to take an interest in what a girl has to say. It is not hard to discover from her conversation if she is being used as the household drudge, and there is usually some way to be found for alleviating even the most dreadful circumstances if there is someone around to look for it. A teacher with the real interests of students at heart can be that someone.

Ann was a girl who benefited from such a teacher. She had spent her first three years of secondary school attending on average three days a week. She was reckoned by her school to be of low intelligence and had gradually dropped down to the fifth band by the time she reached her fourth year. Suddenly her life was shattered by the death of her father in a road accident. With her mother and elder sister she moved to live near relatives. This brought her to a new school for her final two years. Here she found a form tutor who took an interest in her. He recognised that to lose a father at the age of 14 must be a shattering experience and he wondered why Ann had truanted so much in her previous school. So he gave up some of his time to try to find out about her.

He discovered that Ann had been bored at school and had enlisted her mother in conniving at her absences, often getting her to write notes inventing illnesses. Now, however, the home situation had changed. Her mother, widowed and poor, recognised that Ann would have to earn her own living. Ann too was beginning to realise that she needed to get some qualifications; but old habits die hard. In spite of her good intentions she dropped easily into taking off a day or two a week. However, she was not allowed to persist in this.

The form tutor had already decided that Ann was a much more able girl than her reports from the previous school suggested. He enlisted the support of the headmaster and counsellor in an attempt to improve her attendance. This was successful. The counsellor saw Ann regularly and found that with his support she was really keen to keep up her attendance; she needed someone to correct old habits and counteract the lassitude of her mother. Adolescents are in great need of some firmness in life to provide security. The counsellor, by being both friendly and firm, together with the form tutor and headmaster, provided the stability that Ann's home lacked.

Some members of staff felt that too much attention was being paid to Ann because there were other children in the school also in need of special help and attention. Undoubtedly there were, but this did not obviate the need that Ann had for attention. All children should have their needs met in school as far as is humanly possible. Perhaps Ann was lucky because she came across a concerned form tutor. She justified his concern. She worked hard and attended regularly, was promoted to an examination form and was expected by her teachers to do well.

None of these girls was the female equivalent of Huckleberry Finn. None of them had a really worthwhile enjoyable life that school was preventing her from enjoying. The only one with anything like a real home which she might have been expected to want to stay in was Carol, and she was the only one who wanted to go to school but couldn't get herself there. None of them was staying away from school just for the fun of it. Persistent truants rarely do, especially persistently truanting girls. Adolescents need a group: they need a centre for their loyalty. Given half a chance they are happy to make the school into this. They want to belong to society, to be accepted, needed and valued. Girls, even when they are demanding independence, still need adults to support them and make them feel that they belong and are wanted in society. It is easy for adults to perceive only the superficial rebellious behaviour and to fail to recognise it for what it is: a testing out of society to see what it can take.

All these girls, and hundreds of others like them, want an adult society that values them enough to be concerned for them. Being concerned in our society's terms means amongst other things seeing that they get an education. 'Why don't they come and get us, Miss, when we mitch?' 'I'd come back in if they even noticed I wasn't here.' 'Mr X [the headmaster] shouldn't let us stay out should he, Miss? It's his job to see we get to school.' These are a few of the comments of a group of persistent truants from a comprehensive school in a small country town. They were enough in touch with their feelings to know that they wanted to be brought back into the fold, and still children enough to see it as other people's jobs to bring them back.

They may give us a hundred reasons why they truant and there may be another hundred reasons that they cannot give because they cannot yet conceptualise them. They may not just be staying away from school but running away symbolically from themselves. Sometimes they are not running away but running to somewhere: to some imagined paradise or, more mundanely, just some comfort; looking for a warmth that they have missed out on perhaps nearly all their lives. For some, like Mavis, there is a forlorn hope that in each new and ultimately hopeless relationship this will be found; when, inevitably, the shallowness of her contact with others destroys her hope, she looks around again. Only in school, where there should be a stable society run by caring adults, can such children hope to learn again that life can be tolerably secure.

All these girls came from homes where for one reason or another there was not enough of the right kind of support. Those who demanded that teachers took responsibility for getting them into school showed that they had some recognition of the stability that mature and caring adults could provide for them. There is a valid enough case to be made for the viewpoint that this is not the teacher's role and that he has no responsibility to bring the children into school, only to provide an education for them when they get there. Ideally the education should be so enticing that no one wants to stay away and there are teachers around who have the wish and the ability to provide such an education, given ideal conditions to work in. Such conditions are rare, rarer even than such teachers. What we have got, however, is the possibility of tapping the goodwill that is available amongst teachers. If there is no counsellor available in a school to alert the necessary members of staff to the needs of truants, teachers themselves have to be even more vigilant. It is always worth believing that children do not want to truant because this is very nearly always true. Teachers who do believe that have a chance to rescue a lot of children, before the habit of truancy becomes too firmly set, from a lifetime lived without benefit of education. The caring side of a teacher's role should help him to respond to the dependency needs of these children: the teaching side will help him to recognise how unfair it is that children already deprived emotionally should be punished by being deprived intellectually as well.

Chapter 11

Sexuality

Sue is a girl who, like many others at 14, can make no sense of school. Her teachers can make little sense of her: irritating, talkative, inattentive and unable to concentrate, her only interests appear to be clothes and boyfriends. She comes, inevitably, from a home where there is little love. Three older sisters and two half-brothers have already passed through the school. The sisters have been involved in a variety of marriages and divorces, pregnancies and abortions; the brothers are both in care. Sue has called three men father during her short lifetime, none of whom was her progenitor; they have been interspersed with a variety of uncles who have been accorded temporary hospitality by her mother. Sue has not loved any of her family, nor have they loved her. Sue becomes pregnant, as do her friends, because that is what lost, emotionally neglected and generally uncared for girls are doing these days.

Angela, on the other hand, is a model 14-year-old; hard-working and committed, intelligent and conscientious. Her parents are highly respectable pillars of local society and the mainstay of the parent-teacher association; they view their only daughter with pride, if with little else. Angela's father is a successful and extremely busy accountant, her mother an obsessive bridge player. Neither of them has time to notice that there is anything lacking in Angela's life until it is too late: she too has become pregnant. Unlike Sue, she had not had a sexual relationship before; and when she found a boy who was attracted to her, she did not realise how easily sexual feelings could overwhelm her. She had no one to talk to about it because she never discussed anything with her parents.

She took no precautions, partly because she was not sure how to go about doing so, partly because she could not believe that she would ever get pregnant anyhow, and partly because, with the confused adolescent's ability to live with unreality, there was an element in her that made her want to conceive. Like Sue, she needed to be loved; like Sue, at an unconscious level, she believed that a baby would love her. Like so many girls she believed that pregnancies only happened to others. Also like so many of her kind she had a fantasy about love-making that nowhere matched the reality. Perhaps the most damaging aspect of all, however, was her inability to feel that what she was doing was happening to her.

Girls of this sort, who ignore the necessity of taking precautions, do not admit to what is happening to their own bodies because they have never learnt that their bodies belong to them. Girls are still being brought up to be unrelated to their own physical selves. Mothers who have themselves rejected their sexuality unconsciously encourage daughters to do the same by failing to give them a sense of the value of their own bodies and, even more serious, by failing to give them a sense of ownership of their own lives. Daughters, in being allowed to be dependent on their mothers, are also being prevented from becoming self-dependent. Sex is then seen as something outside themselves, something done to them, not chosen. Neither Sue nor Angela believed in herself as an autonomous person who had a right to her sexuality and a duty to care for it.

Angela's mother was beautiful and cold; she lacked feeling for her daughter though she took pride in Angela's achievements at school. She had herself married at a very young age a much older man who dominated her and had come rather to despise her; they were barely on speaking terms. The father retired each evening early to his study with a bottle of whisky. In public they were gracious, intelligent, beautiful and popular: Angela was expected to be a replica of their public image. Her pregnancy was therefore also an extreme act of defiance. She did not tell anyone about it until she was nearly three months pregnant; then, against her wishes, she was made to have an abortion. She had bitter quarrels with her parents after this, and eventually asked to be sent to boarding school so as to get away from the atmosphere at home.

Sue had a series of abortions and then finally, at the age of 15, produced a child which her mother agreed to keep. Sue played with her son for the first few weeks and then, realising that babies need care, that they cry and are not always loving, she rejected the child totally, and had nothing further to do with him. She returned to school and within a month or two was pregnant again.

Marion was the head girl of her school: very well behaved and proper, she was not known even to have a boyfriend let alone to have become pregnant. She was due to take her A levels when suddenly she became withdrawn and unhappy and started to weep. She wept at the slightest provocation and at no provocation. She was advised to speak to the school counsellor, which she did. She confided in him eventually through tears that she had started to weep on what she called 'his birthday'. 'He' was the baby she had conceived nine months ago unknown to anyone in school. Under pressure from her mother she had had the pregnancy terminated, although both she and her boyfriend wanted to keep the baby. The boy, who was away at university, had assured her that they would marry once he had his degree, and they were still in touch with one another. Marion expected to marry him within a year or two, although she was also considering going to university herself. There were no problems in their relationship; her problem was the loss of her baby, and her failure to mourn his loss at the time of the termination. She was weeping now for the birth that should have happened, and that never would.

All girls do not react like this to pregnancy or to termination. We cannot know for certain whether or not these reactions are simply the product of the attitudes of a society which for generations has condemned illegitimate pregnancies and abortions. What we can know is that we have put our young girls into a terrible trap by permitting them the freedom to move lightly into intense sexual experience without giving them either the proper preparation for it or the conditions for living which make such an attitude to sexuality feasible.

South Sea Island girls from time immemorial appear to have enjoyed untrammelled sexuality as part of the normal pattern of life; anthropologists claim that nothing but good comes from this. Captain Cook's sailors could not get used to the notion that girls would have intercourse with them simply for the asking. Such a culture, however, does not encompass the idea of an unwanted child, nor does it give leeway to the girl who wants to do anything other than bring children into the world or provide sexual satisfaction for men. A girl who is instructed at the age of 10 in the art of satisfying a man's sexual desire is not also expected to take school examinations or to develop into an independent, reliable human being who can earn her own living and care, on her own, for her children. To our society's way of thinking, the girls of Captain Cook's islands were trained as competent prostitutes. We do not consider that we are training our young girls for this profession, yet we sometimes seem to do precious little to steer them away from it.

'I think I'm pregnant, Miss' is the depressing statement that has become such a commonplace amongst schoolgirls that it hardly has the power left to shock us. Once more, we are being told that a new human being has been conceived, unwillingly, by a child who is herself not yet out of childhood. Once more we see before us someone who, having undertaken this tremendous responsibility, seems frighteningly unaware of all its implications. For her, it would seem, it might mean anything from 'a bore to have another abortion' to terror lest her dad find out: 'He'll kill me if he ever knows.' To the adults who receive this information it becomes too easily acceptable.

On the young, even those who profess indifference, it is hard to imagine that the experience can fail to make some indelible impression. Those unhappy girls who deny the very existence of the baby until it is actually born bear witness to the traumatic impact that unwanted conception can have on some anxiety-ridden teenagers. Adolescents, with their colossal powers for ignoring the realities that are too hard for them to bear, who can manage to spend nine months totally denying something that is central to their lives, are suffering from a trauma that defies the imagination of most adults. Those teachers who have to teach such girls and help them to re-establish their lives on a normal plane need to exercise imagination beyond average so as to be able to give the support and comfort that is needed. To do this teachers need to recognise some of the factors underlying unwanted teenage pregnancies.

The first thing to realise is that girls who take risks and girls who become pregnant over and over again are not suffering as a rule from lack of instruction about contraception, they are suffering from lack of love. The relationships with their boyfriends are fantasied as loving ones when they are often nothing of the sort. On the boy's part there is quite likely to be a desperate need to prove something to himself about his masculinity, which means for him his own self-worth. On the girl's there is more likely to be an overdependence which leads either to compliance with an unwanted sexual act or to a forlorn hope for a love that she imagines the boy to feel despite little evidence of his ability to be truly loving. Both are looking for what they feel they need from the experience; neither is thinking of what he or she can give to the other.

The loving that they are really looking for, boys and girls, is the loving that they really needed, and still need, from their mothers. This does not make for a true sexual relationship; it represents only an infantile craving for the loving care that was missing at the end when it was most needed.

If a girl is not emotionally mature enough for full sexuality the complete sexual relationship can be destructive for her. It can damage her emotional development by leading her to think, as one girl said to me, 'Well, if this is all there is to it . . . if this is all sex is going to be . . .' and this could stay with her for the rest of her life. So this intense and potentially exciting experience can be a non-event emotionally. This happens undoubtedly in a lot of first encounters, but if both partners are reasonably mature no harm is done. If there is not enough maturity there is little chance of the relationship deepening and developing into something worthwhile. The romantic adolescent who allows herself to be rushed into early sex can very soon find it 'a dead bore, frankly' as one unhappy 16-year-old described it, whilst still submitting to it three times a week.

Submitting was all that she was doing, not enjoying it. Such girls who trivialise the sexual experience whilst still compulsively indulging in it deny any connection between sexuality and feelings. In choosing to have a relationship in which they are subservient but uninvolved, they lose the capacity to make a relationship at a deeper level, the capacity for tenderness which is the essence of concern for other people and so of love.

The average girl at this age is still dependent on her parents, particularly her mother, and if her relationships here are not good she looks for somebody else to be dependent on. She might choose a girlfriend or an older woman to give her a sense of security; if she is unwise she will choose a boy of her own age. Her fantasy is not of having a real hetero-sexual relationship which might ultimately be a procreative one, but of having a kind of infant –mother closeness which she has missed out on. Perhaps she has not missed out on it totally, but it has not been adequate for her.

Janet, whose mother had a baby very shortly after she had been weaned, felt for the rest of her life that she was pushed out of the loving, comfortable relationship a bit sooner than she was ready for it. She spent a lot of her life looking for this warm relationship again. She might have found it ultimately with somebody of the opposite sex but, in her early teens when she was just mature physically but not yet mature emotionally, she got the chance to try to find this relationship with a boy, and became deeply dependent. What she was expecting from this boy was a re-experience of that warm, loving, secure, holding relationship that she remembered physically, if not emotionally, from her very early childhood. And what she got from the boy was nothing of the sort because as far as he was concerned she was primarily an object of physical satisfaction. That is not to say that he was necessarily being rejecting or cruel to her, but simply that the early adolescent boy does not have any more emotional maturity than the early adolescent girl.

A lot of these girls who have early sexual relationships do so with older boys; the second year girls go around with fifth and sixth years, and the third and fourth year girls go around with boys who have left school. Some of these older boys are still emotionally not very much older than some of the schoolgirls and, therefore, find it easier to have a relationship with a very young girl who is emotionally dependent and pliable. The young girls, looking for an adult figure, hope that somebody three or four years older than themselves will be more likely to give them warmth and security than somebody closer in age to themselves, and anyhow as girls tend to grow up earlier than boys do the boys in their age group are not likely to be very interesting as actual sexual partners. For a large number, therefore, the early experience of sex is, as Helene Deutsch tells us, a pseudo-heterosexuality and deeply dissatisfying for both the girl and the boy, because it fulfils none of their fantasies, they are simply using another human being, not really having a relationship.

The girls recognise somewhere that they are being used, and therefore they can come to believe that sex is always an experience in which somebody else uses you. This, if it is established in early years, can be maintained for the rest of their lives. If nothing is done to change the attitude of a boy who discovers he can use a girl he despises (and who expects to be despised), what is to make him into somebody who respects girls and who will respect the woman with whom he finally sets up home? And what will make her into someone who dares to demand respect? An early experience of being able to despise people and treat them with a certain amount of contempt, even if it is not a conscious intention of contempt, is likely to consolidate an opinion which has already been established in his pre-adolescent years, when a great many boys despise girls because they fear them. So the kind of boy who rather despises girls and sees women as inferior beings is somebody who is carrying through his adolescence, and even possibly into the rest of his life, the attitudes which are about 9 years old emotionally. A world full of men who are 9 years old emotionally is a dangerous world: so is a world which is full of girls who are expecting a sexual life to be one in which they are used and who are, therefore, masochistic in their attitude to sex. Girls who don't take precautions when having intercourse are often just such masochists. They may well feel that they deserve the punishment of becoming pregnant because they have done something bad. Sometimes, also, girls are still in the throes of such immature relationships with their mothers that they are envious and unconsciously trying to take over their mothers' role in producing a baby. Sometimes the mother herself will, almost overtly, encourage her daughter to become pregnant; the daughter will do so to give her mother a present of the baby. For some girls the dependency in which they have been reared has taken such a grip on them that they do not feel strong enough to contend with all the competitiveness that a career in the world entails; having a baby is imagined to be a way out of it all. The discovery, too late, of the fallacy of those notions is not much help to them.

Girls like Sue, who imagine that they can own a child, are especially frustrated. They get pregnant so as to satisfy a need for a love object, a mobile cuddly toy that also represents a second self that can be cherished vicariously. Having no real ideas about the true nature of babyhood they demand equal love from the baby. Sue, being too emotionally starved herself, had nothing to spare for her child when the hideous reality of broken nights and curtailed freedom dawned on her. The insistence on keeping their own babies made by such girls must always be regarded warily; so often they will end up deserting or even battering the child.

Angela, on the other hand, had no wish for a child. She was one of the girls who acquiesced in the sexual act; having learnt that girls and women should be submissive, she gave in. Such girls have no clear idea of their role: they have lost any perception of themselves as viable human beings.

These girls make up a large proportion of that 50 per cent of girls who are reported to have lost their virginity by the age of 16, and who contribute to the nearly 2,000 illegitimate children and the 3,000 to 4,000 pregnancy terminations that are recorded each year. Our over-worked social services have the task of dealing with much of the trouble that underlies these statistics, and can be forgiven for reacting at times with exasperation towards girls who produce one pregnancy after another. Often the schools too are reluctantly drawn into these problems and sometimes they are not as helpful as they could be, although mostly through lack of knowledge rather than lack of goodwill.

Teachers, whatever their views on the sexual revolution, feel more than exasperation, something nearer to despair, when faced with one more example of what they might variously interpret as carelessness, folly, stupidity, tragedy or sin. Whatever their standpoint they will need to approach the subject from two angles: that of dealing with the immediate problem and that of deciding what if anything to do about what lies behind it.

The immediate problem often starts with 'Why has she come to me?'. The answer is because she trusts you. She will only talk about her pregnancy to someone she feels safe with. The temptation to feel flattered into thinking one can therefore deal with it all on one's own must be strongly resisted. A girl is a member of a family and, however much she may be rejecting the family by choosing a teacher rather than her parents to confide in, the family has to be involved. Any child she may produce will be a member of that family. If she chooses to have the pregnancy terminated under the age of 18 she would normally require parental permission.

Although some medical practitioners have considered that they have an obligation to withhold from parents information about a daughter's pregnancy, teachers should always urge a girl to confide in her family because in the vast majority of cases there is, underlying the rejection of the family, a great longing to be able to accept it and belong to it. Only those few totally alienated girls whose parents have lost nearly all contact with them will really prefer to go through with the whole process without telling them, and even they, when they tell a teacher, are looking for a parent substitute. Patience and sympathy applied consistently will rarely fail in the end in getting the girl to trust you enough to accept your advice. That advice must always be: 'Tell your parents, they're going to get to know anyway.'

As the law stands at present, any adult can give information about how to obtain a termination, that is, to go to a doctor or clinic, even to a girl below the age of consent, but no one may go so far as to take the girl to such a place without parental permission. It is unwise for any teacher to embark on discussions about termination, or indeed on any advice at all other than that of pointing out the need to involve the family. If, however, the girl herself raises the question of solutions, such as termination, adoption or keeping the child herself, teachers should listen and encourage her to talk. Those who hold strong views, or have absolute convictions, will no doubt feel obliged to express them, but it is always as well to remember that there are often good people who think differently from ourselves. Honesty, however, is always important and it is far better to tell a girl exactly what you believe yourself than to pretend to a position that you think might make life easier for her. If you can manage not to try to persuade her towards that position you will be more help to her. Advice is so rarely taken that it should be given sparingly, and only on essential matters; then it is likely to have more impact.

The second aspect of a teacher's approach to this problem is the consideration of what might be given to this girl subsequently. She is liable to be in need of at least a sympathetic hearing, and often a great deal more. Any teacher with the time and the goodwill, who knows that there is no one more skilled available like a trained counsellor or social worker, can do a great deal by offering to listen for brief periods of time. Long arduous sessions are not so valuable, after the first crisis has been dealt with, as ten minutes or so at fairly regular intervals. These will give a girl a chance to realise that someone understands what she is going through but knows that she must cope with it herself ultimately.

Many girls need much more than this in the way of professional help, but if this is not available the concerned amateur who is prepared just to listen can do a great deal. One of the important aspects of this process for a girl is that she can often then sort out her relationship with the father of the child: something it is often impossible to do with even the most understanding and sympathetic mother. Mothers are naturally angry with boys who make their daughters pregnant, yet the father of the baby, so often left out of this whole business, perhaps matters a great deal to the girl, and maybe the baby matters a great deal to him too. Teachers who can be neutral and non-judgemental on the matter can do a lot to help distressed young people who have been made to feel wicked by all the adults around them.

There are, of course, still teachers who will hold to the view that a girl who is so uncontrolled as to get herself pregnant has only herself to blame, and is therefore worthy of no sympathy. Such an attitude fails to take into account the responsibility of the adults in society for the behaviour of our young. Perhaps we have to ask ourselves what we have been doing, those of us who care for the young, to let this happen to them.

Surely never before in the history of mankind has the conception of a child by the totally immature and unsupported been accepted so much as a matter of course. It is true that in the past many millions of unwanted children have been conceived, born and often disposed of after birth with a callousness that makes the worst of present-day practice look totally humane. But society has always at least set up a structure which made casual conception seem to be something that it was possible to avoid. The concomitant of this structure was undoubtedly such misery for those who failed to avoid conception that the letting down of the barriers in the 1960s seemed to some of us a glorious revolution. Now, as we see the carnage that has been wrought in the lives of so many adolescent girls, those of us who hailed the loosening up of the sexual rules as a triumph against hypocrisy have sadly begun to think again.

Something has gone wrong. Not choosing precisely to encourage unwanted pregnancies in young girls, we have singularly failed to discourage them. Could it be that, in line with so much of our current attitude to our bodies, by handing the whole matter over to a pill and breathing a sigh of relief we missed out on the real significance of the whole process of sexual initiation, intercourse and conception?

We call it, euphemistically, love and leave these children to get on with it, yet we might well be laying down the foundations for very disruptive relationships between the sexes, which have nothing to do with love. The sexual freedom which is now so commonplace, far from giving everyone contentment seems actually to have produced considerable sexual discontent amongst the young. Contrary to expectations there seem to be more, rather than less, young people who have sexual difficulties, who are unhappy with their sexual lives. I have been saddened by the number of intelligent, well-educated, beautiful and apparently socially successful young girls at university who have admitted to a barren and unrewarding sex life that gives them a feeling of worthlessness but that they cannot give up. Having first had intercourse at 16, because everyone else was doing it, they go on repeating an unsatisfactory experience, in the hope of getting it right, without realising where it went wrong in the first place; they had not been serious enough about their sexuality.

In the past a series of rules and conventions, whilst undoubtedly at times diabolical in their restrictiveness and often degenerating into hypocrisy, at least gave a girl some guidelines. Nowadays girls despair as they receive the bland response from the adult world 'you must make up your own mind'. What help does such a piece of advice offer for finding some form of control? Precious little.

The unfortunate girl whose mother said to her, after she had had intercourse at the age of 15 with the very first boy she had ever gone out with, 'Virginity is an overrated asset', had little chance of taking her own sexuality seriously. Such girls are the not uncommon products of mothers who themselves have never come to terms with mature sexuality; often the mothers are casualties of an over-puritanical upbringing against which they are still in an adolescent kind of rebellion. They are perhaps typical of a considerable proportion of the parents of adolescent girls we now see in schools.

So it seems that somewhere society has to start looking again at what it meant by giving adolescents freedom to make their own decisions about their relationships. We do not see them as mature enough to make a lot of decisions about their lives, nor do we see them as mature enough to go out and earn their own living; we have to ask ourselves then why we take such a cavalier attitude to this most important area of their lives. We do not expect them to make such decisions about the food they eat; about how they should spend their days; we say they have got to go to school and work. We do not allow them to make decisions about things like driving cars: we say they are not old enough to drive cars at 14 because it is dangerous. But we do not tell them that they are not old enough to have important sexual relationships because they can be dangerous.

It is certainly possible that it is not true for everyone that a full sexual relationship is necessarily dangerous at the early age of 13 or 14, but it seems highly probable that it will be. Our society is not structured in a way which makes it very easy for somebody to have a good and loving experience at that age. It is not certain that, in fact, driving a car at 14 is always dangerous; some 14-year-olds will be much better drivers than some 40- or 50-year-olds, but the vast majority of the young are not to be trusted with such lethal weapons. It is also, therefore, worth the adult world considering whether these young people are to be trusted with the intensity of sexual encounters which are going to affect them for the rest of their lives.

'If she told me what to do I wouldn't take any notice, would I? I'd just do the opposite.' So said more than one adolescent girl when asked if she wanted her parents to give her guidance as to her sexual life; a powerful argument, some might think, for not telling her what to do. Yet the young have always threatened to do exactly the opposite of what they were told, and in many cases, it must be admitted, have done so with excellent results. They did know, however, that they were being told, and the old had no doubts about their right to do the telling. The difference that is so marked between present-day parents and those of surely any other known society, is that so many of them no longer feel they have the right to tell their young.

'If only they would tell you. I wish I'd had someone in my family who cared about my sex life.' 'They should have told me not to; that's all I wanted.' 'They could have let you know how amazing it would be.' These, and others as critical of the parents who said 'You must decide for yourself', were quite as frequent responses to my questions as were those which demanded complete freedom from adult restraint. The difference was that this group of comments came mostly from the older girls. The younger they were, the less they wanted control; the older they were, the more they appeared to wish they had had it. We, in our generation, whose parents by their silence implied that there was simply no problem to be solved, no advice needed, since everyone knew that sex outside marriage was wicked, could not have foretold that this next generation would find themselves so lost without the structures of what seemed like an outmoded code of practice. Yet now they say: 'Everyone else was doing it so I thought I'd better.' 'Everyone else' is in fact their only guideline as to how to behave when society and parents provide none. As everyone else is also an immature adolescent this seems very shaky support for young people undertaking one of the most momentous decisions of their lives.

There is, of course, a point of view that this decision is not momentous, a view that will receive possibly more general credence as the act of intercourse becomes, as seems likely, even farther separated from the process of reproduction. Perhaps if the time comes when the only form of offspring is the clone, sex will merely become a game. However, although for some boys it would seem that sex has been only a game for a long time, for girls the experience of intercourse will, if it is allowed to, still have significance beyond all the excitement and pleasure, for the foreseeable future; it will remain in the category far removed from mere games. Their own bodies are being penetrated, and they are by having intercourse taking on the role that their mothers took before them. The possibility of becoming a mother can never be wholly eliminated.

The majority of girls, whatever front they might show to the world, do not appear to take sex lightly. We, the elders, should be grateful to them for this, since we have done so little ourselves to help them to develop a more serious approach to the subject. Whilst we are busy promoting a healthy open attitude by multitudinous person-relationship programmes we turn comfortable blind eyes to the unhealthy exploitation of sex that surrounds them in every direction. Findings from research into young girls' ideas about abortion undoubtedly suggest that there is a sizeable minority of girls whose attitude to the whole process is one of indifference. Having sex is part of everyday life from age 13 onwards, and abortions are the easiest form of contraception. Such girls exist, and one can but hope that they continue to use effective means of contraception, since it is hard to imagine that such a cool response to one of the great mysteries of life would augur well for their attitudes towards any children to whom they might give birth; we could well do without them as mothers of a new generation.

Undoubtedly some adult attitudes towards the sexuality of the young, whether male or female, can be due to their own personal difficulties, and some to mere custom and habit of thought. Females having intercourse are still considered indecent by a surprising number of people; they should have it, they believe, only in the marriage bed when their husbands wish it. If girls even have the misfortune to be forced into it against their wills by a rapist they are still likely to be treated as though they have themselves committed an indecency, if not a crime. The cruel fiction that it would not have happened had they not wanted it is evidence that this pejorative view of female sexuality is more common than many would like to admit. For young people the problem is that they do not, of course, share these notions. Few females under the age of 40 would subscribe to them and, those with specific religious convictions apart, hardly anyone under the age of 25 would do so.

The result of the impact of these two radically opposed points of view, one that it is all right and you do what you want, and the other that it is all wrong and only men do what they want, can, not surprisingly, be confusing. It is confusing for parents as well as for their daughters.

Teachers who can take a more objective view than parents can sometimes do a great deal to help. Bearing in mind that the inevitable immaturity of some parents has given their daughters a poor start in learning self-control, teachers can help them in adolescence to re-learn the necessary sense of self-worth to attain to self-regulation. Adolescence can be valuable for re-learning many of the only half-learnt lessons of early childhood. These years, when sensitivity is at its height, when consideration for others, generosity and altruism can be at their zenith, are the best ones for learning to care in a truly loving way for the opposite sex.

Teachers who are sensitive to this openness to learning on the adolescents' part can help them to re-learn the most important lesson of all — respect for self and others. The egocentricity of infancy that sometimes reappears at adolescence can be helped into becoming other-centredness by adults who can make sense for the young of the virtues of concern for others and control of our own inclinations.

Inclinations might not seem a strong enough word to describe what, by the adolescent, is felt with such passionate intensity. But very often the feelings that lead to that life-changing experience of conceiving and perhaps bearing a child are so transitory as to be unworthy of the title of passion. Passions exist, Romeos and Juliets exist at as young as 13 years of age, but no society other than ours has considered it impossible to curb their passions till at least a time when it can be recognised whether what is being felt is really some kind of love, or merely a passing sexual urge. Teachers who can recognise this distinction can be a great help to the young in their charge.

Sex is a personal and private subject and needs to be treated with discretion in a moderate degree of privacy, so small discussion groups work better than large ones. Sympathetic adults who, despite holding clear views that they can justify, will allow others to hold different ones, and those who can give other people space to air their own anxieties and convictions, provide the sort of ambience that can make sex education meaningful for the young. If teachers can provide such a setting, and can decide with conviction what their own views are, they can do a great deal to help adolescents sort their ideas out.

Girls, in my experience, are more than willing to talk about their sexual lives to people who are seriously concerned. They are also much more willing than a lot of adults realise to listen themselves to the views of people they can really respect. They will, of course, listen most to adults whom they recognise as honest. There is no likelihood of their listening, any more than we of the older generation did, to those adults who continue to preach a mindless acceptance of an ill-thought-out creed. Nor are they likely to want to hear once more the refusal to commit themselves to any point of view that is so characteristic of those timid adults who abdicate from their responsibility and give no guidance at all rather than lose favour with the young.

Most of the girls I have spoken to, whether bright or dim, liberated or conservative, have shown a very encouraging attitude towards sexuality even if their actual behaviour has not lived up to their aspirations. They feel that ideally their sexual relationships should be real ones, not just 'one night stands'; that promiscuity is a mistake and that what matters most of all is that the girl and the boy should both be concerned for each other. 'They should not think about it differently; men and women should feel the same', said a 16-year-old, echoing a more profound statement made nearly eighty years ago by Rainer Maria Rilke writing to 'A Young Poet'. Looking forward to the day when women would have 'stripped off the conventions of mere femininity' as well as freeing themselves from the need to be 'imitators of masculine ways', he saw the possibility of the love experience becoming 'a relation that is meant to be of one human being to another, no longer of man to woman'; a relationship that would 'fulfil itself, infinitely considerate and gentle, and kind and clear in binding and releasing . . .'. If this is the kind of sexual life that our young girls are really looking forward to, we should be helping them to reach it, not leaving them floundering.

Chapter 12

Girls Who Have Been Assaulted

Zoe, a 15-year-old, came to see the counsellor at her comprehensive school after a year of troubles and rows at school. She had been suspended at the beginning of the year for bullying. Since then she had made an effort to control her temper, but there were still outbursts, particularly against staff when she felt that she was being talked down to. Zoe could not bear to be treated like a child. She had a twin sister who was much better liked than she and who was far more childish in her behaviour than Zoe.

But children for Zoe still held such gruesome memories that having given it up early she did not want to have it resuscitated. At the age of 10 two men had raped her, each holding her down in turn whilst the other had intercourse with her. The subject was never mentioned in school or at home, although it was well known in the district. The only way Zoe's parents could cope with the horror of the episode was to blot it out of their minds completely; no doubt they hoped that this way they could blot it out of Zoe's mind as well. Unfortunately memories do not work in this way. Whilst everyone was pretending that nothing had happened to her, Zoe was grieving away silently to herself. The conspiracy of silence did nothing to help her, it simply confirmed her in her beliefs. She saw herself as guilty, unlovable and worthy only of death.

Adults, as well as children and young people, who suffer from sexual assaults are liable to react by feeling guilty. It is as though they themselves have committed the crime that was actually perpetrated against them. Receiving obscene telephone calls, for example, often creates a sensation of guilt as well as anger in the recipient.

To prevent herself from being overwhelmed by such feelings, a girl will frequently deal with them by denying their existence. In doing so she puts a kind of moratorium on all strong feelings so that she seems dull, withdrawn and unresponsive to the people around her. Such children are likely to lose the power to concentrate or pay attention. Their thoughts are so frightening and so painful that they are blotted out almost as soon as they reach consciousness.

We call this depression. It is not the only form of depression but it is fairly typical of the state of mind that results from an overwhelming feeling of guilt. What teachers see in such a case is a girl who is morose, sulky, uninterested in her work, feckless because she does not concentrate and much less intelligent, therefore, than she was originally thought to be. Such girls are dominated by the need to suppress all conscious recollection of an experience that is too horrific to think about, yet impossible to forget completely.

It is difficult for teachers to know what to do about girls who show all these symptoms and it is easy for them to assume that a depressed girl is just a lazy one. Any disparity between expectation and performance, however, justifies a more careful assessment of what is really happening. The inability to concentrate, for example, is rarely due to intentional lack of interest; much more frequently it is due to a need to keep the mind occupied with trivia so as to force out any more troubling ideas. As this is not done at a conscious level the depressed person is not aware of what is going on, only of her misery.

Often children in school will show this misery by a variety of bad behaviour as well as by work failure, as did Zoe. They are also likely to get themselves entangled in unsatisfactory relationships because, feeling worthless as they do, they are desperate to find someone who will love and accept them.

Zoe's first request of the counsellor was that he should help her to accede to the demands of her boyfriend who was threatening to end their relationship. He was angry because she was afraid to ask her GP for permission to take the contraceptive pill. Zoe knew well that her parents could not be broached on this subject, and she dared not visit the GP without them. Although ostensibly she intended to try to comply with the boy's demands, she also retained a hope that with the counsellor's support she could resist them and still maintain the friendship.

This tragic dilemma is one into which young girls are constantly being pushed by a society which provides no firm support for a girl who wants to say no, much as she is tempted also to say yes. An outrageous degree of subservience is still recommended to young girls by most of the teenage literature that continues to encourage them to concentrate the bulk of their energies on discovering how to attract boyfriends. Zoe's dilemma was exacerbated by her own damaged personality.

'After all, it is my duty to take precautions, isn't it? You see I feel that I want to give him everything I can,' she said. The number of young girls who allow themselves to be bamboozled into believing that it is the girl's duty alone to take precautions suggests that a high degree of self-denigration is quite commonplace. Apart from the fact that if more boys took more precautions there might be less sexually transmitted infections, the implication that irresponsibility is a male right is very serious.

Girls often cope with their guilt about sexual wishes by being self-punitive. Guilt about sexuality is not unusual in the young (or indeed in the old) in our society, in spite of the relaxation of rules. At present young girls often try to conceal their guilt because present-day mores suggest that guilt about sex is itself a reason for feeling guilty. Whether its roots are of a neurotic nature or are part of the natural human response to life can never be proved conclusively.

Zoe, who in her better moods had ambitions to be a journalist, made most of her communication with the counsellor through writing stories and verse. She depicted herself always as totally unlovable and unworthy of any love. She wrote stories in which she was hanged because she was so evil and would certainly kill people if she were not herself first killed to prevent this. She longed for someone to love her but knew that all her suffering was her own fault so she must bear her punishment in silence. Her twin sister was all that was good and perfect, and wept at the gallows as Zoe died. She did not deserve such concern because of her wickedness. Her greatest wickedness was that she was still attracted to boys.

Zoe's first experience of intercourse had been so terrifying that it would have required a great deal of sensitive adult support to help her to re-establish any normal attitude towards her sexuality. Unfortunately at home this support was not forthcoming, only silence. The silence must have seemed to her, at 10, a confirmation of her worst fears, that she was sinful; that having taken part, however unwillingly, in such an act, that it was better never to mention it again.

Meanwhile as she grew older she unwittingly re-enacted the previous experience. She chose a boyfriend several years older than herself who bullied her into submission by demanding intercourse as a prerequisite of maintaining the relationship. This is not an uncommon demand; it is fortunately not quite so common for a girl to feel that it is her 'duty' to comply. Zoe felt it her duty to comply because the demand for intercourse on terms which included threats of rejection was really felt by her to be a kind of rape. One way of dealing with a frightening situation is to try it out, like testing an aching tooth to see if the pain is real and can be borne.

At school she was also re-enacting the scene in another way. Bullies are all too often people who have themselves been bullied and dominated by others. What more complete experience of being dominated could a girl have than being raped? Zoe's reaction of bullying others needed a much more sympathetic treatment than it had received – a girl who had already been so punished by life was not going to learn anything of value from the rejecting experience of being excluded from school. On the contrary, what Zoe learned only confirmed what she already believed: that she was worthless.

Zoe refused the offer of psychiatric help which the counsellor offered to arrange for her because only mad people saw psychiatrists. It is true that she was not mad, but she was certainly in need of help to sort out the confusion and unhappiness that were dominating her life. Her aggression and depression, both part of the unresolved anger and fear that she had been concealing from herself and everyone else since the time that she was raped, needed to be looked at and dealt with.

She did manage, however, in time and with the help of the counsellor, to gain a good deal of insight into her own behaviour and motivation. She moved out of the tough bullying phase that she had been going through and at the same time was able to assert herself more realistically with her boyfriend. Her work improved and she was accepted in the sixth form, unlike her twin sister who now left school. She began to feel herself more acceptable. It is likely, however, that Zoe will have further problems later in her life with which she will need some help.

One problem about girls who are raped is that they arouse such anxieties in others that the temptation to deny that it has happened, or – as is still often the case – to suggest that somehow it is their own fault, is still strong. Zoe at the age of 10 could not possibly be blamed, yet she was not given the attention and understanding that she needed. If someone had been able to help her to talk through the incident and grieve in the way that was necessary, she would not perhaps still have been bearing the burden of it many years later.

There is one burden that girls can carry for the rest of their lives if it is not dealt with at the proper time, and that is the effect of incestuous attacks; often the worst kind of rape. Incest can always be defined as rape since the element of consent can never be really present in a daughter. Step-fathers sometimes delude themselves that they are not criminal since they have no blood relationship with the girl. The criminality consists, of course, in the damage that is caused by the tremendous emotional pressure that is put on a girl; she is rarely able to resist the attraction of sexual conquest of her mother's husband, and equally rarely able to sustain the guilt that this engenders. A middle-aged woman who had been seduced in her teens by her father stated recently in a television programme that she had not passed one day of her life without remembering what she had gone through.

Monica at 17 was under threat of exclusion from school at the end of her first year in the sixth form, because she had done virtually no work for a year. Some of her teachers had seen her as lazy, others as unhappy. She was an intelligent girl who had shown great promise in the first and second forms, but had since deteriorated. She had managed nevertheless to obtain enough O levels to get her into the sixth form, but it was evident to all her teachers that she was not going to get any A levels if she did not start to work soon.

Monica had once harboured an ambition to go into town planning, and was taking maths, economics and art with this in view. By the time Christmas had arrived her maths teacher was perfectly willing to let Monica drop the subject, and move over to psychology; she had done no work and made no contribution in class. Monica was not well liked by the school staff. She was a well-dressed girl from an obviously well-to-do background, and her lackadaisical attitude and scanty work output did not endear her to them. Hard-working teachers who were trying, in a predominantly underprivileged inner city area, to encourage girls and boys to aim high, work hard and break out of the poverty trap that held so many of their parents found her irritating.

The psychology teacher, who was also a trained counsellor, soon after taking her into the class, however, recognised that she might well be suffering from depression. When some work was actually handed in it was good, and when she could be cajoled into responding in class she did so with intelligence and perception: but she could rarely be so cajoled. One day, during a discussion about human growth and development, the onset of puberty was mentioned. Monica astonished everyone by leaping up and dashing out of the room.

Monica came from a strongly fundamentalist religious group who lived in the area; a sect which tended to treat sex as a necessary evil, not to be mentioned except in cases of extreme necessity. She had not had much sexual instruction at home and the teacher presumed that Monica had been shocked by what had been said. Some hours later her teacher tracked her down and persuaded her to talk about the episode. Her guess proved wrong; however, when she suggested to Monica that there might have been something disturbing in what she had said, Monica said bitterly: 'Dont worry, I know all about sex.'

Eventually the story was unfolded, unwillingly at first, but later in a welter of detail. Monica, since she was 12, had been plagued by her father with sexual attentions. She found these impossible either to prevent or to resist. Whilst they frightened her they also excited her. She gave way to her father, only, later, to be filled with guilt and remorse. Being a deeply religious girl she felt that she was offending God, and after this had been going on for about a year decided that she must try to find someone to help her to stop it.

Monica went to the minister of her church and, having extracted a promise that he would keep her secret, told him about what was happening. Unfortunately the poor man was unable to give her the comfort she needed. He reacted with shocked horror which Monica saw as disbelief. She went away less than comforted and continued her downward path into depression. She found herself unable to concentrate or to sleep, and by the time she was 16 and taking her O levels it was obvious to everyone that something was wrong with her. Her mother advised a visit to the doctor to get some tranquillisers to help her over her exams. Monica found a sympathetic GP in whom she eventually confided her problem. He advised her to tell her mother, but this she could not bring herself to do.

She explained to her psychology teacher that the reason for not talking to her mother was that she really believed her mother knew and even condoned what was happening. The counsellor helped her to see that the GP's advice was quite sound and worth considering. Finally Monica decided to talk to her mother, who unfortunately reacted with alarm when she heard that Monica had talked to her teacher: 'We'll all be prosecuted by the police', she said. Later Monica found herself being bribed by her mother not to say anything to anyone.

Not surprisingly, as Monica went on to reveal, this was a family where everything had to be kept secret. Sex had never been discussed. Monica had gleaned what knowledge she had from schoolfriends, not from home. When her father first made advances to her she was frightened but also flattered: she was pleased to attract his attention away from her mother. Later, when she became frightened and wanted to tell her mother, she found that she did not dare to discuss such a hidden subject. An only child, she was left with no one to talk to and was driven in on herself.

Withdrawal, solitary behaviour, inability to concentrate on work and lassitude, all symptoms similar to those shown by Zoe, were evident signs to the counsellor of severe depression. With her help Monica was eventually able to break away from her father and acquire a boyfriend. She had unsatisfactory sexual relations with him, however, and like many girls who have suffered in this way felt that she would never be able to have a proper heterosexual relationship with anyone again. The combination of confusion about parental and child roles, fear, excess emotion and sexual excitement laced with terrible guilt not surprisingly drives many, probably most, girls who have suffered in this way into some form of neurosis. Unfortunately the incidence of this sort of incest is much more common than is usually realised. Ignorance of its prevalence leads to the kind of shock that Monica's minister expressed. Monica was in fact relatively well treated compared with some girls who are forced into sexual activity by fathers or step-fathers who feel no real affection for them, only lust. Yet the combination of affection and lust can itself be damaging because it arouses confused and ambivalent feelings in a girl. Many an adolescent girl, like a 4- or 5-year-old, feels a secret guilty delight in attracting her father's attention away from the mother. This is commonplace when it stays in the level of fantasy. When it becomes a reality the guilt is liable to be overwhelming.

There are a wide variety of reasons why men commit incest; central to them all is immaturity. Immaturity of emotional development goes along with an inability to withstand stress or to tolerate opposition to one's wishes; like the 3-year-old, the man who is emotionally immature will have something equivalent to a temper tantrum if he does not get his way sexually. If he cannot get satisfaction from his wife he will turn to a daughter who is far more malleable and unable to stand up to him even if she wants to. Usually she is sufficiently flattered and titillated not to want to resist his advances, in spite of the fear and guilt that accompany them.

We still live in a society that frequently sees men's sexual wishes as of such importance that they should not be denied. In a recent case of wife-battering a man who had, amongst other heinous cruelties, dragged his wife up and down stairs by the hair, was excused, from the bench, on the ground that she was frustrating him sexually. He received a brief suspended sentence. In such a climate of opinion fathers can very easily deceive themselves into justifying to themselves and their wives the rape of their daughters.

The wife who deludes herself into believing that she cannot prevent her husband from playing sexual games with her daughter is abdicating from her responsibility as a mother, though perhaps consciously she is just abdicating as a wife. The supreme selfishness of such parents looks like a denial of all human decency; and indeed their children often experience it as such. However, to condemn people for immaturity is a futile occupation. Many an incestuous father is looking for the same fantasied pure young sexual partner that he dreamed of in his youth, who he feels will fulfil all his needs, because he has failed to come to terms with the sexuality of females. Often such a man had a bad relationship with his own mother, who was either rejecting or over-involved, perhaps herself seductive in manner if not in deed to her son.

In the same way the wives who so often appear to tolerate, condone or even encourage the ill-treatment of their daughters are no doubt the victims of circumstances. Condemnation is not so much in order as the finding of some solution. Such parents who are using their children for their own ends are clearly not sufficiently emotionally mature to be entitled to be responsible for the rearing of other immature creatures. Only when we can teach girls the seriousness of conception and birth will we be doing anything very positive towards preventing these practices. With more awareness wives should be able to stand up to the husband who puts his own needs before those of his child.

To condemn such people is a temptation but it would be more fruitful to offer them some help in growing up. So far this is seldom available, though in parts of the USA help for incestuously inclined parents is being given on a growing scale. Help for the children is offered here in child guidance clinics and other child-oriented settings. What is usually needed is the re-establishment of a healthy attitude in a girl towards her own sexuality. Besides this, however, she needs to be able to find her way towards developing an improved relationship with her parents that is neither totally condemning and rejecting nor over-involved and dependent. It is hard for a young girl to feel tolerant when she has been abused; it is equally hard for her, in many cases, to break the intense attraction for her father that this close relationship has engendered. Only with adult guidance can this be achieved.

With more general awareness of the incidence of this kind of family constellation there might be less need for girls to keep their experiences secret. If they learn that others suffer in the same way, they will be able to seek help; and if the people from whom they seek it are better informed they will be less inclined towards the shocked reaction that Monica encountered. Monica's teacher did not find the information shocking because as a counsellor she had been trained to cope with such situations. Whilst not, of course, divulging any confidential matters she was able, with Monica's blessing, to alert the headmistress to the danger that the girl was in. She in her turn, whilst not being prepared to have a girl's private life bandied about in the staffroom, was able to advise the rest of the staff that Monica's home difficulties were responsible for much of her work failure, and to encourage them to deal with her more tolerantly.

The responsibilities of schools in these matters therefore rest first in helping girls who have suffered in this way to come to terms with their difficulties and face up to their depression, and secondly in laying a good foundation for future partnerships by giving boys and girls a chance to discuss and discover the implications of marriage and child-rearing. More open discussion can do a lot to help the immature and frightened boy, and more information about what children need from their parents can impress on future parents the need for a sense of responsibility towards their offspring.

Chapter 13

Girls and their Health

Surprisingly large numbers of present-day teenagers seem to have health problems. The National Children's Bureau report *Britain's 16 Year Olds* found that 65 per cent had visited their GPs during their sixteenth year. Almost certainly a count of the notes sent by parents to excuse their teenage children from school would produce an even higher number of complaints not necessarily reported to GPs. Discounting those which are fraudulent or merely collusion with a bit of malingering, we still find a picture of an excessively high sickness rate for a society that has a built-in health protection service.

Little difference was found between the excuse notes of boys and girls but there are nevertheless specific illnesses that are either exclusively female or more commonly found in girls that crop up in adolescence. The most obvious are those related to menstruation. Another, anorexia nervosa, is more often found in girls and frequently involves disturbance of the menstrual cycle. Depressions occur in boys and girls equally but currently girls make more suicide attempts than do boys. Hysteria, that rather mysterious illness that has no real symptomatology or known cause, is more frequently diagnosed in girls than in boys. Perhaps one of the hardest crosses girls have to bear is that of excessive perspiration, which might not seem like an ailment to those who have not suffered from it but is the cause of great suffering to many an adolescent girl and is related to anxiety, usually about sexual maturation. Eneuresis and encopresis, found equally in boys and girls at an early age, sometimes last into adolescence and can also cause tremendous misery. All these ailments are either overtly or indirectly considered to be emotionally based; they are amongst those aspects of human suffering that show most clearly how inadequate is that concept of the human animal that divides us rigidly into body and mind, soul, spirit or psyche. As far as teachers are concerned it is the psychological aspect of their pupil's ailments that is of importance to them.

MENSTRUATION

Marianne, a 14-year-old, suffered from the fact that everybody knows that period pains are due to psychological causes and therefore something to be ashamed of. Unfortunately even her GP subscribed to these outmoded notions and gave her no help. Her mother was a brisk young woman who had not only played county hockey in the past but was still given to breaking the ice on the local open air swimming pool in the early mornings. She had never suffered from dismenorrhoea in her life. Between them the mother and the GP managed to convince Marianne that she was an incurable neurotic and so she was well set on the path to becoming one.

She took as much time off school as her mother would grudgingly allow. Because she felt criticised by her GP she would not return to him to get medical certificates, so her mother was constantly worried about the days off and being blamed for Marianne's absences. Her father, whose work took him away from home a great deal, left her mother to cope on her own. As far as he was concerned it was all women's business and a lot of nonsense anyhow. Marianne's work suffered and her termly reports indicated a steady deterioration, partly because of absences but also because for up to a quarter or more of each month she really could not concentrate at all. Marianne suffered agonies for at least seven days out of every month, and spent a lot of the rest of the month worrying about the next onslaught. At school she received more sympathy than she did at home because she was fortunate in her PE teacher. This teacher had long ago abandoned the once-current fashion of teaching girls that it is shameful to suffer from period pains. She sympathised with Marianne's condition as she knew that exercise was not necessarily the best or the only cure. It was with her help, and that of the school medical officer whom she enlisted, that Marianne was eventually persuaded that it was possible for her to change her GP. She did this with good results, was given medication to alleviate a great deal of the discomfort and, more important still, she was given both assurance that she was not suffering from something incurable and confidence in realising that she was not herself personally responsible for her state.

Those adults who have the good fortune to enjoy excellent health sometimes fail to sympathise with the more fragile members of society, yet most women at one time or another have experienced dismenorrhoea. They need only to have done so once to recognise that as a severe and recurring disability it could be totally incapacitating. The unfortunate association between the whole syndrome of tension related to menstruation and emotional problems has made matters worse. Whilst we still live in a society that associates emotional difficulties with sin, or at least with self-indulgence, any suggestion of such difficulties, especially to an adolescent, is experienced as accusation.

For too many people, like Marianne's mother, the notion psychosomatic implies malingering. She really could not imagine that something which for her was a simple and natural process could be a serious problem for anyone else. Equally myopic are those who, admitting that there is a problem, label it psychosomatic, and so see no further need to take action. Research into this aspect of women's lives has for long been neglected because the whole topic has been seen as indelicate. Although currently much more is being done, the findings have not always reached the ears of the general public. Teachers can therefore be very helpful to girls by giving them some hope and some support based on those findings. For example, they can comfort girls who suffer this way by pointing out first how common such suffering is, at least in Western society, and secondly by assuring them that most women experience spontaneous remission. More practically they can bear in mind the evidence for the bad effects that menstruation has been shown to have on a large number of girls in terms of examination performance. It is not impossible to rearrange examination dates and the evidence that girls do significantly worse whilst menstruating is strong enough to support them in their endeavours.

Until everyone, including members of examination boards, develops a healthier attitude to this topic, girls will continue to refer to their menstruation as 'the curse', and large numbers will suffer unnecessary pain because they expect to do so. If menstruation as an aspect of femininity is rejected, then femininity as an aspect of a human being can easily be rejected too: this can lead to pain of a psychological origin: pain actually caused by anxiety about psychosexual development. As open discussion about problems connected with menstruation becomes more acceptable, so knowledge about the real impact of this important aspect of a girl's life will increase.

Penelope Shuttle and Peter Redgrove in their excellent book *The Wise Wound* (which should be read by everyone who has anything to do with health education of girls) have pointed out that there is no real agreement among authorities as to the actual mechanism of the menstrual cycle. They do, however, go on to give a great deal of information and comment which could be of immense value to teachers involved in physical education, child care and home economics as well as health education. If they seem to some to go too far overboard in stressing the superiority of everything feminine, they do at least redress the balance a little in a world which has for so long seen menstruation as a sickness and an evil; they also give some convincing evidence that it is possible that all sickness associated with menstruation might be caused by attitudes which, although inherent in our society, and not just the responsibility of the girl concerned, can be altered if she is willing to accept help, and that all menstrual pain can be abolished. If the prospect of this happening for every adolescent girl is somewhat remote, we can at least in the meantime hope that those adults who will take the trouble to understand these problems will thereby learn to treat them with sympathy.

HYSTERIA

Gloria used to go into peals of laughter with no apparent provocation and in the most unsuitable places: the main hall during assembly or the school chapel during a service. She was accused of seeking attention, which was what she was doing, because she needed it desperately. Anyone who works as hard as that to get attention should be attended to; they are usually either very ill or very unhappy or both.

Having finally announced that she had seen the devil in the corner of the chapel, to the great delight and excitement of her friends, Gloria was carted off and seen no more. By this time she had been in her boarding school for a year, showing increasing signs of unbalance, but, because it was not respectable to be unbalanced, nor indeed was it understood why anybody should be anything so strange, nothing had been done. The poor girl was in fact at a stage of total breakdown, but with a little more awareness the school authorities might well have prevented her from reaching such a state of despair before she received treatment.

Awareness of problems and the ability to be alert to danger signs can be a valuable part of the armoury of anyone who deals with adolescents. So much normal adolescent behaviour is a little mad that sometimes teachers are tempted to ignore the abnormal in the hope that it will just go away. Gloria, however, was manifestly more than just an excitable adolescent. She was showing the sorts of symptoms that are popularly associated with hysteria, but for which she was eventually diagnosed as a schizophrenic. Hysteria, originally thought to have something to do with the womb, has always been seen as a predominantly female problem. Perhaps because girls are permitted more extremes of emotional experience in our society, they are more likely to show this kind of behaviour. However, if they do so they are no longer very likely to be diagnosed as hysteric by anyone in the medical profession.

The term 'hysteric' has a long and ignoble history, and its main role in contemporary vocabulary is often still to describe some girl who is making a nuisance of herself. Without having any exact scientific definition, it implies all those unreliable, unpredictable, over-emotional traits that have for so long been said to be associated with femininity. The more recent medical definition of the term, however, though rejected by many psychiatrists who claim that there is no such animal as a hysteric, suggest more a useful umbrella for a lot of ill-defined symptoms. The connecting factor between these symptoms is that they often show themselves physically, yet, because their origin is unclear, they are assumed to come from psychological causes.

The problem about this sort of definition is that it does not really define, all it does is imply. What is implied above all by terms like psychogenic or psychosomatic is some sort of pejorative comment, unspoken and almost always denied, nevertheless there. It is not very nice to be suffering from an illness that might have a psychological basis and people should be ashamed of it, but it is, of course, just what you would expect from adolescent girls. Whilst years of hard work by associations working for the mentally ill have borne some fruit in that treatment for psychological problems now bears less stigma, physiological concomitants of emotional difficulties still carry overtones of malingering. Any hysteric, therefore, is someone who is not really ill but seems so; she is actually merely a bit neurotic.

Beryl suffered from just such a diagnosis; she arrived at a comprehensive school with it written in to her record card, the clinician concerned being her former teacher. There was a sufficient grain of truth in the description of her for it to be accepted without question by her new teachers at first. Beryl did produce a startling variety of illnesses, and the possibility that all her ailments were conversion symptoms, psychological problems manifesting themselves in physical form, could not, wrote one of the doctors she visited, be ruled out. It might be questioned why there would be any need for this to be ruled out since even the most conservative of medical minds are now opening up to recognition that psyches and somas are rather intimately connected, even if they will not go so far as to toy with the daring notion that they could be one and the same. So Beryl's illnesses, whilst showing themselves physically, were allowed to have some relationship to her feelings, but unfortunately that was as far as it went. No one took the matter seriously enough to offer to help her to improve her feelings in any way, or indeed to recognise that they existed.

Ever since Freud published his early *Studies in Hysteria* it has been recognised by the general public that those people who show conversion symptoms are likely to be doing so because they are out of touch with their true feelings. Usually we stay out of touch with those feelings that it is too painful to remain in touch with. A physical symptom related to such denied feelings might well bear some relation to the nature of that feeling, the classic example being the paralysed arm of some one who is repressing wishes to murder.

Beryl's symptoms, though many and varied, could be generally classified as pain in the gut. This was diagnosed originally as 'abdominal migraine', subsequently as a 'grumbling appendix' and finally, after a few more titles had been added to the list, as 'imaginary pain'. At no time, it seems, did any of the medical people whom she saw question whether this much pain, whatever its cause, might be rather hard to bear and might have something to do with unhappiness. A diet of tranquillisers, however, prescribed after the 'imaginary pain' diagnosis, indicated that at least some attention had been paid to the relevance of Beryl's psyche to her somatic symptoms.

Meanwhile, in a rather sporadic way, Beryl was attending school. If, as is almost certainly the case, few GPs have the time, the training, or, in many cases, even the inclination to unearth the unhappiness that might lie behind what they could classify as the hysteric symptoms of a 13-year-old girl, who else is available to undertake such work? Certainly this hardly seems a teaching job. How many teachers could claim to have any more qualifications or time than a GP to take on so demanding a task? Yet teachers are the only people outside the family who are likely to come into any regular contact with such a girl and who might have any skills at all in the kind of human relations that would be necessary to enable her to examine the causes of her misery and her pains.

It is for this reason that it has been considered possible for teachers to involve themselves in what is called pastoral care, but to take on such work is one thing, to do it is another. Incompetent and insensitive tramping about on other people's feelings by those who believe they have a mission to do good to others is a nightmare that many opponents of pastoral care fear, not without justification. Teachers, like doctors, are not necessarily more suited to the role of confidante to the unhappy, because their normal work makes demands that are of a different order from those made on a counsellor of any sort. Their experience of being efficient advisers and instructors who can organise away difficulties does not necessarily fit people well for a role requiring the more passive acceptance and tolerance that is generally considered essential for any form of counselling relationship. Likewise Carl Rogers's *Unconditional Positive Regard*, recommended originally, and wisely, as central to the counsellor's role, is a lovely concept which might well, if practised by all teachers at all times, bring havoc into many an erstwhile peaceful classroom. Yet is is at the centre of all counselling work. It is for this reason that however good, kind, loving and tolerant teachers may be, unless they learn when trying to counsel the unhappy to dissociate themselves from their normal role they can do more damage than good.

It is sometimes thought that because they possess no medical knowledge teachers should not be trained as counsellors but, as most honest psychiatrists will admit, it is not medical skill which is necessary in this kind of work but skill in interpersonal relations. This can be taught to people who are receptive to it, but however receptive they are by nature they still need to be taught. Training in counselling is essential for anyone who is going to give help to deeply disturbed and unhappy adolescents, and can be of immense value to those working with all the normal adolescent problems. However, even without training those teachers who have the interests of children at heart can do a great deal if they can learn first of all to admit that theirs is a didactic role, however much they would like to see it otherwise, and secondly to shed it when they are taking on counselling-type activities.

Beryl had the good fortune to attend a school which employed a full-time counsellor. After a series of long absences he managed to persuade her to come to talk to him about why she had been away. Having catalogued her various illnesses, she then went on to pour out to him the misery that she had been bottling up for years. With a phrase familiar to so many counsellors, 'I've never found anyone I could talk to like this before', she opened up a picture of the nightmare that her life had become.

She lived with a mother who was clearly psychologically very ill – they moved from town to town every few years to escape, Beryl believed, the wrath of neighbours. Her mother was a kind of prostitute in that she kept herself and her daughter largely on money that she was paid by a variety of men who would come to live with them for a while. They invariably left after being subjected to one of her maniacal rages in which, claiming that they must pay maintenance for the child that she had conceived, she hurled abuse at them. After this she would tell Beryl that she had had an abortion, going into graphic and probably totally fictitious details.

Beryl's first six years had been spent with her mother and father and two older brothers in a town at the other side of the country. She had left with her mother and now at nearly 14 she had lived in four different towns. She fantasised that her previous childhood had been idyllic and longed to return to her father's house. She was not, however, unsympathetic towards her mother who was mostly kind and concerned, especially when Beryl was ill. She thought that her mother's menfriends were really cruel when they left her and was deeply anxious about the series of terminations.

Beryl's mother, who depended emotionally as well as financially on these men, was at pains to conceal her real age from them. She insisted therefore that Beryl pass herself off as her sister instead of her daughter. This produced such confusion in Beryl's mind that she felt as though she had no identity, no mother and no place in the world. She had recurring nightmares about men attacking her and invariably woke up from them with abdominal pains.

Her ailments, centring on her abdomen, might well have borne some relation to her anxieties about her mother's abortions. Certainly they were connected with her unhappiness. These patterns of recurring illness were not inventions on her part, they were genuine. Quite a lot of the time she was really ill and always she was in real pain. The illness was a way for her body to cope with the anxieties that she could only experience otherwise in her sleep in the form of nightmares. The constant attacks that her mother was making on her own body in fantasy if not in reality, through all these abortions, gave Beryl a basis for her fears. When she was able to talk about her feelings her anxieties could be relieved.

Within six months of Beryl's first visit to the counsellor, whom she continued to see regularly from then on, she began to improve. Her illnesses did not disappear overnight, but diminished gradually, her school attendances became regular and she settled down to something like a normal adolescence.

The turning-point had undoubtedly come when the counsellor had, with the co-operation of Beryl's mother, arranged for her to visit her father. She spent a week with him and her brothers, enjoyed herself, but decided that she preferred life with her mother. This life would never be simple or straightforward, but it was already much better, and she was able to cope with it. As she commented herself, having someone to talk to made all the difference. A member of the pastoral care staff, given time, might well have been able to help Beryl in a similar way. What was necessary was to realise how much she was in need of an adult who would listen to her, give her support and help her to adjust to the rather grim reality of her life.

ANOREXIA

Some psychiatric help for Beryl might well have been useful but it was not available; for some problems, however, it is imperative that someone makes sure that medical and psychiatric help is called in. There is one type of abnormal adolescent behaviour that is currently prevalent amongst girls that must not be ignored: anorexia, which means a refusal to eat. This illness comes under the heading of hysteria because it is one in which there is a strong denial of reality. It is also much more common in girls than in boys, though not by any means unknown in boys.

Hilary was a fairly typical example of a serious anorexic. She developed this illness when she was 12 years old. It was not diagnosed at first as there were at the time still GPs around who had somehow not managed to hear about it; there are probably few of these now, but for Hilary the increased knowledge of this subject has come too late. She was an extreme case and is still, in her early twenties, spending a large part of her life in a mental hospital. Nowadays others are more likely to be spotted earlier, especially if those responsible for pastoral care in schools are on the look-out for them.

Hilary was an intelligent girl, the only child of a very ambitious mother who had great hopes for her career. Her father, less intelligent than either Hilary or her mother, had a great attachment to his daughter with whom he used to spend hours when she was a little girl. Where her mother was obsessed with Hilary's gaining excellent marks for her work, he would encourage her to develop her physical as well as her mental skills. He took her skating, enrolled her in a gym club and drove her all over the country to compete, and win, in point to points. Whatever Hilary did, intellectually or physically, she got the message that she must succeed.

When they moved into a town Hilary was of an age to leave her private convent school so she was enrolled in the nearby comprehensive school. An only child, she had had little to do with boys so she found her encounters with some fairly tough specimens in her new school very frightening and more than she could cope with. She complained about the behaviour of the boy who sat next to her, saying he was nasty. She began for the first time in her life to dislike school. She made excuses to stay away, complained of sickness and pains and spent a lot of time in bed. Meantime she worried endlessly about her work; dropped all her out of school activities; and rejected all her father's attempts to revive her interest in the sports that she had enjoyed so much in the country.

Hilary was eventually seen by an educational psychologist who, discerning the state of hyper-anxiety that was developing, recommended that she spend some of her time at one of the withdrawal units that had been established in the town. Here, under less pressure, Hilary was able to talk about the anxieties which were reaching such a pitch that she was almost afraid to be in the same room as a boy. She felt that she was going to be attacked.

After Hilary had spent some months in the unit the teacher in charge realised that she was losing weight. She discussed the matter with Hilary's mother who revealed that she herself, worried about the weight loss, had taken her to their family doctor who had said not to bother about it, it was only temporary. After this her teacher started to encourage Hilary to eat at the mid-morning break, but found that she was not interested in food; attributing this to Hilary's state of anxiety she decided that medical attention was called for. Further discussion with the mother revealed that Hilary's periods, which had started when she was 11, had ceased within the last year. She reported that Hilary was glad, as she hated having periods, and that she was trying to prevent herself from developing physically by wrapping bandages made of torn-up sheets around her body, particularly round her breasts, to prevent her shape changing. It was when she heard this that the teacher decided to press Hilary's mother to insist on a psychiatric assessment.

This rejection of female sexuality is characteristic of anorexia nervosa. There is such a tremendous anxiety about this whole area that both consciously and unconsciously femininity is rejected by disguising the feminine aspects of her figure and by actually ceasing to menstruate. The rejection of her father and the criticism of the boys at school as nasty represents a characteristic aversion to the opposite sex. She refused to do PE at school, as she later revealed, because she did not want her figure to be seen in the shower.

Hilary went from bad to worse; she showed all the classic behaviour of an anorexic: refusing to believe that she was losing weight, yet in fact hardly eating anything at all. Her after-meals exercises were a typical anorexic's attempt to get rid of the fat that she feared she had put on, although she might only have eaten a morsel. Anorexics believe that they are fatter than they really are and when shown themselves in a glass and asked to assess the width of their bodies they always over-estimate it. They believe themselves to be fat although they become in fact as thin as rakes. She would run up and down stairs fifty times to take off weight. Alternating with this behaviour she would go on what anorexics usually call a binge – eating enormous quantities, especially of chocolates and other sweet, fattening foods.

Her teacher eventually managed to persuade the mother that she should insist on a psychiatric assessment and as a result treatment was inaugurated. Hilary was sent first to a general hospital where she manifested another characteristic symptom. She refused all the food that she was offered, but every day bought a large box of chocolates from the trolley, saying that she was buying them for her mother. She took them to the bathroom and ate them. She finally ended up in a psychiatric ward after she had had serious rows with her mother who by this time was threatening to turn her out of the house. Had her case been recognised in time it might have been possible to prevent this serious deterioration.

Other girls with a lesser form of this problem do not show all these symptoms. Frequently their periods cease and they have anxieties about their appearance and their work. Very often they are highly intelligent girls with a serious attitude towards study. They often suffer special anxieties about examinations and worry that they are not doing enough. They can be helped if their problem is recognised soon enough and, with help, will be able to adjust their diet and learn to cope with school in a more realistic way.

One of the commonest precipitating factors is starting to slim. There is no doubt that obesity is one of the serious hazards in our society, and slimming will always be important as a way of maintaining health as well as a fashionable figure. A good many sensible girls recognise the need to keep to a diet with a limited carbohydrate content and a maximum of fresh fruit and green vegetables. Unfortunately the constant bombardment with propaganda about the necessity of a slim figure on television, in newspapers and journals can have too powerful an effect on some not too stable girls. They take to ridiculously unbalanced diets, lacking essential ingredients, and this can lead to the habit of rejecting food altogether.

But although dieting is the principal feature of the illness, anorexia is by no means correctly called the slimming disease. It is not dieting which usually causes it in the first place, much more often some instability of temperament. Serious anorexia needs specialised treatment, usually hospitalisation, where psychological as well as physiological treatment is available.

Teachers who for any reason at all have suspicions that a girl is not eating enough should look very closely at her behaviour. They should report their suspicions, even if they are only slightly based, to someone on the staff who is responsible for pastoral care. Ideally there should be a counsellor who is trained to recognise the symptoms and would know how to set in motion the process of getting the girl into treatment. If not, whichever member of staff has responsibility for these matters should make inquiries as to the girl's eating habits. Find out if she eats lunch at school. If, as so often happens, she is presumed by her parents to be doing so, but is not in fact eating her lunch, there are good grounds for making further investigations.

It will be necessary for a responsible member of staff to contact the parents at some time. This has to be done with great tact because there is a high probability that her parents will already be extremely anxious people, so any comment by teachers on their daughter's behaviour may come over to them as a criticism of their handling of her. Undoubtedly many girls with one or other form of anorexia have difficult relationships with their parents, but not all do so. It is always wiser, however, to be prepared for difficulties rather than to be surprised by them.

Sometimes there will be a temporary rift between the girl and her parents, a commonplace in adolescence, which might be wrongly interpreted as a severe problem by those expecting to find family difficulties. Sometimes, however, the textbook picture of the sort of mother who has an anorexic daughter may emerge. There are undoubtedly mothers who because of their dominating and cold attitude create in their daughters tremendous anxieties. Such a mother will be likely to resent intrusion into her family affairs by any outsider. Members of the school staff need to show that they are interested only in making sure that her daughter is happy and successful at school and that everything is being done to ensure this. The mother will then usually admit to being relieved that someone else besides herself is concerned at her daughter's behaviour.

What needs to be done next is to find out what medical help has been sought and to give the parents as clear a picture as possible of the girl's behaviour in school and the reasons for the school's anxieties. Sometimes the girl shows more symptoms in school than at home and the school's evidence will therefore be useful for the parents who might need to convince a hesitant GP that this really is a serious situation.

Sometimes the parents will be so overwhelmed with guilt about their daughter's condition, feeling, as parents always do, that they are to blame, that they will find it hard at first to talk about it. Most parents keep their anxieties to themselves and as a result exacerbate the tensions in the household. When at last they find an understanding listener in a teacher or counsellor who knows and understands their daughter, they can gain enormous relief of tension and a renewed hope and stability. Help given to the parents by just listening to them can go a long way towards helping the daughter.

Listening, however, is not enough. The girl nearly always needs some kind of psychological help and always needs to be seen by a physician; this is a physical condition and a serious one. If you do not eat you die. Prevention being better than cure, the school health education projects have most to offer in dealing with the problem. Girls should be given the facts and encouraged to discuss their difficulties and anxieties with understanding members of the teaching staff so that any tendency in the direction of eating disorders can be attended to before it gets out of hand.

Hilary's anorexia, Gloria's even more serious schizophrenia and Beryl's hypochondria, because they had an aura of unreality about them, tended to antagonise the adults in their lives. It is these irrational aspects of adolescent behaviour that are often the most difficult for people to understand although at a less serious level they are characteristic of a great number of normal adolescents. What we need in schools is as many teachers as possible who feel that they can at least try to understand enough to be able to recognise serious difficulties when they arise. Where there is no trained counsellor in the school teachers need to discover for themselves how to go about making sure that the children get professional help outside the school. When such problems are not attended to they do not go away, they grow. Yet in many cases there is help available if schools will make use of it, and a great deal can be done if problems are dealt with soon enough.

Chapter 14

Suicide, Depression and Suicide Threats

'She's taken an overdose, Miss' is a Monday morning greeting that some school counsellors have come to expect. Despite its familiarity it never fails to cause a sinking of the heart. Whilst taking an overdose can mean the swallowing of anything from a few aspirins to a dose of mother's barbiturates, it could always mean death; and this the counsellor and others who deal with such matters can never forget.

The incidence of suicide in all age-groups throughout the world is on the increase. The incidence of suicide attempts by adolescent girls is most marked. In some schools it seems almost to have become a fashion to play this bizarre form of Russian roulette. Of course a lot of these attempts are not intended to succeed, but evidence seems to suggest that they sometimes succeed when they are not intended to do so. Al Alvarez, in his moving book on the subject *The Savage God*, suggests that a high proportion of suicides might belong in this category. Certainly in adolescence the concept of death itself can be so confused that some attempts at suicide look like experiments rather than acts of tragedy. Tragedy, however, is always inherent in the act and no such attempt should ever be taken lightly.

There is no doubt that death has a fascination for many adolescents; often the loss of life does not seem to them as serious as it does to older people. Where young warriors are no longer the fashion we have young hooligans instead riding motorbikes or driving cars in a suicidal and sometimes murderous manner. Dicing with death is a common adolescent pastime and so is thinking and talking about it. Death, in fact, a difficult concept for most of us, is often in the teens very attractive. It has the property of excitement that is attached to all danger, and it has that quality of mystery that accords with so much of the imaginative thinking of adolescence. So it is something to be played with, but since the playing can often accidentally spill over into reality, never should even the slightest move towards suicide be ignored.

The only known way of dealing with a person who threatens suicide is to find out what it is that is troubling him or her. This will not necessarily get rid of the trouble as such, if it exists outside the imagination of the person concerned, but it is the first step towards helping her to cope with the trouble.

Adults sometimes treat the attempted overdose as an irritating game, but this is a misunderstanding of the phenomenon, for however trivial the attempt of the young person may seem there is no frivolity there. No one makes a suicide attempt, however inept, who is not suffering from some kind of despair. We might be right in assessing that the attempt is intended only to attract notice to herself. We have to ask ourselves what has been done to a child that she has to go to such extremes to gain the attention that she needs. What kind of a world have we presented to the young if they want to leave it at a time when their lives are just beginning? A suicide attempt is never just a light-hearted game of chance; it is also always a rejection of life.

The life that is being rejected might well be one that none of the adults around would like to live; or it might, at least on the surface, appear to be a perfectly satisfactory one. All that is certain is that it does not contain enough promise to fire the imagination of the young person concerned. To retain hope in life we need some security either from within provided by beliefs and commitments or from without provided by a supporting environment. It is the inner security that we find is absent in the present-day young; when the outer is lacking too, what basis have they for hope? The illusion of certainties and security with which so many societies of the past have cushioned their young against realities are no longer available to many. In an age which has casually thrown away centuries-old supports and retained only a fantasy that life can be lived totally on a rational plane (despite all evidence to the contrary), to be young is very difficult.

If the adults in adolescents' lives have a workable philosophy of life, however simply expressed, they can survive the uncertainties, recognising them in some way as part of the human condition. If on the other hand the young live, as they do in such increasing numbers, amongst adults who themselves see little meaning in life, the struggle to find a reason for believing that life is worthwhile becomes increasingly difficult as adolescence advances and reasoning powers develop. Hume told us that all beliefs are irrational; this did not prevent him or any of the rest of the human race from finding anchors for their need to believe something; when, however, these securities are pushed away from under the young by the old, how can the young find anchors? Some run straight for the securest, most fundamentalist belief that they can find around and give themselves thereby the necessary security. They discover that being irrational in Hume's terms is not such a bad idea; it does appear to have been a characteristic of the human race as far back as we have records. Others, perhaps with equal irrationality, opt out. They say to themselves in some way 'I can't cope'. They are indeed often irrational as they tend also to retain a belief that once they are dead everything will change and people will be nice to them from then onwards. 'Then they'll be sorry and won't treat me like that any more.'

It is within the context of this uncertainty that we have to find our sympathy for the suicide attempt. Without such a context the response tends to become one of irritation, and the feeling that they are simply looking for notice begins to predominate. It is a worthwhile axiom that when the young demand attention it is perhaps because they need it. Often they really are sending out distress signals.

They indicate this by the euphemisms that they too use for death. They don't always talk about 'taking my own life', but say something like 'I feel like doing what John did' referring to a contemporary who succeeded in killing himself and so getting a headline in the national press. Tina Wilson, whose tragic death alerted, for a while, so many teachers to the need to keep a watch on children, left a note to say that she had been bullied. She had indeed been bullied. She had also given warning that she was going to kill herself but the warning was not recognised so not heeded. The child who says 'I've taken seven aspirins' does not sound like a potential suicide, she sounds like a typical attention-seeker; and if her life looks, as Tina's did, for example, to be a contented happy one, if she seems, and indeed is, well provided for in a good home, there seems little ground for believing that she has really any serious intentions to take her life.

But we can never run the risk of making assumptions. The best home in the world may be a purgatory to some child for reasons of which we know nothing, and of which even her parents may know nothing. We should accept the evidence before our eyes and not be tempted to reject it because it seems inappropriate. If a girl says she feels like killing herself she should be believed.

There are, of course, times when it becomes positively fashionable to take small overdoses, and in schools where this has become the case it is important to bring the topic out into the open and discuss it with all its implications. It is rare, however, that those who take the overdose do not actually need some help. So each case must be looked at individually. Sometimes, as in Martha's case, the act is just one of despair in the face of intolerable conditions.

Martha was not a noticeable problem in school. Martha's mother herself had a history of mental illness and had made several suicide attempts. Two of her three older sisters and her father, who no longer lived with them had also made attempts. Martha lived in dread of her mother's rages when she would be beaten with a strap. By the age of 15, well used to the idea of suicide, she herself took an overdose of her mother's tranquillisers. She was admitted to hospital and when she returned to school she told the counsellor that she could no longer put up with her home circumstances where her step-father was not interested in her and her mother was so unpredictably cruel.

In class this despair had not been too evident. Martha was first seen as a rather solitary, somewhat unkempt child. As she was quiet and retiring no one had taken much notice of her. In fact, she was too solitary, having only one friend with whom she had a somewhat unstable relationship. She was not exactly unpopular, just isolated.

All the relevant social agencies were contacted. The counsellor discussed Martha's case with the headmaster, she was seen by the school educational psychologist who arranged for a visit to the school medical officer and she was found to be suffering from severe bruising. The social services eventually offered to try to find a place for her in a foster home, but in the end she remained in her own home. The counsellor and the school medical officer saw the mother, and the rest of the school staff were alerted to Martha's needs, so that she got more attention and consideration. In time she began to develop a more realistic attitude to life and even to see her mother as someone deserving of her sympathy.

It is often the quiet, rather subdued and somewhat isolated child who is suffering from the greatest despair. Teachers are sometimes so busy that they are grateful for any child who is quiet and undemanding but these are the ones who might be most at risk. It should be possible and could be essential for teachers to aim at having a word with every child in every class that they teach. On the face of it this might seem too great a demand to make on a teacher who is dealing with a different group of thirty children every fifty minutes or so. However, it will soon be found if this aim is put into practice that there are some children who always have something to say and will not let themselves be ignored. The Marthas will then become conspicuous to the teacher just because they do not seek or command attention. A child who is consistently withdrawn and solitary should be observed a little more closely. Teachers who find such children in their classes should alert the members of staff responsible for pastoral care and discuss the children with the school counsellor if there is one.

Perhaps the most evident sign of depression in Martha was one which is not always recognisable as such: her unkempt appearance. Failure by adolescents to take care of their appearance is a sign of discontent with themselves as well as with the world at large. At an age when appearances are perhaps more significant than at any other time of life, this signal should not be ignored.

Adults sometimes feel intuitively that they are being got at by adolescents who dress scruffily or fail to keep themselves reasonably clean. This is a valid intuition; there is often a great deal of anger, usually unrecognised, underlying the adolescent's rejection of the world's standards. There is sadness too, however, and the anger cannot be reached until the adolescent has been able to get through the sadness. This usually involves help from someone else, someone who will listen to the adolescent and understand, perhaps even remember, the loneliness that is so common at this time of life.

Loneliness is endemic in human life, but for those who are just about to set out on their own and both wanting and not wanting to grow up and be independent it can be devastating in its effects. The over-intense but brief friendships that we see in the early teens are often not recognised by adults for the important part that they play in helping to give at least an illusory sense of security against loneliness.

The sad, lonely, angry girl who has no belief that life has any meaning or purpose and no parental support to help her in looking for such a belief has two possible modes of behaviour for dealing with life. She can sink into her sadness and maybe end in suicide or she can run away from it and go to the other extreme – she can dress in dirty, untidy and gloomy clothes and moon about or she can be wildly defensive. The first response is easier to recognise; the second is more difficult, but just as important because it is still a product of depression. It includes such unlikely behaviour as running away from home, driving recklessly, drug-taking, wild party going, promiscuity and delinquencies of all sorts.

Depression in adolescents can show a lot of improbable faces, the most improbable being the artificial gaiety or manic excitement that it the exact opposite of the true underlying feeling. Adults can attune themselves to their own intuitive responses to this behaviour – if it seems false it probably is so; the feeling is as likely as not the adolescent's incompetent attempt to get away from the sadness of depression. A society that is so terrified of sadness and psychic pain that it spends millions of pounds a year on anti-depressants is not an easy one in which to face your own sadness. The temptations to run away from it are held out on every side. Running away can be literal or metaphorical; a lot of the girls leaving home never to return again are running away from themselves only to find themselves all too sadly, wherever they run to. They are also running to some imagined Shangri La which they are less likely to find. Adults who have the courage to admit to their own sadness from time to time will find that they can help depressed adolescents who are in most cases more than willing to look at their true feelings if they discover that someone else believes in them too.

Depression sometimes has physiological causes, sometimes psychological ones; more often than not the cause is not known for certain. Sometimes in adolescence the brief bouts of depression seem to be just part of the growing-up process. However, because sometimes they can be the signal of the beginning of something much more serious they should never be ignored. Occasionally a depression can be the first sign of a severe illness, psychological or physical. For this reason it is always worthwhile to suggest a visit to a GP by a depressed adolescent.

Because there are physical concomitants to depressions, in particular in girls when, as mentioned already, the menstrual cycle is involved, possible physical solutions should never be ignored. There are less GPs now than there were in the recent past who would be willing to prescribe anti-depressant drugs immediately on meeting a depressed patient, mostly more circumspection can be relied upon. But anti-depressants should not be discounted as a first step in the cure of depression. In the end the patient has to do the essential work but a wide variety of psychotropic drugs have been manufactured which, so long as they do not become objects of dependency, can do a great deal to help people over the first stages towards recovery. The danger with adolescents is that they are too prone to find escape routes and for this reason they need sympathetic adults around who can help them to work out their own solutions. Because often the troubles underlying the depression stem from home, it is at school that most adolescents might hope to find these adults. Teachers need therefore to look out for depression amongst their pupils.

Another fairly standard suicide-attempter was Alex who was in personality diametrically opposite to Martha. Alex left nobody in any doubt as to her misery; far from hiding it under a quiet exterior she blazoned it about her school. As the school was a highly respectable, rather old-fashioned girls' grammar school with a tradition of academic excellence and impeccable behaviour, Alex managed to get herself noticed. The general feeling amongst the staff was in fact that they noticed her so much they wished she would go away. By the time she was in the sixth form the headmistress was being put under pressure to suggest that she be removed and sent to the local sixth form college where her strident demands for attention would not be so much out of keeping as they were within the ivy-covered walls of this respectable edifice. Though she was intelligent, she was not using her intelligence. She was after all only doing music and art, not real academic subjects; it was not as though she would bring any credit to the school by getting to Oxford.

Alex took a dramatic overdose of her mother's sleeping tablets along with a good deal of alcohol and a few aspirins. She was hospitalised and subsequently seen for a while by a psychiatrist. She returned to school and had a short-term success as a martyr and romantic heroine because she claimed to have tried to poison herself because of love: a kind of twentieth-century Juliet. Her days of glory did not last because Alex did not have the temperament to hold people's sympathy or even attention. She was too self-centred and too demanding. The other girls soon tired of the self-dramatisation which had been the pattern of her behaviour since she entered the school. She was not a popular girl. Those who demand too much attention seldom are. After her second attempt Alex's form tutor tried to take her in hand and had some success. She pointed out to Alex how she was alienating even those who had sympathy for her and gave her the opportunity to talk about how she herself felt and about what she believed.

Alex, inevitably breaking down and weeping copiously, nevertheless was able to be a bit more honest with this teacher than she usually was. She revealed that she was well aware that she alienated people but did not know how to stop. She claimed to have been very happy until she was 10, and certainly up to that age she had been no trouble in school; on the contrary she had been exceedingly bright, had passed the 11-plus with one of the highest marks in the county and had looked well set for a brilliant career. She could not at first recall what had happened at the age of 10 but eventually it transpired that it was at 10 years of age that she first became disillusioned about her father – a clergyman who appears to have had a drink problem and who was ultimately unfrocked with a degree of public scandal.

Alex realised that she had been spoiled and allowed to do anything that she liked, and that somehow this had been of no help to her. She now felt riddled with guilt and full of self-hatred. She expressed this as 'I hate people – all human beings; that means I hate myself'. What she hated herself for most was the fact that she could no longer bear to be with her parents, she could not communicate with them at all. This was generalising to other people and now she was finding it increasingly difficult to make contact with anyone.

The outbursts of wild exhibitionist behaviour that her teachers so resented were actually a desperate attempt to make contact with them. She felt so unacceptable as her real self that she acted a part in the hope of at least getting a little notice. Those who feel totally alien to their fellows will look for any attention, even punishment, rather than be ignored. Alex felt truly alien because it seemed to her that her feelings were totally beyond her own control. To her teachers she was just a nuisance, to her the teachers were goddesses whom she was prepared to worship. She perceived for herself that she was looking for some woman to attach herself to, as she had no feeling left for her mother who seemed to have withdrawn into herself since her husband's disgrace. Alex was worried because she felt that her attachments to these teachers, of which they were in fact quite unaware, were too strong and too sexual.

Alex was in need of a lot of help and the fact that she alienated herself from other people by her behaviour made it hard for anyone to offer it to her. Teachers do find it hard to bear with girls who overdramatise themselves, especially when they do so to the point of suicide. Very few people are not afraid of death and most of us feel that the bell might toll for us. But Alex was acting a part that was not difficult for a sympathetic teacher to see through. She had suffered a tremendous blow to her security when her adored and admired father had been publicly disgraced. Even before that the over-indulgence of her parents had failed to prepare her for facing any of life's inconsistencies. So, as she had run away from reality into a false personality, now she was running even farther away into death. To have shipped her off to another school would have been to confirm her in her feelings of worthlessness and that at least was prevented.

Girls who overdramatise themselves should not be too easily dismissed as self-centred nuisances with too high an opinion of their own importance. Often enough they are covering with their behaviour a welter of misery that they do not know how to cope with. The mood-swings which characterise this age-group, often rapid and extreme, tend to occupy the centre of the adolescent's mind so that rational thinking takes a poor second place. The feelings of the moment must be attended to; reality can come later. This results in behaviour that can look light-hearted and frivolous to an observer. To the adolescent it is neither; it is often desperate.

Adolescence is a time when feelings can overwhelm; not since infancy as a rule has anyone been so strongly in the grip of feelings which seem to have little to do with reasonable thinking or sensible behaviour. For those young people whose lives do seem to be dominated by the intensity of their feelings, there should be words of encouragement rather than exasperation from adults, because the very fact that the feelings are so powerful can itself be salutary. Given a bit of sensible adult guidance the young can learn that through the intensity of their feelings they can sort out a great deal. Because of the very transparency and openness of their feelings adolescents get a second chance to experience some of those unresolved problems that all of us carry with us from childhood.

Used properly, Alex's depressions and dramas could help her to face up to what she really felt about her father's débâcle and her mother's despair. Her dramatics were a call to the adult world for just this sort of help. Martha, too, given the chance to look at her behaviour and the feelings that underlay it, was given the opportunity to rediscover some positive attitudes towards her mother in spite of the cruel treatment that she had received. Adolescence has been seen as a time of recrudescence of infantile experiences which can be, as it were, taken out and looked at again and given a second chance to get themselves straight. A lot of the adolescent behaviour which looks so infantile is in fact just this sorting-out process.

At times, when the overwhelming feeling is one of depression, which is common amongst even the sanest and most stable adolescents, the temptation is to indulge in avoidance behaviour rather than face up to sadness or disappointment; the depressed young girl will rush into love affairs which have no real meaning for her; promiscuity is often the outcome of despair. She will also indulge in wild behaviour, joining in any kind of delinquency that is currently fashionable: she will steal for the thrill of the risk involved, so as to give herself some kind of sensation to counteract the deadness of feeling that depression can induce.

Only too often she will at least think about suicide and often talk about it. Adults have to keep re-learning the necessity of standing back and taking the young at their own evaluation. This is especially hard for teachers who are used to making the running and, indeed, are obliged to organise the learning processes of those they teach. It is nevertheless an important part of their role to know those they are teaching enough to be able to recognise when there is a need that is not being met.

All teachers are not able to find the time or the skill to listen to the kind of depressed or over-excited girl who announces in one way or another that she wants to end it all, but all can develop enough awareness to be able to recognise that some help is needed. Any teacher can spot an unhappy child; all that is needed is an admission that unhappiness in children matters. Those who do not feel that they can go any farther than recognising the unhappiness do not need to do so. All they need to do is to contact whoever in the school has the facilities for doing something about it. The teacher who thinks a child is in danger should warn everyone who might be concerned or might be able to help.

Ultimately, whoever is finally responsible in the school for home—school relations should always, as a matter of course, involve the parents or guardians at least to the extent of inviting them in for discussion and alerting them to possible dangers of severe depression. Some parents will be less interested than others but the vast majority will be shocked to realise the state that their daughter is in. The daughter herself, because she has been making signals with some, perhaps not too conscious, awareness that she is wanting help will be grateful if she can find someone to whom she can eventually talk about her worries.

Chapter 15

Stealing

One of the biggest problems for those who live in an acquisitive society, but who know that they have a less than average chance of acquiring much for themselves out of that society, is what to do with their envy. The simplest reaction to a society that puts people in this position is to steal from it. But the stealing done by young people is very often not simply an avaricious attempt to acquire more goods; it is more than that. Very often, to the young, it seems to be an act of aggression against what is felt to be an unfair world. It is also, in very many cases, an attempt to replace symbolically what is missing from life in the way of affection and security.

Stealing, in fact, is probably the most frequent act of aggression by both boys and girls against the adults in their lives. But where boys break and enter, girls simply lift what is around. Shoplifters and pilferers are a never-ending menace in schools and a high proportion of them are girls. Even the most law-abiding will steal from Woolworth's or from the school itself; an impersonal institution does not seem as likely to suffer as a person. This is such a common attitude that some feel it can hardly be blamed on the young people themselves.

Stealing, however, should always be taken seriously because ultimately every child knows that it is wrong and needs to find a society that will uphold this belief. This can only be done if that society is prepared to find out why someone does what is known to be wrong. Girls, who are likely to have a stronger sense of morality inculcated into them from an earlier age than boys, are usually well aware that they are doing what they themselves believe to be wrong when they steal. Mothers are still expecting, and therefore getting, a higher level of compliance from their baby daughters than from their sons and this remains with them into their teens. Girls stealing money therefore should be taken seriously. It is generally more than just a bad habit.

Dinah was the sort of thief who is part of nearly every school population. She stole from classmates, from pockets in cloakrooms, from shops and from anywhere where anything was lying about. One day a teacher left a purse on her desk and Dinah stole that. After being confronted by the senior mistress, she returned the money but would not actually admit to having stolen it. She did, however, agree to talk to this senior mistress quite happily. She talked to her about home, which she contrasted unfavourably with school: in school she was happy, she did not want to leave because here people were nice to her. At home she was unhappy because no one was nice to her.

As the oldest of four children living with their mother, and no father, Dinah's life included a good deal of hard work. Her father lived elsewhere with another woman, whom Dinah did not like, and rarely visited. Dinah felt that this woman disliked her but as she felt that everyone in her home disliked her it was possible that all this antagonism might be just part of her own unhappy perception of life. There was no doubt, however, that Dinah was capable of liking people. In school she was surprisingly popular with both teachers and pupils, in spite of her known habits. She was an attractive girl, lively and friendly and quite open about everything except her stealing.

Her home life was, like that of many an eldest daughter of a family living in straitened circumstances with a single parent who went out to work, full of chores and responsibilities. Her mother went out early to work as a cleaner and came back in the evening two hours later than Dinah and the other children. Dinah had therefore not only to get the others off to school but to feed them when they got home and often to shop for their food during the lunch-hour.

It was during these shopping expeditions that she did most of her stealing but she did not steal for the family, only for herself. She took sweets and soft drinks. Her mother remained unaware of these activities until the purse episode when she was called into school. She was of course deeply upset but also genuinely surprised. She saw Dinah as a useful member of the family but had actually taken very little notice of her for years. Harassed by the burdens of rearing a family of four single-handed, receiving no maintenance from her feckless ex-husband and doing two tiring and badly paid jobs besides running the home, she had little time or energy to notice her eldest daughter's needs. Dinah resented this. Seeing the younger children getting attention she felt left out; having to cope with them in her mother's absence, she found them a burden. They were always quarrelling and resented Dinah's no doubt inadequate attempts to control them.

This life-style, not an easy nor attractive one, is nevertheless not uncommon and is coped with by many a girl without resorting to thieving. It was not the demands that were being made on her time and energy that were undermining her. Great though these were and little though most of us would relish them, they were not impossible and could be survived. The rewards inherent in having a responsible role and playing a meaningful part in society have been shown often to outweigh the misery that can be caused by the drudgery that such a life entails. It was not the drudgery that upset Dinah, it was the feeling of not being loved. Unconsciously, in stealing foodstuffs she was filling the empty gap that she felt was left by her father's departure and her mother's preoccupation. She was also trying to attract attention to her needs: this she did by her almost public theft of a purse that she knew would be discovered.

Thieves often steal because they feel psychologically empty and because they want to attract punishment to themselves. The food that Dinah stole temporarily assuaged the psychological hunger and the punishment that she brought on herself coped for a while with her guilt about what she experienced as greed. So she had both her needs fulfilled but not yet in any permanent way. That had to come about by her facing up to the realities of what she was doing. Her senior mistress helped her with this by listening to her and encouraging her to talk.

It is not easy to help people who are unhappy to see how inadequately they are dealing with their unhappiness, when its source cannot be removed; it takes time and patience to allow them to come to their own realisation of what they are doing. Blatant delinquency like Dinah's, however, is such an obvious attempt to make a communication about feelings that it is always worth following up. Dinah took time to get around to admitting that she was a thief, even to herself. She got there through the roundabout route of talking in the third person about 'this thief who stole a purse'. It was important that at no time should she be either rushed into admitting that the thief was really herself, or allowed to escape from the route that would ultimately lead to her making this admission for herself. She got there through a slow process of gradually substituting an 'I' for a 'she', and finally raising the problem of her stealing of her own accord.

In time she was able to make the connection herself between her feelings of emptiness and deprivation and her need to fill herself up with sweet things. The visit by her mother to school had also been a great help as it revealed to both of them a lot that they had not been aware of, both of Dinah's unhappiness and her mother's genuine concern. A mother—daughter relationship is based so much on the identification of the daughter with the mother that its success depends to a great extent on how much the mother can make her daughter feel that she is taking on the mother's way of life successfully. Dinah had taken over really the whole of her mother's role in the home but she did not feel that at any time she had been successful, as her mother seemed to give her no praise or affection.

A changed atmosphere at home, together with the lifting of a load of guilt at school, helped Dinah to a new approach to life. She did not in fact ever steal again. She was one of the fortunate thieves in that she achieved what she had aimed at: gaining the attention, and ultimately the affection, of her mother. This was not a conscious aim; if it had been it would have been acted out at home and not at school. In fact school was a safe place to play her part, because there she felt wanted and cared for. Compulsive thieves are not aware of what they are doing but if they can be helped to become aware they can often control the stealing.

Girls who steal are very often in Dinah's category, girls who are looking for their mother's affection which they feel they have lost. Some, however, come into that more tragic and less tractable category, those who come as did Lilly from backgrounds where thieving is endemic. Lilly's mother herself had been charged with shoplifting innumerable times and had once served a prison sentence when she had been caught teaching her children to steal.

Lilly had spent time in care whilst her mother was in prison and remained deeply antagonistic towards the authorities who had been responsible for this disruption of the family life. Unlike Dinah, Lilly appeared to feel little compunction about her stealing when she was caught, and tended to deny it furiously even when she was found to have a locker full of other people's property.

Lilly too, however, revealed on closer acquaintance that she recognised only too well the wrong that she was doing. She was ashamed of her mother but loyal to her. She loved her and wished that she would not steal. She would like to stop stealing herself, but it had become such a habit that she did not know how to break it. She too had no father, at least none that she knew about. She had a couple of older sisters who no longer lived at home and two younger sisters. They lived in a haphazard manner, with an occasional temporary boyfriend of her mother's claiming the paternal role in the house, but little attended to. Unlike Dinah, Lilly found little satisfaction in school. It was not surprising, therefore, that her school could do little to help her to conquer her bad habits.

Both Lilly and Dinah illustrated the need for a firm source of morality in their lives. Morality, however, can only be learnt from those who are respected. Dinah learnt it at school because there she felt respect for the people in charge. Lilly, unable to find any meaning in school, could not accept the values that it presented.

Yet it is the moral values that are represented by schools that are often more important to children than the actual knowledge that they acquire there. Neither of these girls had any doubt that stealing was wrong, both wanted someone stronger than themselves to help them to break the habit. Few even of the most hardened criminals have any doubts that what they do is wrong; neither of these two girls was a criminal, both lacked stability and a firm supportive background of morality at home. Perhaps the fact that both lacked fathers was not irrelevant. We still tend to put fathers into the role of law-giver and law-upholder. A family without such a figurehead does not necessarily produce thieves but it can produce insecurity. The strain of running a house, earning the money and acting as both stern law-upholder and loving comforter can prove too much for one woman to cope with on her own. If she is coping with this in an uncaring society she may well fail. This is what happened to Dinah's mother, but through the help given by the school she was able to put things right. Lilly's mother came up against the stern morality of the law but this was not sufficient to change her pattern of behaviour.

Lilly herself would have benefited from more attention at school to compensate for what was lacking at home but she was one of many thieves in a difficult school. It is very hard for teachers to keep a track on all the stealing that happens yet it is really important that somebody should do so. A society that teaches its young to take stealing and being stolen from for granted, at the same time as preaching the paramount importance of the acquisition of material goods, is not building a very sound foundation for the future.

Although ill-treatment of human beings is a far worse crime than stealing, our courts give much more severe sentences to those who offend against property than to those who offend against even the life of others. Train robbers are sent to prison for thirty years whilst we read (*Guardian*, March 1979) of young men who, having kicked another to death, receive a two years' suspended sentence. Perhaps this sort of legal practice is a measure of our desperation.

Stealing, however, needs to be seen by rational human beings (rather than by those who pronounce such sentences) as an offence against people. Both the person who is stolen from and the thief are damaged, and when an institution or a state is stolen from society is damaged by having its structure undermined. Without an agreed morality that needs no justification we are in great danger. Girls who are going to be the mothers who will have to teach morality to the next generation need in particular to have standards to work from. If they do not get such morality at home there is only school left to give it to them.

A society with its hand in the till is a depressing one; schools inevitably contribute to the building of a society, whether individual teachers see this as their role or not. There is nowhere else where children are going to learn values different from those at home, when the home ones fail them. Churches which used to teach the virtues are no longer attracting the Lillys. Yet she too needed to be taught. She needed more than just to learn that stealing is a punishable offence; she had been made only too aware of this through her mother's experiences. She also needed to learn something about her own worth if she was ever to learn to have respect for other people and therefore for other people's rights to their own property.

We are so shocked by people who steal from us that we find it hard to remember that the theft has been done by a person. Yet unless we can respond to the person in the thief we will not be able to cure the stealing. Good teachers are always aware that it is people whom they are dealing with, but it is easier to remember this when their students have some positive attributes and give some evidence of wanting to learn. The Lillys are harder to like than the Dinahs, yet they are as much in need; too easily both these girls could have been dismissed as incorrigible, their thieving being taken as an inevitable and tiresome aspect of life about which nothing could be done. Fortunately Dinah was strong enough and intelligent enough to make sure that this did not happen to her. There was enough evident goodness in her for her teachers to pick up and respond to.

Whether a girl is attractive or not, likeable or not, she is still a person and is still it must always be remembered a potential guardian of other persons as a mother of the future. As a thief she is likely to be a person with little sense of her own worth and therefore more than ever in need of help from the adults around her.

More likely to attract the attention of teachers than Lilly is the not unusual girl who, after a blameless career, suddenly starts to shoplift sometime during her adolescence. Sometimes this is just a brief episode that comes about through association with more practised thieves or more emotionally damaged individuals. Sometimes it is a response to a life in which the pressure has become just too much to bear.

Janice, who came from a very different background from Dinah and Lilly, was a student of great promise in a grammar school. At 16 she appeared to be a cool successful girl, rather pleased with herself and somewhat contemptuous of anyone who acted impulsively or showed any excess of emotion. Her parents, well-respected members of the community, appeared to provide a secure and supportive home. Her father had visited the school to discuss her future and had impressed the fifth form tutor with his perception and concern. He seemed a pleasant, reasonable and intelligent man who could be relied upon to do the best for his daughter.

The school counsellor was therefore very surprised when Janice turned up one day in a highly emotional state. She confessed that she had been caught shoplifting. She was adamant that no one at home must be told, not, it transpired, because she was afraid that they would be shocked, but because they had 'too much to bear already and any more would break them. As she began to give a picture of her home life it appeared that maybe she was really afraid that anything more would break her.

Once more it was the lack of a supportive and reliable father that seemed to be at the root of her difficulties. Janice's father, contrary to appearances, was far from filling the picture of the ideal family man which he had presented at school. It seemed he was locally notorious, the neighbours having on occasion felt the need to call in the police because of the violence that they could hear him perpetrating on his wife and family. He was a man of extreme moods, subservient and trampled on at work according to Janice and physically violent at home.

Janice's older brother had left home for good two years earlier after a fight in which his arm had been broken by his father. Now her mother was threatening to leave and take the three younger sisters with her. Janice was to be left to look after her father. She appreciated her mother's viewpoint and also had some understanding of her father, seeing a great deal of him in herself. She recognised that the cool front that she put on covered the same kinds of violent swings of emotion as her father's facade when he visited the school and meekness whilst he was at work. She also recognised the quality of falsity in all this. She realised that her inability to be aware of what she was doing when she was shoplifting was another way of pretending to herself that all was well, just as her behaviour was intended to pretend to the world that her life was smooth and successful.

Unfortunately for Janice the world at school, having believed that all was well, was inclined at first to be deeply shocked by the discovery of something closer to the reality. The headmaster of the grammar school which she attended could not conceal his astonishment when he received a request for a school report for the juvenile court at which Janice's case was to be tried. After her interview with him, Janice came to the counsellor in tears but was consoled when she learnt that the counsellor was willing to talk to the head and, with Janice's permission, explain the stress that she was being put under at home, but not to reveal it to the rest of the staff – at her request.

Meanwhile, before the court case came up, Janice had to cope with mock O levels. Her mother was still undecided as to whether to leave her husband or stay; her father was still having outbursts of unpredictable rage followed by bouts of morose penitence. When Janice failed all her exams her teachers were justly appalled at the deterioration in her work for which they could find no explanation.

With patient work the counsellor managed to help Janice to see that if she could let her teachers know that her life at present was a bit more stressful than she could cope with they would treat her with sympathy rather than with the contempt that she feared. As she needed their support if she was to be allowed to take any O levels after the fiasco of her mock exams, Janice could not but agree. The resulting change in attitude of the staff was such a revelation to her that Janice really began to recognise that the cool indifference that she had cultivated as a cover for her misery was redundant. There was no need for her to pretend that all was well when it was not.

Janice was one of the many children whose stealing seems so out of character that it is hard for the adults around to believe in it; as a result they sometimes act more punitively to such thieves than they do to someone from whom stealing money is more to be expected. Yet Janice was deserving of the concern that was shown to her. This syndrome of perfectly acceptable behaviour suddenly interrupted by a burst of delinquency is a sure sign of undue stress. It is commonest amongst those whose parents themselves suffer from emotional problems. At times the children appear to be acting out the parents' delinquency whilst they themselves present a respectable front to the world. This vicarious delinquency on the part of the parents is frequently found in those whose lives appear highly structured and overcontrolled but who are unable to cope entirely with the impulses of their own inner natures. Some part of such parents seems to condone the child's delinquency. Janice's father kept his front perfect for the world to see; he at no time broke the law, leaving that to Janice, but his behaviour was divided between conformist submissiveness and wild irresponsibility. Although Janice had survived under this pressure for years, the extra tension caused by the imminent family break-up was too much for her.

Janice's fall from grace was produced by an acute form of the stress that was chronic both for her and for Dinah and Lilly. Attacks on society's institutions by the young may well always be a response to some form of stress and we need to look carefully at the causes of these attacks. Stealing may not seem to some people to be an attack on society, yet it does not only threaten people's property it threatens their security. The less confidence we have that we can trust our fellow men, the less we can ourselves contribute to a society.

Schools are themselves societies that provide structures which are intended to give shape to the lives of their members. If these structures are not strong enough to control thieving, both the thieves and those who lose their property suffer. As most of the culprits, especially girls, will be aware of feeling guilt about their actions, the guilt needs to be acknowledged; punishment of some sort is the only known way of assuaging guilt; it is a necessary part of the ritual, though there will always of course be some who show little guilt, and there may at times be fashions in stealing which affect half a school's population when the whole process is seen as fun and not taken too seriously by anyone.

Some adolescents steal a great number of things although the actual nature of the objects is of no interest to them. These are sad children, very much in need of help. They steal for no gain at all but as a way of responding to an inner urge that they do not understand; they have emotional problems that will not go away simply because they are ignored. Like Dinah they are unconsciously filling a gap in their feelings; unlike her they are a long way from knowing what they are doing or why. As what they steal is of no value to them, their reasons for stealing have no basis in rational thinking, and are therefore harder to come by. Such children need a good deal of specialist help to sort out their emotional difficulties. This kind of stealing appears to work on the basis of some infantile logic. Young children love to get presents in large quantities and presents represent the fact that they are loved, and the quantity often supersedes quality in importance. An adolescent who steals this way is functioning at an infantile level of irrational thinking: something we are all capable of doing if we become very distraught.

When we are very young we do not know the difference between mine and yours. Infants feel that anything is theirs and very young infants act as though everything is a part of their own bodies. Stealing by adolescents can therefore be related to a recrudescence of this infantile sense of incompleteness, a need to restore wholeness.

When we see that an object is stolen which is manifestly of no interest in itself to the thief we can understand more easily the theory of researchers like Dr D. W. Winnicott who interprets the theft as a search for the mother herself. He sees the child as having rights over the mother on the grounds that in infancy the child's omnipotent fancy is of having created the mother, and on this basis sees such stealing as a hopeful sign. The child is showing what he calls 'a tendency to self-cure'. But because the object stolen is not exactly meaningful or useful to the thief it must be assumed that it has some symbolic meaning for her. On this basis it is well to remember that unless she is helped to make use of this symbolism she will not easily relinquish the habit; referral to psychological investigation is therefore always indicated in such children.

The regressive nature of stealing is evident in many cases even when there is an immediate clear-cut advantage to the thief in acquiring what she has stolen. There is very frequently a two-fold meaning to her in the act of stealing. If she can get in touch with the infantile aspect of the act she has more chance of getting control over her tendency, though the getting in touch does not always have to be at a conscious level.

If a girl who is feeling bereft of the loving care that she has needed for much of her life finds someone who can offer concerned interest she can use that person as a means of substituting in fantasy for the defecting parent without behaving to a teacher, say, as though he or she were a parent. She can feel the kind of support from that teacher that as an infant she might have expected to get from a mother. As this is a symbolic rather than an actual mother—child relationship, whether the teacher is male or female is immaterial.

There are some who steal so as to give to others in the hope of buying friendship. This is a more straightforward attempt to find a place for themselves in the world. Since most girls steal to gain some fantasied sense of security, schools can provide some of that security by being firm about not tolerating stealing and by letting it be known that it will not be tolerated. This in itself is not enough: unless some substitute can be provided for the care and concern that is lacking in the lives of those who make their protest by stealing, some children will never cease to be thieves. Our response to stealing money as a society is frequently to throw up our hands in horror; this despite the evidence that is available of how much delinquent adolescents are the product of the delinquent aspects of the society into which they are born. Whilst this does not obviate the necessity of curbing the delinquency it does provide food for thought for all those who deal with adolescents and deplore their anti-social acts.

Teachers, whose dealings with adolescents should come second in importance only to those of their parents, need to know with some clarity where they stand on such issues. Mindless punishments without regard to the needs of the thief are no more valuable than the ignoring of the theft of relegating it to the responsibility of someone else.

Since as a society which values property we set great store by protecting it, it is appropriate to consider those who attack it as delinquent; but we have seen in these three cases, and we find it in most, that the thieves themselves are also victims. Whilst bearing in mind, therefore, that stealing must be curtailed, and punishment as a deterrent is our usual method of curtailing behaviour, the punishment itself should never be seen as a solution, nor should it be delivered in such a way that it is considered to be the most important aspect of society's response to the victim/thief.

It is not necessary for every teacher to be able to help every child who steals to sort out the reasons for the stealing; it is, however, essential that there should be someone in the school who has the time and knowledge to do this, and it is important for all teachers to be alert to the needs of both those who steal and those who are stolen from. Both are at risk if the problem is ignored.

Chapter 16

The Hand That Rocks the Cradle Drops the H-Bomb

'Home is so sad' wrote Philip Larkin in his collection of verse *The Whitsun Weddings*. Home is sad, the product of 'A Joyous Shot at how things ought to be, Long fallen wide', and it is the centre, the heart of most women's lives. Mr Larkin would have us share his gentle melancholy, tinged with contempt ('that vase'), on contemplation of the home from which everyone has departed. The woman left in such a home after the children have gone, with more than half her life in front of her and nothing to put into it, turns in her thousands to a bottle. Alcohol or tranquillisers might stem for a while her despair at the desert that stretches in front of her. This is the future that we can promise to our girls leaving school if we do not take their education seriously. Women escape into the dreariest of work rather than stay in their sad houses, despite being encouraged on every side to invest most of their hopes in them.

What is a home then that can cause such sadness? First it is a woman's world: she makes it, creates in it and is important in it. Secondly, it is where her children grow up, learn to love and to go out into the world. Thirdly, it is where a woman can do her final growing up, where she realises that she has to live inside herself and not in her husband or children.

Nancy Friday, in her book *My Mother Myself*, suggests that few women in the Western world ever really achieve this second stage of maturity because they are too dominated by their own mothers. She presents a good case to support the view that women must change their attitudes towards the rearing of their daughters if this is to be altered. Girls on the brink of motherhood could benefit from examining Ms Friday's ideas if they aim to provide a better life for themselves and their children than that which many of their own mothers have had. Currently only those who escape the conventional pattern of Western women's ordained destiny manage to design their own life's structure. But they too are affected by the expected pattern when they have to struggle against it in order to live their chosen lives. They too have homes, but by learning not to be exclusively dependent on them they can enjoy them.

Homes are not of their nature sad; we make them so only when we expect of them more than they can offer. If we see them as the only source of our satisfaction, few of them can live up to our expectations. But virtually every woman will want to run some kind of home and, however inadequate this is, it will often represent for her the only possibility that she has of being someone in her own right, someone who matters.

It is time therefore that those who design and carry out the curriculum looked honestly at how much attention is paid in schools to helping a girl to prepare for home-making. This means preparing her for putting that home in perspective in her life, seeing the rewards that are inherent in good home-making and good child-rearing and recognising that marriage is more than the 'settling down' that so many girls imagine it to be. It means also preparing a girl to recognise that her life will have different stages and that the pattern of it will change as she grows older. At present neither as a housewife nor as a mother, and perhaps least of all as a middle-aged member of the unemployed, do we prepare a girl for what is ahead of her; so easily do we lose sight of the future and get sidetracked by the present. We see A levels, O levels and CSE as important goals and forget the lifetime that is to follow them. Not only do we take too lightly the immediate work prospects of girls who are leaving school, we also forget the conception, parturition, child-rearing and goodbyes that make up so much of the average woman's life.

A girl's future career as a wife and mother has long been used as an excuse for downgrading her chances in other work, invalidated though this is by the realities of thousands of women's lives in which child-rearing occupies perhaps 25 per cent of her working life, and perhaps far less. This view is further discredited by the evidence of the devastating inadequacy of the preparation that girls are given for child-rearing during their education. If this work is so important that it supersedes all other, and there is an excellent case to be made for such a viewpoint, why does it get so little recognition in our schools? Cost-effectiveness, the current justification for limiting girls' training in industry, could at least be defended if she were given training in the work that she is more or less certain to do: running a home.

There are, then, three important matters to be considered in looking at the education system as a preparation for the real shape of a girl's adult life. The first is training for the work of child-rearing; the assumption that child-rearing, like home-making, comes naturally to all girls, despite massive evidence to the contrary in terms of bad homes and badly brought-up children, is still a useful basis for evading responsibility. As Nancy Friday points out, there is little evidence for a maternal instinct in humans; mother love itself often has to be learnt. The second is the recognition of the three-fold pattern that many women's lives will follow: career, child-rearing and either second career or depression. This depression need never arise if a woman really has a career, as a happy occupied housewife or as a happy occupied worker outside the home. The third is the impact of a mother's thinking on the development of her young, the significance of her education in the narrowest concept of the word. Too easily is lip-service paid to a mother's influence on her children, whilst the realities of the influence are ignored.

In the chapter on careers I shall set out possibilities that might make women's lives before and after child-rearing more meaningful and worthwhile and consider how schools can contribute towards this. In the final chapter I shall consider the significance of learning itself in its effects not just on the girl who 'has a taste for it' in Lady Mary's words, but on all girls and on their children. I shall look briefly at how girls are discouraged from learning, whatever their tastes, bearing in mind the figures from the National Child Development Trust study which show that a mother's education has a statistically more significant impact on her children's future educational achievement than a father's. So a well-educated mother increases the probability that the child will also respond well to education. Children whose mothers went on to further education after leaving school are more likely to do so themselves, and all children benefit from having a mother who has learned to use her mind.

I shall look for the rest of this chapter at that universal role of women – child-rearing and home-making – and examine what teachers do and can do to prepare adolescent girls for it. There are academically able adults who consider that schools should only teach academic subjects. They would protest against accepting any responsibility for other aspects of education on the grounds that parents should do such work. Parents do not, however, show in abundance a great deal of knowledge of what constitutes normal good child-rearing, as has been revealed by the above-mentioned study by the National Child Development Trust.

This important and disturbing work should be in the hands of every teacher of social education, child care or home economics. It is important because it is full of information that should be available to every teenager, boy and girl, since virtually all of them expect to be parents. It is disturbing because it reveals the serious impact of the failure of education in preparing children for parenthood, but especially in preparing girls for motherhood in the present-day world. If it is true that all that is needed of knowledge about child-rearing is born naturally into every mother, we do have to ask ourselves how it is that so many mothers turn out to be inadequate in the ways documented here.

In the days when families were large and all but the youngest children witnessed childbirth and child-rearing as a matter of course, and anything that was done for a child was done in the home, no doubt almost every girl had at least the opportunity to learn what there was to know about the procedures involved: this does not necessarily mean that she could learn all that there was to know; knowledge has advanced since those days. Nowadays very few children are born at home and, when far more facilities are available outside the home itself to ensure children's continued growth in good health, it is clearly not enough to somehow hope that knowledge will be picked up. Girls themselves rarely want these matters left to chance. In Fogelmann's summary of the National Child Development Trust study *Britain's 16 Year Olds*, a clear picture is presented of adolescents' perception of their lives and their education. More than half of those spoken to wanted to know more about the care of babies and practical problems of family life. Yet more than half of them would be leaving school at 16, so where were they going to make up this lack of knowledge? Few of the others who stayed on for any kind of sixth form work or further education would be likely to have much of that kind of study included in their timetables.

In our research with girls who were about to leave or had left school, although a small number of girls said they knew enough about child-rearing through watching siblings or cousins grow up, a frightening number admitted that they knew next to nothing about babies and young children. A good many had been subjected to 'social studies' where these matters were touched upon theoretically, which was virtually unanimously declared to be a waste of time. Social studies altogether throughout our sample tended to be derided, or at least seen as a pleasant diversion because it was usually taught by nice teachers; at worst it was a boring waste of time because no one took it seriously. As a non-exam subject it was recognised as being of low prestige amongst both teaching staff and students. Only when it touched on sex education or, for some, politics, did it have any real impact amongst the girls to whom I spoke. Those interested in politics, mostly the inner city girls and particularly the black girls, rated social studies as one of their most enjoyable classes, but they saw in it no relevance to their lives as housewives and mothers. They considered that child care and home economics should give that sort of preparation but claimed that they mostly did not.

To alleviate their anxiety when questioned about their knowledge they would say things like 'I suppose it all comes naturally'. More frequent was 'I wish I could have done child care, but I couldn't fit it into my timetable': or 'I wasn't allowed to choose that option, I'm in band one, or set three or four; only the fifth and sixth sets can take that'. Most distressing of all were the reports from those girls who were studying child care right up to CSE level: 'What are you doing in it now?' I asked one group on the eve of CSE exams. 'Making a baby's bib' they replied, with some scorn. Maybe they had previously learnt something a bit more useful than that, I suggested. 'Not that we can think of,' they said. 'This has taken us three weeks.'

No doubt most child care teaching aims a little higher than wasting girls' time on making what can be cut out of a piece of plastic for nothing if it is too expensive to buy; but this is not an unfamiliar story. Child care is usually relegated to the less able and probably, as with so much of the teaching aimed at poorer students, expectations on the teacher's part are low; and expectations from the pupils soon sink to the same level.

So somewhere those in charge of these aspects of education, home economics and health education, as well as child care, need to see how they can go about getting essential data disseminated. If we really expect that girls will learn their child-rearing processes at home, as they did in the past, why do we not also expect them to learn everything else at home as they did in the past? If at the same time we expect that most girls will not, unlike the women teachers who teach them, have any career outside the home but only that of child-rearing, it would be reasonable to expect that we would put enormous resources into the child-rearing part of their education, and that it would form a major part of the curriculum. Probably all the girls encountered in schools could benefit from some guidance about running a home and caring for a baby.

Some will be fortunate and get a lot of help from their mothers or other relatives; some will do pretty well with Spock. But a high proportion of the population will not be so lucky. Many of these will have no competent parent around and many will never have developed that peculiarly twentieth-century Western idiosyncrasy of gaining all their information from the printed word: quite a number will never look at a printed word except under duress for the rest of their lives after leaving school. But all these girls will be responsible for the lives of those most vulnerable members of our society, their babies, and not only for keeping them alive but for educating them too.

In past ages high infant mortality rates were taken for granted, along with brief life expectancy, and an acceptance of poor physical health and a low level of intellectual functioning. Within the last forty years or so dramatic changes have taken place, and a complacent attitude is no longer taken to early death, poor health or inadequate educational attainment in children. It is evident that amongst the poorer and less well-educated members of society there is still a lot of improvement to be made very largely because mothers do not have enough knowledge about good child-rearing practice. And schools are the only places where girls have any chance to attain such knowledge.

In every sphere investigated in the National Child Development Trust study it was found that the vast majority of the most needy children in society received the least of the care and services that were available. This was not because of any refusal on anyone's part to offer this care, but because the children's parents did not know how to go about getting it for them. Their mothers, for the most part, had been educated in the lower streams, bands or sets in their schools. They might have studied child care but they had certainly not acquired the necessary skills for finding out how to use the society that they lived in; how to read and fill in forms, how to discover what benefits they were entitled to, and how to go about getting them. Worst of all they had not acquired that basic knowledge which would help them to realise how valuable these benefits could be to them, and to their children, and how essential it is for a mother in this society to use the system and to get the best for her child.

The uneducated do not know how to find out what is available because they do not read advertisements when they exist and often, of course, services are not advertised; it is simply taken for granted that people know about them. People cannot know what they have not been told; they cannot know the importance of such services if they have not been taught why they are important. Readers of *New Society* can learn all about how complicated and difficult it is for the poor to extract from the bureaucrats all that they are entitled to, and the *Guardian* can give advice about how to do so. Not many poor read either journal.

So ante-natal services and clinics which are so crucial for the future of mothers and babies are least attended by mothers from poorer homes. Presumably such mothers do not deliberately put their own and their babies' health at risk, they simply do not understand how important such clinics can be. They do not know, for example, of the findings of the National Birthday Trust Fund research which showed that the social class differences in incidence of infant mortality are actually widening instead of diminishing; that whilst it is a rarity in social classes I and II for a baby to die within days of its birth, it is still relatively frequent in V and VI. Only when the mothers of those infants are properly educated in the care of their own and their children's health, both before and after birth, will these figures change.

At a later stage in the child's life it was found that the incidence of various disabilities such as dental troubles, aphasia, hearing difficulties and even emotional disturbances were significantly more frequent amongst the poorer than the wealthier members of society. Yet all the services which deal with such problems were far less frequently used by just these people who needed them so much, than by the wealthier who could have found private treatment if pushed. The properly educated mother knows the importance of, for example, dental care to a child's health; all our future mothers should be properly educated, yet far more wealthy parents take their infants for free dental check-ups than do poor ones. If the children of the poor have a higher probability of showing emotional problems, their mothers need education not just in the use of services to deal with such problems but in how to attempt to prevent them arising in the first place. They need in fact to be taught how to care and why to do so.

In far-off days in simpler societies, legend would have us believe, children were brought into the world and brought up without any such modern aids as health visitors or immunisation. History based on stark facts rather than colourful fantasy will tell us a different and much grimmer story; so will some of the more enlightened novelists of past ages. At present we have in fact a society which, for all its short-comings, still provides the best opportunities for rearing children, and yet we continue to allow a high percentage of our girls to become mothers without educating them in the means to make use of those opportunities.

Theirs is the hand that will rock the cradle and that will bring the next generation to whatever realisation it may glean of what life is about, yet how seriously do our schools take this future role of motherhood on which so much adulation is showered? What kind of a philosophy of education is it that, whilst discouraging girls from seeing themselves as a significant factor in the workforce of the nation by not taking their careers seriously, at the same time ignores the need for any education in the child-rearing that is seen to be their major role in life? Too easily do we blame the parents of children for the misdemeanours that we have to deal with in school, and too little do we admit that the next generation of parents is our responsibility sitting there in front of us at their desks. If we fail the less intelligent girls we do not do much better by their brighter sisters.

Presumably expecting them to be more closely in touch with their instincts than the less able, we consider them to be even less in need of instruction in home-making and child-rearing (even in the making of bibs) than those in the lower strata of schools. I know of a girls' grammar school in which parents of third year students are told that there is a choice between Latin and home economics, and that the more intel-ligent girls are naturally expected to take Latin. Whilst it is good to hear that girls are still being encouraged to study the classics, there is a tragically familiar ring about this kind of pronouncement. In it we can see the residue of that early battle fought by the pioneers of women's education who, in great need to convince the world that girls could be clever too, assumed that to be learned meant to eschew the domestic arts; yet it is precisely these girls who, when they have their babies, will terrorise themselves with a multitude of contrary instructions from the baby books and agonise about whether to go out to work or not, because they have not thought about these matters seriously before.

This need to pander to the pretensions of intellectualism is presum-ably responsible for the abysmal state of home economics teaching that I personally have seen in some schools. At one extreme we see an A level home economics syllabus that is, as one hard-working and conscientious teacher complained to me, so much like a chemistry course that she could not possibly let any of her non-scientific students attempt it, they would get too discouraged and most of them would fail. At the other is the depressingly common experience of one group of children after another taking a mandatory term or two of cookery during a second or third year.

When it is known that this miniscule portion of an adolescent's life is all that is going to be devoted to learning the essential facts about how to keep alive and healthy, one can be justified in imagining that the information that will be given will at least be sound and simple, though inevitably very basic. When we consider the research that has gone into the dietary needs of the human body and the evidence that has been produced about the effects of different foods on health and even on behaviour, it should not seem too unrealistic to expect that some of this information would have percolated down to the children in our schools through their home economics lessons.

The fortunate few do learn a great deal about how to use the products of the earth that they live on. Many more take dull and meaningless notes on these matters and actually learn little. Thousands of schoolchildren, however, leave school having done nothing more than dabble in the use of that abominable collection of commercial products called 'convenience foods' which they appear to be actually encouraged to use by some of their teachers. I know one adolescent who was forbidden to bring fresh fruit to school to make a depressing concoction called a fruit crumble; she was told that she must bring tinned fruit, as fresh fruit was too time-consuming to deal with and was not as easy to handle as tinned. This was not an isolated case.

In a world becoming increasingly aware of the need for resourcefulness, proper use of the fruits of the earth, and the value to physical well-being of fresh and properly prepared food, the inculcation of such attitudes towards 'cookery' seems to me to be near-criminal. The excuse that I have heard that parents use these foods anyhow and that they are all that the children are familiar with, except for a few snobbish middle-class children whose parents might be cranks, amounts in my opinion to a further level of irresponsibility. If it were true that children ate only such food at home there would be even more obligation on the part of schools to teach them something better, so that they at least would be able to bring up their children to better dietary habits.

There is nothing snobbish in teaching children that tinned, frozen and packaged foods are more expensive than fresh foods because they have been processed and packaged and have therefore had labour costs added to the cost of raw materials: that they have by necessity to be given what is known as 'shelf life' which entails the addition of various non-nutrient and sometimes not particularly beneficial substances. There is nothing cranky about helping children to enjoy the excitement of making food from basic ingredients, especially ones which they can at some time see growing, even if they will never get the chance to grow them themselves.

It is of course much more difficult to teach this way, and with huge classes at times it may well seem impossible. Some teachers unfortunately have themselves been so badly taught in their colleges that they have not learnt how to teach the important basic essentials. One well-known college has been known to give instructions on how to lay a tea tray, complete with tray-cloth and triangular sandwiches. I have known a home economics teacher pass this valuable knowledge on to children in the East End of London during precious school time. Yet the popularity of cookery courses on television must itself give power for thought to some home economics teachers. Why is television doing what schools should be doing?

Perhaps the answer to that question is that television producers do not have a headmistress or headmaster looking over their shoulders. Heads of schools, in almost all cases (though unfortunately not absolutely all), are academically able. Whilst being academically able does not preclude being practical, sensible and in touch with reality it sometimes encourages the more ambitious and vain amongst us to value academic learning above all other forms of knowledge. This leads to a devaluation of those other important aspects of life without which ultimately no learning of any sort could take place. So the skills of home-making, like the skills of child-rearing, are relegated to a secondary role by such people; instead of being seen as complementary to intellectual life they are seen as an inferior alternative.

Teachers of these non-academic subjects therefore often have to brave the disapproval, even disdain, of such heads, and fight for what they know to be right: the chance to educate girls and boys in the arts and sciences of making homes healthy and happy places to live in. This means that they have to be prepared to argue the case for taking seriously the future domestic lives of boys and girls. They themselves will have to think too about how much they believe in the importance of teaching people how to support themselves by proper feeding and how to support the children they will produce. Boys as well as girls run their own establishments and need to know how to cook for themselves and for their families. Girls, more than boys but not exclusively, will be caring for families, but both boys and girls should learn the essentials of home and child care.

If we want girls in schools to face up to the realities we must also recognise that when some women go out to work, sometimes others will be needed to care for their children. A great many more girls could well be trained in doing just this to their own and to society's great advantage. A high proportion of girls from all intellectual levels will, if given the opportunity, say that they would like to work with children. In our research vast numbers of those with not too impressive academic attainments expressed this wish, but nearly all concluded that, for one reason or another, there was no chance of their doing so.

You have to have four 'O's and go to college: I couldn't get that.

I wasn't allowed to do child care . . . I'd have loved it though: I want to look after children . . . but I'm in the O level stream. I'm going to do a secretarial course.

In spite of the large number of women who would like, and indeed need, help in caring for their children, there are few openings for these girls. 'College' trains girls in specific work oriented towards either expensive nannying or residential work with children in the care of the local authority. Despite the overwhelming evidence that the isolated nuclear family and the single-parent family are crying out for some kind of help (both of these being difficult, often unsuitable and occasionally impossible, places for rearing children), nothing has been done so far to enable the mothers in need of even part-time help to tap this well of resources.

Perhaps a start could be made by careers teachers examining what the real possibilities are for more girls to train and to undertake such work, and maybe thereby effecting a revolution in our society's attitude towards child care. Another start could be made by courageous heads of schools who would dare to make child care and home economics, properly taught, a compulsory subject for boys and for girls.

Teachers are in a strong position to effect some sort of revolution in the whole of the country's attitude to child care. This could include the recognition of the plight of adolescent girls, the dual role that society demands of them: that of hard worker in school, competitive and aspiring; but dependent, gentle, uncompetitive seductress out of school. It will involve bearing in mind that if teachers emphasise a girl's need for preparation for home-making and parenthood they risk being categorised as sexist and unenlightened; if on the contrary they emphasise the need for girls to prepare for their two careers, face the fact that there is a momentous decision to be made as between child-rearing and other careers, they will of course be faced with further problems. For every individual who, like myself, urges them to think of these girls as people with the possibilities of having careers, as well as being mothers (just as many teachers themselves are), there will be at least two who will be fulminating against the whole idea. If girls are going to be mothers, how can they think of career prospects?

Latchkey children; Borstal as the inevitable destination of the off-spring of working mothers; neglect, delinquency and maladjustment; these are just a few of the prognostications that any teacher will come across. Before taking them too seriously, however, teachers of adolescent girls might consider their value as useful excuses for ignoring a great deal of reality and not necessarily contributing much to the well-being of children.

For example, as one enlightened 16-year-old, a Londoner who had no illusions about the security that life would offer to her once she had left school, said to me:

> Girls' careers are more important than boys', because they've got to keep a home going;

and another:

> She'll be the one left holding the baby so she'll need to earn enough to give it a home.

Latchkey children belong to the poor; professional women are not condemned for being barristers, pianists or politicians, in spite of having a family. There is plenty of evidence that many happy, healthy, stable children had mothers who went out to work at some time in their lives. Marie Curie, Golda Meir and Mrs Beeton (who reared some twenty children and ran a racecourse besides writing her cookery books) did not do too badly. Clearly it does not do to be dogmatic on these matters. John Bowlby, in his original report to the World Health Organisation subsequently published as *Child Care and the Growth of Love*, startled the world into consciousness of the importance of the relationship between the infant and its caretaker. The subsequent controversy which has raged, and is still raging, amongst child psychologists has tended to obscure the enormous benefits that have accrued to many millions of children as a result of this work. The care of children who for one reason or another have had to be looked after by those who were not their natural parents has improved beyond recognition in the Western world. The most committed opponent of Dr Bowlby's views would be hard put to it to refute the claim that this was at least set in train by his magnificent work. The extrapolations from his research that have been made by those who would still entrap women in a place that is sometimes only euphemistically called the home is another matter altogether.

As Katherine Whitehorn pointed out in the *Observer* (December 1978), women are as prejudiced as men about other women who work outside the home, especially the successful ones who do not have to do their own housework; and teachers sometimes come into this group. Do such women, she asks, demand that Yehudi Menuhin do the washing-up, as well as being a good violinist? Margaret Thatcher, carrying a shopping basket down the King's Road, Chelsea, as part of her election campaign presumably recognised that they do. Jim Callaghan noticeably failed to carry a shopping basket, but maybe had he done so he might have been returned as Prime Minister instead of her in 1979. Yet Margaret Thatcher had quite as much work to do outside her home as any other politician has, and what goes into a shopping basket matters exactly as much to men as it does to women.

For teachers of adolescents the important question is how much help they can give to boys and girls in understanding the significance of these issues. Clearly, for example, those who have no option but to go out to work despite having children need at least to consider what is the minimum length of time for which a baby needs the undivided attention of the mother or the mother surrogate.

This is the sort of question that every adolescent girl and boy should find time to discuss as a natural part of the education process. Without the knowledge of what babies need there is a considerable risk that easily averted damage could be done to young children by their unwitting parents. Recent research is suggesting that infants are responding to their environment even before the moment of birth, and the evidence of researchers like Martin Richards and Leboyer confirms that the mother—infant relationship can be extremely important during the first months of life.

For many years the late Dr Donald Winnicott, who probably watched more mother—infant interchanges than any other known pediatrician, tried to convince the world of the need for a mother to 'go mad with her child' during at least the first three months of her baby's life. By this he meant, in more mundane terms, that given the freedom and the necessary feelings of security a mother can abandon all other cares and allow her own secret self to predominate during these first few months, so that she and the baby can enjoy their life together, living at an intuitive level that may seem quite irrational to outside observers, and carrying on the symbionic relationship that they have had for nine previous months. This, he believed, would gradually dwindle naturally as the child adapted to being outside the womb and was able to welcome with enthusiasm the challenges of being inside and part of a much larger, more stimulating, more exciting world. A mother, Winnicott suggested, who can do this for her child, an ordinary 'good enough mother' who is by no means claiming to be perfect, gives her child a safe, secure and solid foundation on which to build his or her future life. From then on for the rest of the child's life as such the mother's role is one of weaning. Increasingly research findings are supporting Dr Winnicott's viewpoint.

By adolescence the weaning should be complete and the female child should be ready to consider preparing for taking on this role herself. Adolescent girls who have reached this stage need to learn about this and be helped to consider that somewhere between this three-month stage and adolescence the mother has to decide when weaning is sufficiently accomplished for the child to cease to see itself at the centre of the mother's life. If nature is left to itself that time might well be within a year of the baby's birth, since it is possible for a younger sibling to be born then, and the mother's attention to be diverted from the, at least physically, weaned infant to the next child. It would seem that nature does not demand that a mother give her whole undivided attention to her baby for longer than the first few months of its life; it can clearly survive on a good deal less.

Girls whose own mothers went out to work in their infancy can take heart from teachers who can reveal to them, for example, the researches of Hoffman and Nye who shown that the claim that working mothers are liable to produce delinquent children is invalid. What is important always is the quality of the child-rearing that children are subjected to. Some studies indeed have shown that there is a correlation between high intellectual and social development and having a mother who goes out to work. The rationale given for this finding is that working mothers stress independence. There is also evidence that these mothers can often be more concerned about their children, giving them on average more interested attention than do some mothers who stay at home with their children and get bored and frustrated by them. This does not in any way imply that all mothers staying at home will damage their young, only that those going out to work might not do so either.

From the point of view of those who are educating the future mothers of children what is important is that these sorts of questions should be discussed with them in their adolescence and that they should be given access to the information that is available rather than simply fobbed off with prejudices. Amongst the girls whom I interviewed there were few who had not contemplated the prospect of having children and few who thought they would want no children ever. They recognised that for part of their lives they would be wholly occupied with their children, and most of them realised that child-rearing might be the most demanding and most important work that they would ever undertake. They could see as far into the future as that date when they might become mothers; few girls in adolescence can be expected to see beyond that. Yet such a time will come.

Once the main rationale for the existence of the home has been threatened, that is, when the children have grown up and have gone to set up their own homes, the importance of the work in the house dwindles. In women whose homes represent their main source of power and importance, the feelings of significance that went with being the mother and housewife diminish as the significance of the work they do diminishes; and as the importance of the work that a woman does in her home disappears, so do her own feelings of self-worth. Her children, by making the biggest demands, are most likely to have given her the biggest rewards and her greatest sense of importance. Her husband will often not be an adequate substitute.

Caring for a husband in practical terms means largely feeding him and looking after his home. With years of practice the skills required for this work soon become negligible, and so therefore does the self-esteem to be gained from doing it well. Cookery can be a glorious and exciting art form, as can sewing or making a house beautiful; but everyday cooking for two people does not usually constitute a day's work, and neither do the everyday household chores. Sewing has become almost exclusively an art form for a great many women who no longer find it profitable or rewarding enough to make clothes. So what is there left of the traditional home-making skills that can keep an active, even only moderately intelligent, woman going on day after day?

The tragedy of the middle-aged woman where children have gone from home is that, unless she has a special interest in entertaining or has enough money to make her house an enthralling hobby, her work can become so meaningless to her that her life can seem to have no purpose.

Country people are better off than town dwellers, whatever their class or intelligence, because society in the country provides more activities that can still make the household arts meaningful: but the vast majority of people, both middle and working class, live not in the country but in towns and suburbs.

The middle class have devised self-employment like gardening and voluntary work for those who have no professions, but the failure of such activities to satisfy more than a handful of the more intelligent women is becoming increasingly evident. Working-class women rarely have gardens that are big enough to provide a life's work and have less of a tradition of creating a meaning for their lives by doing good works. It is usually necessary anyhow to have enough money yourself before you feel tempted to spend valuable working hours giving your time freely to others; and not too many working-class people have all that much money to spare.

Work, then, meaningful work, for at least a part of their lives, is what most middle-aged women are asking for; just as it is also what an ever-growing body of younger women are asking for. Middle age as represented by the departure of the children from home can come as early as 35.

Few adolescent girls can envisage being as ancient as 35, but their teachers can. They can therefore encourage girls to take a sensible attitude to their future lives by using their present lives for learning as much as they can that will help them both to run their homes better and to enjoy their work outside their homes. Encouragement must come from teachers because there are few other sources for it. Only if teachers themselves believe in the realities of their responsibilities to their students will they be able to give them this encouragement.

Chapter 17

Careers

Her voice was ever soft, gentle and low, an excellent thing in woman; and one about as likely to get her a good job as Cordelia's was to get her a just inheritance, or for that matter even to keep her alive. Perhaps the biggest single obstacle to a woman's career is incorporated in Shakespeare's beautiful phrase. The image that it presents, of what a young girl should be like, is as seductive as it is deceptive. It includes the possibility of being loved for not making too much effort and admired for being self-effacing, submissive and uncompetitive; it contains reminders that a woman's voice, if it is raised, is called strident; and it tells a girl, subtly, that if she does not achieve excellence as defined by a man her chances of being accepted by the world are slim.

Because there is admiration and sometimes love awaiting those who live up to these kinds of expectations, women as well as men subscribe to this image with alacrity, only to recognise too late that the price they pay for it may be a lifetime of drudgery. Not that drudgery, let it be said immediately, is the prerogative of women. Men too in any industrial society can become drudges, but they are not expected to enjoy the experience. Men are at least given to believe that they have a right to aim higher; they can move upwards from the servile position, though perhaps at some cost to themselves. They are always in danger of being despised if they do not move upwards. Where women are not allowed to succeed, men, in an achieving society, are not allowed to fail.

We have here a dilemma that is facing the young as they come to the end of their school lives. For girls the question is, are they to be satisfied with a fair amount of drudgery but spared the horror of the race that is rather unfairly ascribed to rats, but is more properly perceived as human? or are they to take the risk of joining the race? Are they to accept the role of second-class citizens that a lot of them have seen their mothers succumb to, or are they to join the militants and rebel against it all?

This problem includes the whole area of marriage and children and the complex decisions that have to be made about priorities. On top of these are the difficulties posed by society outside school where so often girls are not taken seriously as workers just because they are expected to be gentle and submissive.

Too many girls find themselves inadequately prepared to tackle these serious issues and too often the structures designed to help them is not just inadequate but is actually militating against their true needs. The result is a loss to the country of work the girls could do, and a tremendous loss of enjoyment for girls who do not find a rewarding career.

A girl who represented a sadly typical waste of potential amongst possibly the top 2 per cent in intellectual ability was Jean. She did in fact become a teacher for a while, a career that is so well suited to those who hope to bring up children that it is tempting to girls to take it up without thought as to whether they are suited to it or not. Teachers themselves are in the best position to know this, yet there is still a steady stream of Jeans flowing into the profession. Jean was neither interested in nor good at the work.

She was a pupil at a rather select girls' grammar school. Though coming from a poor home she had managed to acquire many of the trappings of middle-class culture and some of its aspirations. She had also accumulated some very good O level results, nine in all and most of them grade 1. However as she had parents who although intelligent had not stayed at school beyond the statutory leaving age, no one at home felt competent to advise her about her future. She herself had no doubts; she wanted to be an architect. She was intelligent, good at maths and art and expected to gain three good A levels. Nevertheless, when her father came to the school to discuss her future, it was suggested to him that he advise her to lower her aspirations. 'Architecture's a man's job. Jean wouldn't fit in; she'd never get on in it.'

Jean's father had been proud when his daughter had gained a place in this prestigious school, and was annually humbled before the might of the capped and gowned staff in their serried ranks on the Prize Day platform. He could not argue with such erudition and duly capitulated on Jean's behalf. Her mother showed little interest in her daughter's career. She worked full-time herself as a cleaner and, with her eldest son an apprentice engineer and the next studying at a college of further education, Jean's attendance at a grammar school was in itself as much as she could support by way of break from tradition. Although a bitter argument ensued, Jean complied with her father's wishes; she felt her inferiority as a mere girl before him, and a mere ignoramous before her teachers.

Jean suffered from three blatant disabilities: she was poor, she had parents who had neither the knowledge nor the wish to further her prospects and she was a girl. It was not sufficient that she had managed to overcome the not inconsiderable hurdle of adapting to an alien culture and beating it at its own game, she had also to try to drag her parents and her teachers after her into the twentieth century; in this she failed.

Her mother and father, though both loving and intelligent, were thoroughly imbued with ideas that have no class barriers: they believed that the careers of girls were of secondary importance, and that the wisdom of the elders must take precedence over the wishes of the young.

The teachers who gave Jean advice were affected by similar stereo-types of thought, with the addition of unconscious class bias. Had Jean's father been an architect, or maybe a doctor or lawyer, no obstacles would have been put in her way. Had they been dealing with a boy there would have been little difficulty. It would be hard to imagine a highly intelligent middle-class boy who had acquired nine O levels with good grades expressing a wish to study architecture and being discouraged by his teachers. Indeed, in the improbable event of such a boy's parents opposing his wishes it is to be expected that the school staff would do their utmost to support him in his career plans. It seems somewhat unlikely that they would have acquiesced easily in his ending up, as Jean finally did, in a college of education.

The unconscious prejudice and class bias that Jean's teachers showed blinded them to her real worth. A girl higher up on the social scale would have found less indifference to her career, although if such a girl had chosen perhaps engineering as her target she would no doubt have found similar opposition.

When she lacks family backing a girl from a lower rung on the social ladder has far less chance. When she also lacks her teachers' backing she has virtually no hope of standing up to the pressures. She must accept that she is expected to know her place and stay in it. So despite all her earlier successes, followed in time by three good A levels, Jean did not even apply to university. She took the less intellectually demanding route into teaching, through a Certificate in Education, that was being followed by so many of the working-class girls in her school. She did not want to teach, yet in taking this training she was closing the door to virtually every other profession. Had she taken the B.Ed. that was available in her college she would still have had little chance of a career outside teaching. As it was, she hurried through her course as quickly as possible to acquire the minimum qualification. She did not enjoy it.

Three years after starting her career she gave it up and went into a drawing office. Here she earned less money, and had less chance of promotion than as a teacher. The office was run by men younger and less well-qualified than herself who, because of the structure of the organisation, would move steadily upwards in salary and status. Jean and the other draughtswomen (there were no draughtsmen) had a separate scale of pay which reached a ceiling within a few years; there were no other openings to better jobs.

The work itself was moderately interesting, and closer to Jean's interests than teaching had been, but it did not stretch her to capacity and she was often bored. From being a bright enthusiastic sixth-former Jean, when I saw her last, was turning into a rather idle, discouraged adult with not too much commitment to work. Jean was intelligent: she recognised what is now being admitted openly, that marriage is the principal determinant of a woman's social position. Without a husband she was nobody. She was determined therefore to get married to a man with a decent job. She no longer saw herself as a person who was valuable in her own right. No one had taken her career seriously except herself; now she had given up too.

In her position Jean could not battle single-handed against so many convinced and convincing people. To get married was the obvious way out; a way of perhaps gaining a place in society and of forgetting her disappointment. Not to get married meant a life of continued frustration and increasing boredom with a low social status and little chance of improving it.

After adolescence has passed and hopes have been dashed greater strength of mind is needed to take up the cudgels again; only those with a sense of their own worth can continue to fight for their rights, and few girls in Jean's position can have this sense. She had from infancy known her inferiority to her father and brothers. The fact that she had demonstrated that she was more intelligent than any of them did not really register with her, and she was not going to change her attitudes easily.

Whilst all girls do not receive such inept careers advice, far too many still do. Parents like Jean's, knowing only the world of semi-skilled labour, have no means of assessing the guidance that is given to their daughters in schools. When they too have spent their lives in a society that uses the term 'women's work' in a pejorative sense, it should not surprise us that they fail to take their daughters' careers too seriously.

Since bright girls from this sort of background run the risk of having their capabilities underestimated by their parents, they are dependent on their teachers in a way that those from more privileged backgrounds may not be. Unless their teachers can present them with a picture of women which is more realistic than that held by their parents, these girls have either to do battle on their own, or give way to pressure. That large numbers still give way is evident from the vast army of women who occupy low-paid posts and who are receiving a decreasing proportion of the country's wealth as the years go by.

Nevertheless despite all these difficulties girls in some ways appear to be more blessed than their brothers, in that, although most of the best careers may not be open to them with any great welcome, at least one career, that of not going out to work at all, is still theoretically available. Women who do not want to enter the struggle for worldly success and who prefer to take life more gently can count themselves fortunate that they have not always all had competition in work forced upon them. If they can afford to, or if their husbands can, they will have been allowed to live lives that have often been closer to the human realities than those of the majority of men. The work that they have done at home, given reasonable circumstances, will often have been creative and enjoyable. Their most important work, child-rearing, is generally accepted as one of the most fulfilling activities that a human being can undertake.

The number of men who are able to do work that really satisfies their inner needs, seems important to them and makes them feel like worthwhile people, as child-rearing can do, is manifestly small in the present-day world. The majority are occupied in dull and demanding work with no expectation of reward other than the pay-packet. Relatively few men find that their work can develop their sensitivity, their humanity and generosity in the way that motherhood can. Not many men are given such a golden opportunity to recognise their capacity for concern, tenderness and gentleness, characteristics which we think of as quintessentially human, and which are as normal in males as in females.

Unfortunately quite a number of women, given this opportunity, have not always found it an unmitigated joy. Imaginative women like Marie Stopes first braved public wrath in the 1920s to reveal facts which threw a slight shadow over this idyllic picture of motherhood. She made it known that women of the poorer classes, that is, the majority of the women in Britain, by the time that they had had their fifth or maybe their fifteenth child, were somewhat disenchanted.

The size of the average present-day family, now that choice is available, does not indicate a desperate wish on the part of most women to repeat this rewarding process of child-rearing too frequently. Meanwhile if they are not given adequate guidance, the price they are likely to pay for spending some of their youth so enjoyably occupied will be to be excluded from most other enjoyable occupations for the rest of their lives. It is true that they will have had the satisfaction of doing a really worthwhile job. If they have had reasonable circumstances for doing it in they will have discovered that they can grow in stature inwardly through the daily practice of caring for another more than for themselves. Their husbands meanwhile are more than likely to have left behind all their generosity and concern as they set out on the ruthless struggle to reach the top of the ladder, or maybe simply to stay in the place where they are. This struggle might well be a necessary contribution from a father; the joys of child-rearing are somewhat diminished if there is a poor family income, or indeed none if the man is unemployed.

Which is preferable then? To be committed to aiming high in the external world of success and power, but dubbed as inferior if you fail to reach the heights; or to be allowed to find your own inner level of existence but to be prevented from achieving external success? Is it worse to be a woman who is, as most of us are, excluded from real power in a man's world, or a man who, unless he conceals from the world whole areas of his feeling self, might be castigated as feminine, that worst of all insults? Should a careers teacher advise adolescent girls that to go out into the cold of a winter morning to spend all the hours of light at a factory bench or an artificially lit office desk doing repetitive, unexciting work is better than staying in your own warm home and working at what you feel like doing when you want to?

If this were the true picture there would be no doubt which was the better life. How is it, therefore, that so few men choose to stay at home and do housework whilst their wives go out to earn the money? And why is it that so many wives, even from the most luxurious homes, make such efforts to get away from them? The fact is, of course, that staying at home and working at your own pace is by no means as delightful as it sounds. Some adolescents will be aware of this; others will not. To those who have not thought much about their mother's role in life, she might well seem to be a lady of leisure. Others with more experience and more perception will recognise that, for example, for many a young mother isolated in a tower block on her estate, or even in her beautiful detached villa, child-rearing can be a frightening and lonely job.

With a limited experience of what such a life can do to a woman, too many girls leave school with completely false notions about what running a home is like, because too few of them are involved in any way in running their own homes. Whilst they recognise that non-stop physical labour down a coal mine, for example, has few psychological rewards built into it, the hard physical labour of child-rearing and housework is not evident to many young girls. The fact that babies' needs can never be ignored and that sleepless nights can take away all capacity for enjoyment rarely crosses the mind of the dreamy adolescent. The further problem that this work is nowadays often undertaken in an isolation that amounts almost to solitary confinement is also easily ignored. It is pleasanter to be seduced into the belief that child-rearing is sacred and beautiful and that that is all there is to it.

The fact is that for many women the attractive and easily run home that increased prosperity has brought can become a prison of tedium; such houses often demand work that would occupy less than a fifth of any intelligent person's energy and interest. For those millions of women whose homes are very considerably less than attractive and for those whose homes are not always even dry, let alone warm, there is precious little excitement in housework.

Trying to make a meaningful existence out of doing what is not only repetitive and boring, but often as physically demanding as a great deal of factory work, and ultimately hardly as productive, is made worse by the fact that it is unpaid. Housekeeping money does not constitute a wage, it has too many emotional strings attached. Most women love their husbands and children, and do not want to be paid for loving them; they do however want their contributions to be recognised as work.

Hard work is not of its nature unattractive but there is no doubt that a more realistic assessment of what is really involved could prevent some devastating disappointments. Housework can, of course, be an enjoyable and psychologically satisfying activity, and child-rearing is fun for a great many women. For more than half the female population of this country, however, it is evident that the fun is not enough; or why would these women not only go out to work but often do so for much less money than most men are paid? The answer to this question, posed in innumerable research projects, is always the same: women go out to work because they are poor, lonely or bored, and mostly because of all three. If they remain at home they can do nothing to change the style of their lives; if they are unhappy in that home, housework, commanding no salary, can become slavery.

Those women who are fortunate enough to go out to work because they enjoy it usually do so in the teeth of, rather than with the support of, popular opinion. They might well also be amongst those who enjoy the creative aspects of house-running and child-rearing too; in that case they are fortunate, if occasionally a little overworked, because they have two jobs, or sometimes three, which they enjoy. They are in the minority and are almost always middle class.

Nevertheless, staying at home when home is pleasant can, of course, be much more fun than going out to work, as every schoolchild knows. Family activities are being valued increasingly these days, by men as well as by women, as the most rewarding part of life. But neither home nor family can be enjoyed so much when two fundamental elements are missing: those of choice and of self-respect. A man who chooses to stay at home feels very different from one who is forced to do so by unemployment, for example. A woman who elects to stay at home because she wants to rear her children, care for her husband or run her home can enjoy the work too. When she has no choice but still has to do this work and when, in addition, she is poor or feels that her status in society is diminished by the very activity that society demands of her, she not only has little chance of finding her work enjoyable, she can also see no end to it. She is caught in a trap which is not of her own making, and from which there seems to be no escape.

There may well be, or at any rate have been, societies in which women in their own homes rated as much status as the men out at work. Ours is not such a society. Few of the girls in our sample thought so. In talking to them about their futures, I found large numbers who had firmly embedded in their minds the notion that women on the whole did not work. When asked if their mothers worked, far more than half (above the received national figures) said 'Yes'. But they qualified this in two ways: they did not consider their mother's work a career, it was just a job; and they did not in any way see running a house as work. They were well indoctrinated with the popular idea that women do not work, though all of them saw themselves as planning to have a job of some sort.

Women have in reality always worked. Sometimes they have been paid for doing so, more often they have not. Work that is not paid for can easily be overlooked. Switching on my radio recently I heard, to my astonishment, a voice telling me that Mrs Handley 'only works part-time'. She has a family of four children at school, two others under 18 and a husband (presumably handicapped) who cannot even cut his own bread. Mrs Handley, whoever she is, works I guess harder than most of us have ever done in our lives; what she does 'part-time' is work outside her home after she has done her more than full-time job in it.

The majority of women for many years now have not been the idle passengers who dominated fiction in the prewar years. The upper- and middle-class Western woman who played bridge day and night has only ever existed in minute numbers in relation to the female population as a whole. It is true that amongst the upper classes, within living memory, a gentleman was someone who did not need to work and a lady someone who would not know how to. She could not even envisage the possibility of doing anything more demanding than directing her servants, except voluntarily in times of National Emergency. The First World War sounded the first death knell of this attitude and the Second finished it off completely. Since then a momentous revolution has taken place for girls of the upper class who can now respectably embark on careers and, being generally well or at least expensively educated and backed by sound finance, are doing so with great success.

Amongst the lower orders little change has taken place. Many of them since the beginning of the Industrial Revolution, and often since long before that, have worked not only in their own homes but outside them as well. Whatever work they have done outside, or in other people's houses (and this is where huge numbers of them worked as servants) they have also always had to do a good deal of hard work at home.

The root of the problem is a set of beliefs that is still prevalent even, sometimes, amongst teachers. The beliefs are not held consciously by the girls they teach, but they are surprisingly easily inculcated. Girls when they leave school act only too often as though they also subscribed to them. They fall into three categories. The first of these is that women do not need to work because their husbands will support them; when they do work, therefore, they do it for money with which they will buy pins. As they do not have to support their families they do not need such well-paid jobs as men. Secondly, even when they get the chance to work they will not choose interesting jobs; they are not ambitious and will not apply for promotion. Thirdly, as I mentioned in Chapter 16, women should not go out to work anyhow because their place is in the home; those women who do work neglect their children, all, that is, except the Queen who manifestly works very hard and cannot possibly have neglected her children because one of them is going to be king.

There is a sufficient element of half-truth in all of these beliefs to enable most of those who hold them to avoid seeing the facts that render them untenable. Let us then examine the validity of some of them. We will leave aside the last as it has already been looked at. The first depends entirely on the assumption that all women will get married and will stay married. The men they marry will all live as long as their wives do, will never be unemployed or incapacitated and will always earn enough on their own to support a wife and family. Furthermore, all women will always want to be kept by someone else and none of them will ever have any right to want to be independent. But, as most girls now know, independence and marriage have at last been established as not incompatible.

Only a very few girls in our sample said that they did not expect to get married, but there were frighteningly large numbers of them, especially amongst the less sophisticated, who still saw marriage itself as the ultimate accomplishment: the end to all their aims and ambitions. Despite the fact that they themselves in many cases came from broken homes, they still clung to the notion that marriage was for ever. Not so the inner city girls, they had their feet more firmly on the ground. Perhaps those from backgrounds where long-term marriages have never been seen as the norm have a better chance of coping with the contemporary fluidity of marital relationships. West Indians, for example, who frequently come from homes with a strong family orientation and a stable and supportive community but who, as a result of their past history, do not necessarily see marriage as an essential for child-rearing, can take in their stride the reality of marriage break-up more easily than can some of their English contemporaries. They see no need to delude themselves and can be realistic about their expectations: they will marry if they find someone they can rely on, they will try not to have children till they have found such a person but they will not expect that marriages will last for ever. 'How can you know you are going to go on loving someone till the end of your life? That's nonsense, till death do us part, it isn't honest,' they said.

They are more in touch with the reality that they are going into than are those who imagine that wedding bells mean the end of responsibility and the beginning of leisure. They recognise that in the first place all women do not get married and that those who do not can always be condemned to a lower standard of living than men who do not marry, as long as society works on the principle that women do not need to earn as much as men.

Equally important, and much more cruel than the financial handicap is the lower standard of respect that unmarried women can expect. This is built into a society which assumes that all women should marry, and has by no means been resolved by legislation. Try asking anyone to define spinster and bachelor and you will soon discover the prejudices that lurk just below consciousness in most of us. Because of such attitudes unmarried women need not be taken seriously; they have not fulfilled society's requirements, so society need not reward them.

Girls need to realise that one in three is the current figure of marriage breakdowns, and that family finances are automatically reduced when two homes have to be provided for. Women with children remarry less easily than men, partly because they have children and partly because they are likely to be older than the unmarried men around. Men who make second marriages have been shown to be most likely to marry younger women. So these ex-wives, although having children to provide for, are also condemned to a lower income because they are women with only less well-paid work available to them. Most single-parent families are headed by women, and these account for probably the greatest number of people below the poverty line.

As we have already seen, one woman in five in the UK is the family breadwinner; in the USA the figure is one in three and, as we are inclined to follow trends from across the Atlantic, in all probability the figure for the UK will continue to increase. Since the average income for women workers is actually decreasing in relation to that of men, we automatically condemn one family in five to a lower and diminishing standard of living when we fail to take the careers of women seriously.

Where there are two parents the fantasy that a man earns the wage and a woman, if she works at all, earns only pin money, or higher up the scale that a man has an income and his wife graces his table, is equally ill-founded. A large proportion of that 50 per cent of married women who go out to work do so to supplement, if not substitute for completely, the husband's income. When the woman's earnings are not required for the necessities that keep body and soul together they are, more often than not, used for those luxuries which we have come to think of as necessities; they provide school uniforms and pocket money, sometimes bicycles and, for the better-off, holidays.

The saddest reason for going out to work, as so many do even in the dreariest of factories, is loneliness. Companionship, including that represented only by the sight of other people, the sound of them being drowned in the clatter of machinery or blare of music, is preferable to the devastating solitude of home. The sunny picture of the happy housewife with her smiling children, even if it represents a genuine experience in some women's lives, is not universal: it is also not unending. Children grow up and that episode ends in most women's lives long before their capacity for work is exhausted.

Whilst few young girls can be expected to imagine that they will end up in the category of unhappy housewife or depressed spinster, it is surely the responsibility of those who are guiding them to put some of the realities of life before them. Only if they see their lives, as their brothers do, as to some extent in their own hands, can they prevent themselves reaching this same impasse. Without help from teachers many of them will not begin to think seriously about their jobs and will not be able to imagine that work can be rewarding and interesting.

If we look at the picture that schools around the country present at this moment in attitudes to the careers of the girls they teach, we see that it is not a happy one. Too rarely will teachers consciously help girls to move away from the soft-voiced submissive model; even more rarely do they seem to encourage them to be courageous in their job choices. Indeed, some teachers still do not seem to think it is part of their job to concern themselves at all with what girls do once they leave school.

The girls in our sample, from the brightest to the dullest, from the richest to the poorest, whether from secondary, grammar, comprehensive, public or private independent school, gave, with really only a handful of exceptions, a very dismal picture of the careers guidance that they had received. This included not only guidance from a specific careers teacher where one existed, but advice from form teachers, year tutors, heads of house and headmistresses themselves who above all should have known better. The bright reflected the conveyor-belt attitude to examinations and university places that gave them no leeway and left unexamined their own inclinations. The less bright resented the stress on examinations as the source of all good jobs, knowing that their own potential as successful exam-passers was limited. The dullest had mostly already given up hope. Somewhere teachers, especially career teachers, have to examine these attitudes and see if they are paying enough attention to all the facts.

Lest there be any thought, however, that it is only in schools that this failure to take girls' careers seriously exists, we need only take a glance at some of the advice given elsewhere – at home, on television, in journals and worst of all, in further education establishments. Try getting into an engineering course, for example, if you are a girl, or a typing course if you are a boy. Girls, it is said, will not take up engineering apprenticeships even when these are offered them. They will not indeed until they can be reassured that they will be safe from the prejudices of both tutors and students, which is not often currently the case, and unless they have found acceptance early in their school lives for their interest in these supposedly male subjects.

Boys are unlikely to demand to take typing courses in any large numbers. And here perhaps we have the paradigm for the most widespread attitude towards girls' careers. There are women's jobs, and girls should be satisfied with them; for most girls office work is the simple solution. How many male graduates can expect to be advised by university careers services to take a secretarial training as a standby? Yet plenty of girls who are expecting to take good honours degrees, or indeed who have already obtained such qualifications, are still receiving this advice: and it is true that it is sound advice from one point of view. A girl at present does not need to be unemployed if she can type. There are still openings for those trained in office work, but they are not openings to higher things. However, the truth is that typing, valuable though that skill is, rarely leads to well-paid jobs. Few directors of ICI started as typists.

But do girls during their adolescent years want to be directors of ICI? For the most part, certainly not. Later in life, perhaps, when it is too late to do anything about it, quite a lot of women might well wish that they had at least had the opportunity to apply for the post. They will not get the chance until they learn to start from the right place. They will not do that until someone shows them where it is; and that is not in the typing pool.

As a part-time filling-in post, typing is an excellent occupation. As a career it is full of hazards for the unwary. Once set on this road a girl has precious little chance of getting off it. As a career it is rewarding only for those few who are gifted enough and fortunate enough to find real secretarial work that provides interest and demands skills. For the many it is low-paid machine operating under another name. Only for the very few does it lead on to anything more adventurous or creative.

This has nothing to do with the work itself, only with the fact that it is female work. When the typewriter was first invented, typewriting, as it was called, was considered to be men's work, too difficult for the feeble female intellect to grasp. No doubt the ambitious young men who took it up went on to greater things; not so the women who followed them. Typing and secretarial work, like so many jobs designated female, have their own little career structure in almost every organisation, parallel to, but hardly ever interacting with, the main structure, and always reaching a peak well below even the middle, let alone the top, of the average career-ladder.

Teachers of office practice, business studies and such should be honest with their students. Typing is a valuable skill, so is book-keeping and so are other business-related activities. When taught in conjunction with economics they can be an excellent foundation for working in commerce, especially for setting up one's own business, surely an admirable ambition for any boy or girl. As an interesting skill like playing the guitar, or hang-gliding, it can be useful and profitable as well as fun. As a basis for temporary part-time employment, until micro-electronics does away with secretarial work entirely, it is unparalleled. Women are fortunate that such work is still available. They should, however, be warned by teachers of the pitfalls. No girl should leave school without having been made aware of how easy it is to let this useful craft blight her whole career if she allows it to be misused.

If, however, a girl recognises that as a typist she has the chance to be a machine operator in a pleasanter setting than the usual factory bench, she might make this choice. She should be helped to see that this is the choice that she is making. The notion that she is in something called a 'white-collar' job will often be more appealing than the larger income that she might earn in a factory. This is a valid and sensible choice to make; but she should know what the choice is, and she should know its limitations.

It is not usually the machine operator girl who chooses typing, though; it is more likely to be the girl who is interested in a satisfying career, and it is this girl who is going to be most frustrated by the barriers to success that typing can create. As she already has the barrier inherent in being female to contend with, she should not be encouraged to ignore the dangers of this further handicap.

The other great obstacle that girls have to overcome is the fact that most of them expect to have a baby or two and popular mythology sustains the myth that this makes a career impossible. For the girl herself there is no point in denying that babies can cause conflicts; it is often hard to make decisions about having a career versus having a child at some particular point in life and it is hard to decide how much a career can be allowed to dictate the sort of child-rearing that is to be undertaken. This, however, is the province of the baby's parents not the mother's employer or potential employer.

It is well known that, although the law forbids these matters to be taken into account, young married women are constantly asked at interviews if they intend to have a child and are equally frequently turned down by interviewing panels in case they do. The rationale for this is that having babies will prevent them from working their way steadily up through a career structure from the bottom to the top, on the assumption that every man will do so without a break.

In fact, of course, most people change jobs rather more frequently than women have babies. People who move from one career to another, businessmen, members of parliament, civil servants and university lecturers, for example, can bring knowledge and experience with them from previous work that will enhance their contributions in their new role. Those who occupy the most powerful posts in industry, government or research have rarely remained in one occupation; it is much more likely that their careers will have spanned a wide range of activities. Even the Einsteins do not follow a straight and narrow path uphill.

Women who devote a few years of their lives to raising a family are no less likely than these men to be able to engage in responsible work subsequent to their child-rearing. They too can bring to their new careers some of the insights and growth that their demanding activities have produced in them. In most cases, however, if someone is so rash as to make having a baby or two one of her careers she is likely to find this a deadly handicap to future success. It has been found that child-rearing is the last activity that should be mentioned at interviews, despite its obvious value in training people to be responsible, accepting of the demands of others, resourceful and hard-working. The popular myth that this interlude in a woman's life in which she bears and rears children automatically precludes her ever having the ability to do any really demanding work again (except when we are short of teachers, despite the fact that teaching is the most demanding work of all), keeps prejudice firmly in power. Here is a useful means of excluding from interesting work all those people who have no choice but to change their job for a while if they become pregnant.

Whatever laws are passed, the myth will remain unless women fight against it. They will, it is said, take time off not only to have their babies but to attend to their sick children. In a civilised society men too might be allowed time off to attend to their children at birth and during sick-ness. Child-rearing is another job which (as Barbara Castle said recently) is a valuable way of spending a few years but does not set the seal on a girl's career. Girls in school should be helped to see it in this perspective, as should the boys who will father future children. 'What if Margaret Thatcher got a bun in the oven?' was a reason given to me by a 15-year-old boy for keeping women out of the important work that only he as a future man was fit to do.

More sinister is the myth that women are altogether so dominated by their bodies that they are incapable of any work that demands strenuous exercise or commitment. This has never prevented women from being employed as railway porters during wartime, or nurses at any time. It is used, however, when convenient to keep girls in a state of sustained under-estimation of their own capabilities. The sickly young woman who is always either pre-menstrual, pregnant or attending to a sick child is in later years superseded by the menopausal neurotic of popular fiction. One notorious American politician is reputed to have gained his first foothold in the state legislature by putting it about that his female opponent, manifestly more reliable than he, was menopausal and therefore unstable.

There is nothing that anyone can do about such attitudes except wait for those who hold them to meet their deserved fate. But there is something that teachers can do to help girls who are likely to go into low paid jobs to have sufficient self-respect to resist such bullying and to demand decent payment. Too many women convince themselves that to work below the standard rate is virtuous because it means putting what they see to be the needs of their families before their own, thus confirming their secondary role. They ignore the fact that in doing so they put their families' needs before those of society. Is this virtuous? Women are hard to unionise for this reason. Unions, dominated by men, have responded by not showing too much interest in furthering the rights of women. Careers teachers who are really interested in the futures of the girls in their schools should be able to inaugurate, and sustain, debate about the pros and cons of unions, particularly amongst the less academically successful who will be the most at risk. It is these girls, even more than the brighter ones who might get into the professions, who are going to be at the mercy of any economic crisis that might affect wages and work. They need to be taught that such matters are their concern since for so long they have been told otherwise.

Let us now examine the proposition that women do not choose interesting jobs, are not ambitious and do not seek promotion. Most teachers will have seen girls like Jean leave school after showing great promise, and having plenty of intellectual success, only to end up in a career well below their recognised level of intellect and potential achievement. Never mind, they say, she will get married and have children, the solution to all female problems.

We have seen that the more intelligent girls frequently justify the accusation that they are not ambitious; they have not been encouraged to be so. Ruthless ambition does not appeal to many girls anyhow, and this is to their credit: Shakespeare too saw it as a dangerous fault, but the wastage of talent that results from so many girls' acceptance of the inferior role can never be justified. Margaret Hennig and Anne Jardin in *The Managerial Woman* comment that the US labour force is 40 per cent female but has only 5 per cent of women in a managerial capacity. In the higher salary brackets, 2–3 per cent are women, and 97–8 per cent are men. A similar picture would emerge from an English study. The parable of the talents, it seems, does not apply to women. The only talent that they are allowed to develop is that of bearing and rearing children.

The characteristics that Hennig and Jardin found in most of the women they saw, even amongst those studying in Harvard Business School, were lack of confidence, timidity and fear of taking risks; hardly the best endowment, one might have thought, for marriage and child-rearing. A significant factor besides those was the fear of appearing too intelligent before the male students. As this is a problem that intelligent girls have always had to battle with it is time that teachers helped them to see what nonsense it is.

Not only do fewer girls than boys go to university, far fewer take technical training, hardly any go in for apprenticeships, and far less stay on at school after the statutory school-leaving age. Those who do go into higher education tend to aim at the less lucrative occupations with lower status. So the degree of freedom that a university qualification gives and the attendant valuable opportunities to broaden their learning are what these girls who settle for the minor feminine professions miss out on.

Because girls like to help, to care for others and involve themselves with people rather than things (and whether this tendency is genetically determined or culturally indoctrinated, it is a good one and worth preserving), they tend to find themselves classed as helpers, and therefore second class and not worth taking seriously as potential students of abstract ideas. Nursing rather than medicine, a teaching certificate rather than a degree, physiotherapy and speech therapy, both badly paid jobs and socially highly regarded for that very reason (a nice girl does not demand high pay) are all cited as viable alternatives to the university study that would follow automatically for most boys with sufficient intelligence to qualify for any of these jobs. The result of this thinking is that girls frequently find themselves making choices of study in school or college which will automatically exclude them from the higher-status professions; they are not expected to want to study any non-humanities subjects. Maths, for example, is well known to be an essential requirement for most scientific work, any kind of engineering and a high proportion of administrative posts in industry, civil service or government. Increasingly university departments demand A level maths for subjects which no untutored teenager could be expected to associate with mathematics; psychology, for example, or philosophy. Meanwhile the computer industry booms and continues to spawn courses as well as jobs that require mathematical knowledge. Yet it appears that girls have not begun to take notice of any of those facts, though they are already beginning to be recruited in large numbers to the lowliest typewriting-like computer work. Have the facts not been put before them by their teachers? The figures do not suggest that they have.

Despite the mythology that girls lack spatial awareness and cannot therefore master mathematical ideas, which makes a splendid base for the tradition of conveying to girls before they even get to school the self-fulfilling prophecy that they will not be interested in such matters, Aletha Stein has shown that when maths is presented to girl children as a feminine activity they do just as well in it as boys. And despite a school-life's history of being gently nudged into a belief that maths are difficult for girls and unenjoyable, a surprisingly large number of girls have still survived to do well in maths when taking the 11-plus, and large numbers still obtain passes at O level. Only a minority of these, however, go on to A level maths, unlike the boys, four times as many of whom have the sense to study this most essential of subjects to as advanced a level as they can manage.

If girls' careers were being taken seriously, the significance of maths as a major factor in opening doors to them would be explained to 13- and 14-year-old girls because it is at this age that attitudes harden and important, and often irreversible, decisions are made. Option choices are too frequently made on the assumption that the compulsory maths element is sufficient to satisfy most girls' requirements. Whilst boys, even those who do not claim great intelligence, will aspire to a worthwhile exam pass, the girls will languish with boredom in a non-exam set till they can thankfully give the subject up. The rarity of female maths graduates and the shortage of good maths teachers, particularly at the primary level, owes a lot to this attitude.

Perhaps the greatest problem that is created by the perception of girls as poor mathematicians is the eagerness with which one who is manifestly good at maths is seized upon by the school. The really disturbing syndrome which I have come across too often amongst students at university is that of the bright girl who, because she is good at maths, spent two or three years in her sixth form studying nothing else. Such a girl is cherished by her school and encouraged to go up to university to read maths only to find by the end of her first year that three or four years of nothing but maths is already too much. Two more such years ahead are more than she can bear. She wants to do something else; maybe something to do with people or something to do with the arts or just, as one girl said to me, 'anything that has no digits in it'. If she had not been so good at maths she could have done a mixed bag of A levels and still have got into university. But the school has treasured this supposedly rare bird too highly and prevented her developing all her natural feathers. As a result many a potential maths teacher has given up either her maths course, or, much more drastically, her whole university career. This way she can so often let herself down and the teaching profession can lose a valuable asset.

Those girls, however, who reach the end of their education successfully, whether it be at the level of a CSE or post-doctoral research, have by no means surmounted all the hurdles that are created by their feminine upbringing. They still have to find their jobs, and they still have a harder task in doing so than their male equivalents at all levels of employment; and this will be by no means due entirely to male prejudice.

There are two continually recurring reasons given by interviewing panels for failing to appoint women to positions of authority: one, women do not apply; two, if they do apply and are short-listed they do not present themselves well at interview, they are not dynamic enough. The voice that is soft, gentle and low will not be interpreted as an excellent thing by those looking for a head of school or a factory manager. Women who want to get on have got to learn to be assertive. They will, of course, be accused of being aggressive because any strength of purpose or firm conviction in a woman is still described by many people as aggression, but interviewing panels are not concerned about that. They look for those qualities that, when found in men, are called confidence, assurance and strength, and they look for them in women just the same as in men. So teachers, in particular women teachers, should bear this in mind. They should ask themselves how valid is their judgement of the girls whom they see as stroppy and self-assertive; have such girls not also a right to develop the characteristics that, if they were boys, would win them approval? Have they too not a right to try to find good, satisfying work?

In fact, in schools girls are hardly being set an example that will encourage them to aspire to high office. The average secondary school in this country has a headmaster rather than a headmistress, despite the vastly greater number of women than men in the teaching profession. Even independent girls' schools are currently actually priding themselves on appointing men rather than women to their top posts; presumably there is some rationalisation for this, but I cannot recollect that it has ever been extended to the appointment of a headmistress to a boys' public school.

Although state schools make no discrimination in their advertising they are more likely to appoint men than women to the posts of deputy head, year head and such, though there is usually one mandatory female in a deputy post that has something to do with girls' welfare: she often teaches needlework.

So what is the picture that confronts a girl in her formative years? A group of influential adults amongst whom it is taken for granted that men occupy the superior roles. Girls going out into the world will not have had models for an ambitious and self-confident approach to job-hunting. They will not, therefore, always present themselves at interviews as people who expect to succeed, and only too often they will not even present themselves at interviews. They will in many cases convince themselves that they are not capable of doing the work of administration or organisation – man's work. Having been taught to be humble, humble they will be. Even in those other predominantly female jobs, besides teaching, we are seeing the same pattern emerging. In nursing, social work, and the like, the best-paid and most powerful posts are going to men. There are a good many reasons, both sociological and psychological, for this but in the main they have to do with money. As salaries rise, so jobs become more attractive. Girls, still influenced by homes in which the larger income is earned by the father rather than the mother, are easily seduced into the polite fiction that it is indecent for girls to think about money and unladylike to want any power; even when it is evident that having power means being able to do the work well and to make sure that it is done better by others.

Anyone who wishes to alter this trend must look hard at what happens to girls in schools; what they see going on around them and what impact the educational power structure will have even when they are not totally aware of it. Teachers who see the need for their influence in schools, but do not see a way to exert it, should bear this in mind – not just in relation to their own careers, but in relation to those of their pupils too. It is the women teachers having a career themselves, in particular, who can influence their pupils as well as their colleagues to change their attitudes. To do so they must recognise the problem for what it is.

Women teachers are usually the first, and often the only, women workers with whom girls come into much contact outside their families;

these women therefore set an example, whether they like it or not, of how women can be treated at work. But all teachers, not just women and not just careers staff, could give extra encouragement to girls both to believe in their own ability and to increase it where necessary by taking further training so that they can contemplate worthwhile careers. Eileen Byrne, in her book *Women in Education*, gives detailed statistics of how the education system is doing nothing like enough to promote the careers of girl pupils. The girls at the lower ability level undoubtedly do worst; even worse than the lowest ability boys. They consistently choose less valuable options at school, and once they get to work they are discriminated against again by being offered the poorest chances of day-release.

Teachers have a tremendous responsibility to help girls to see how much their own attitudes to work affect the lives of other girls, and will affect the lives of their children and their children's children. They can give their girl pupils a sense of self-worth so that they will apply for top jobs if they truly believe in equality of opportunity. Whilst it is not possible for many teachers to do much about the present career structures in the schools where they work, now at this moment it is possible for them to do something about its future. They are in a powerful position to counteract the myths that dog women's attempts to improve their career prospects. 'Liberation has come in but it just hasn't happened,' said a 16-year-old to me in mid-1979, 'because our headmistress doesn't know about it.'

As teachers have often spent their lives, since the age of 5, in educational establishments and can sometimes therefore be dangerously myopic about the world of work outside the school, they do not always recognise that they see such a small fragment of life from the classroom. They may meet successful women; they rarely meet the unsuccessful in great numbers except in that amorphous mass called parents. Successful women – perhaps because of their relatively small numbers – make headlines; at the top, indeed, women are having more success; at the bottom they are still the largest group of low-paid workers in the country. Schools are designed to give high status to intellect, so even when sufficient support is given to the more intelligent girls there is little hope for their less well-endowed sisters. Changes in attitudes must come from the successful and from those who have had the chance to develop their intelligence. It is not enough to say 'I got here by my own hard work, everyone else must work as hard and they can get there too.' We know that it takes more than just your own hard work to defeat the prejudices of centuries. Support must come from the adult world if children are to make changes. When parents don't support, teachers must. It devolves on the educated females most of all to improve the lot of their less successful sisters, and teachers are highly educated. They must use their education to inform themselves about the world that they live in, and pass this information on.

Teachers must show their pupils that there is no longer a role for women who do not see themselves honestly as part of the workforce of the nation. Girls do not have the right to assume that marriage will turn them overnight into kept women, nor do they claim it. The message that women who demand equality of treatment have to accept equality of responsibility for earning is beginning to get through to the younger generation, at least at the level of paying lip-service. What has not yet got through is that a girl can, if she has the will to do so, earn as much as her husband, do as interesting a job, and take her work as seriously as he does his.

If her teachers, especially her careers teachers, do not believe this, she is going to take a long time in reaching that equality which is neverthe-less now embodied in our law. If teachers perpetuate in their pupils the concept of womanhood in which they were themselves perhaps brought up, and to which many of the girls' parents may still subscribe, they could be doing a great disservice to society. Liberation will come because increasing numbers of schoolgirls are already fighting for it; and as the job market gets tougher these numbers will grow. Whether teachers are committed to the 'liberation' that these girls are asking for or not, they have to ask themselves, honestly, if they have a right to ignore the rights of half their students to gain for themselves a decent living.

Chapter 18

Conclusion – a Mind Like a Man's

There are two kinds of adolescent girl, I was told recently, when I mentioned that I was writing a book about their education: those who want to learn and are worth educating; those who do not and are not. The battle has still to be won. There is one kind of adolescent girl; she is a human being. Whether she is worth educating or not cannot, therefore, be called into question. What is, has been and will be questioned, as long as people feel entitled to such flippant, ill-considered pronouncements, is whether she is capable of accepting the education that she is offered. Still in doubt too, in some people's minds, is whether, if she should reveal a taste for learning, she can be truly 'happy in it' in Lady Mary's terms. Only girls themselves can provide the answer to these questions: in doing so they still have to contend with a considerable handicap. It is this handicap that teachers, ordinary, good, concerned and responsible teachers, can help to mitigate.

The handicap in essence is history: untold generations of child-rearing practices, accepted ideas, social systems, marital customs, established beliefs and received prejudices, all of which weigh against any new-born female infant. Nevertheless, none of these is so strong that good teachers cannot counteract it. None is so deeply rooted in anyone's needs that a little logic, and a lot of common sense, cannot oust it. All of them, however, need to be recognised and faced up to before they can be defeated.

Intellectually, long before she meets a teacher, an infant girl's handicaps are quite likely to be exacerbated, as Nancy Friday pointed out, by her own mother. It was this mother who taught her little daughter that boys do exciting things whilst girls sit by and admire them. She it was who read to her, before she went to school, all those stories about boys flying aeroplanes, driving cars and being extrovert; and about girls helping Mummy or putting a plaster on the boy's leg, cut whilst he was being extrovert. Some 95 per cent of preschool stories were found recently to belong in these categories. But mothers are easily blamed. They did not write these stories or invent these ideas. They gave their daughters the anti-intellectual culture they themselves had received, passed on through their mothers and grandmothers, back into history.

Where mothers leave off, television takes over, with research showing over 90 per cent of top viewing time being devoted to male actors being heroes and girls standing by helping, being girlfriends and wives, playing the secondary role. We in education are meantime doing our bit. J. B. Douglas told us so way back in the 1960s in his *Home and School*, but like so much good advice it fell on closed ears and little notice was taken. Boys in infant and junior schools are still being seen as extrovert, difficult to handle and as a result in need of, and getting, more attention than girls, who still get most praise for sitting still and being compliant.

Women of the Western world are supposed to be freed from the shackles that we condemn in those Middle Eastern countries where they live behind closed doors; but even in that most liberated Western country, the USA, researchers are still finding that little boys receive more instruction than little girls. Daniel O'Leary and Lisa Sarbin reported in *Psychology Today* in 1976 that the boys whom they observed in class consistently received twice as much instruction as did the girls; they also got more attention and more physical and verbal rewards. Whether it was a simple matter like stapling a handle to a paper basket or a more complex one like studying Piagetian conservation, the boys were encouraged to participate, the girls to observe. In the first lesson they describe, the teacher taught the boys how to use the stapler, but stapled the girls' handles for them. In the second she allowed the boys each to take a turn pouring water from one vessel to another; girls were told to wait their turn, but their turn never arrived, they watched what the boys did.

Girls, we are always being told, are no good at problem-solving, they have no spatial awareness. We even have television programmes showing photographs of female rats' brains containing less lines than male ones to prove this. If this is the case, since massive evidence is available to show that these capacities are enhanced by instruction, it would seem reasonable to assume that girls would be given more rather than less teaching in these subjects than boys. Alas, such logic does not inform the organisation of many schools. Dr Eileen Byrne suggests that girls lose interest in mathematical subjects more quickly than they do in verbal ones because at home they can practise the verbal and not the mathematical skills. There is some indication that girls spend more time talking to parents than boys do, but it is at school that learning is supposed to take place. Yet, as Dr Byrne goes on to show, failure to consolidate mathematical learning in girls persists throughout Europe, not just in Britain, right through to secondary education. Sue Sharpe, in her excellent study *Just Like a Girl*, confirms this finding.

Mathematics, problem-solving, all these really intellectual activities that require the Man's Mind that George Eliot spoke of, could be made available, according to Eileen Byrne, to the least able girls by good teaching methods. What is more, she quotes research undertaken by the

Irish Education Research Centre, involving the testing of nearly 4,000 children, which revealed that girls, in that sample, were actually superior to boys in solving the problems presented to them. It does not seem, then, that these areas of learning are necessarily a male prerogative, just that we have accepted too easily that they are, and assumed that most girls will never be able to cope with them.

A great deal of research has gone into establishing that what is assumed to be difficult will be found to be difficult and that what is expected to be impossible will be well-nigh impossible – the four-minute mile being an excellent example. Teachers would do well to remember the fact that as late as the fifteenth century reading was considered to be an almost impossible feat which many an aristocrat did not attempt, and even some bishops were said to have found difficult. A lifetime of unconscious assimilation of accepted mores by teachers may well be responsible for all those girls who give up so easily when the going gets a bit harder. Girls are expected to fail, so, unless they are particularly pushy, or especially encouraged, fail they will.

We have seen what happens, however, when girls get pushy, as a good many are doing at present. They do not necessarily do themselves a lot of good. It would be better if they could be especially encouraged by their teachers. Being obstreperous can be damaging to anyone's school career. Camilla, with her exhibitionism and need to demonstrate how clever she is, finds just as much antagonism in some quarters as the self-effacing Mavis, who only wants to merge with the background so that no one will notice her truancies. Neither is making a great success of life, and both need abundant help from their tolerant and long-suffering teachers. Mandy's more obvious nuisance value, stemming from her determination to find a place for herself in the world, takes the form of imitating her male counterparts, despite her natural inclinations to do otherwise. Torn, like so many girls today, between the Scylla of over-dependence and the Charybdis of rebellion, Mandy opts for Charybdis. The Scyllas remain more acceptable to the adult world; but they lose out in the long run.

Teachers coping not only with the rebellious and the bored, the demanding and the passive, have also to find patience and understanding for another group of girls: the lost. These, only too many in number, products of two generations of the neglect which is called euphemistically permissiveness, are a most unhappy band. It was hard enough to teach in a world where growing up was stunted by an excess of rules. It is harder still in a world where no rules at all are recognised, where the young not only have no idea how to behave but have no idea even what to fight against.

Hardest of all for newly qualified teachers is to know where they stand themselves. They too have been brought up, whether they realise it or not, in a world that still has doubts about educating girls. It is difficult for them to think clearly about giving special attention to girls when they have so many other new problems to deal with. If they do have time to think about such matters they may well feel daunted at the prospect of doing battle with history. But it will be a worthwhile fight. History is not entirely on the opposite side.

The education of girls went on through the darkest of dark ages and always some women managed to keep the torch alight. Celia Fiennes rode her ponies from Yorkshire to Cornwall and recorded her feat with a calm insouciance which suggests no concern that a respectable female, in the seventeenth century, might be thought of as doing something odd in being independent and clever. There have always been intelligent, courageous women who belie the nonsense that is talked about the female intellect. Only one of them is needed to reduce the whole edifice of prejudice to rubble. Teachers can find them every day in the making in their classes, if they care to look. They can also find hundreds of other girls who are not startlingly clever but are full of qualities that can make any teacher's life a joy if they are tapped aright.

Many years ago Ian Suttie pointed out that there is, in our society, a taboo on tenderness. Tenderness is the prerogative of girls; they suffer less from the taboo, and traditionally they conserve the loving and caring aspects of society. Since they have a major problem at present in demonstrating, to themselves as well as to the rest of the world, that tenderness and learning can work together in one person, they need teachers who believe this too to help them.

If girls feel the world is hostile to their development of freedom from past unnecessary restraints, they will be tempted to imitate the stereotyped male who acts rather than feels. The alternative, the gentle nurturing female who feels rather than thinks, is a stereotype that has decreasing attraction. Sensitive teachers are needed to help them to see that neither alternative is necessary.

If girls who are assertive can find teachers who will recognise this for a positive quality rather than label it negatively as aggression, they will demonstrate that such characteristics are not incompatible with loving kindness. Assertive men can be kind and loving; so can assertive girls and women. Strong-minded mothers can teach their own children that strength and kindness are not mutually exclusive; that assertion does not mean destructive competitiveness and that loving does not mean meek masochism. Boys brought up by such mothers will have more chance of developing into men who perceive the immorality of greed, whether between individuals or nations, and the futility of war (between the sexes as well as between great powers). Teachers of adolescent girls can help them to develop into such mothers.

Perhaps what I have proposed throughout this book seems impossible to achieve in present-day educational institutions. I am asking for more attention to the needs of individual girls, more listening to what they have to say and more recognition of the pressures that they are under whilst they are attending school. At the same time I am asking for more responsibility on the part of teachers, more commitment to their adult role, more admission that they know how the young should behave and more determination to demand such behaviour. I am also asking for more interest to be shown in the future of the girls in schools and more concern for what happens both at work and at home when they have left school.

This is making tremendous demands on busy teachers. Schools, after all, are designed for treating people *en masse*, and most teachers will recognise that it is this mass education that militates most against trying to make individual responses to students. When such responses can be made, however, teaching can be enjoyed; especially the teaching of girls, who in spite of all the difficulties mostly still know that they care about people, including their teachers. They know that they want to love and to care for people in general, and for their own children and the fathers of their children in particular. In a world that pushes them into early maturity with its emphasis on sexuality, girls still manage to recognise that, although this is an important part of life, it does not as a rule constitute the whole of it. They can appreciate too that learning is an important part. They can recognise that realistically in the present world having boyfriends is not only just one aspect of life; it might never in fact be any part of their lives, and they are not thereby diminished. In this they are better off than their grandmothers were.

The majority of girls, however, expect to look after families during some part of their lives, and to find that this is important and enjoyable work. They realise that the feminine life to which they have been born has qualities which are different from those that are masculine but, being in no way inferior, can be valued for themselves. At the same time a great many girls are capable these days of being much more tranquil than previous generations of women have been about accepting a world in which they are expected to be self-sufficient. Those who have not learnt to cope with it entirely soon will with their teachers' help.

Back in the early 1900s Rainer Maria Rilke was able to sense the possibilities that were becoming available to a girl who was able to find a place for herself in a new society that would no longer despise the feminine but would value it for its true properties. 'This humanity of women', he said, 'borne its full time in suffering and humiliation will come to light when she will have stripped off the conventions of mere femininity . . . and those men who do not yet feel it approaching today may be surprised and struck by it. Some day . . . there will be girls and women whose name will no longer signify merely an opposite of masculine, but something in itself, something that makes one think, not of any complement and limit, but only of life and existence: the feminine human being.'

Nearly eighty years have passed since Rilke wrote of his hope that this advance in women's status would change the whole of society's attitudes, towards a more honest and more loving and gentle relationship between all people. If those who have the responsibility of educating girls could see how near we could be to arriving at Rilke's ideal, and how far we are in danger of moving away from it, maybe they would feel that they had a solemn enough task to accomplish to merit all the effort and pain that such work entails. At the same time they might recognise that if they will only set out to enjoy their work and to appreciate their pupils, teaching adolescent girls, whatever its hardships, can also be exciting and inspiring and indeed great fun.

Bibliography and References

Alvarez, A. L., *The Savage God* (London: Weidenfeld & Nicolson, 1971).

Anon., *Go Ask Alice* (London: Eyre Methuen, 1972).

Ashdown-Sharp, Patricia, *The Single Woman's Guide to Pregnancy and Parenthood* (Harmondsworth: Penguin, 1972).

Association for the Psychiatric Study of Adolescence, *Journal of Adolescence* (London: Academic Press).

Association for Therapeutic Education, *Adolescence*, journal of the Association, vol. 1, no. 2, 1973; vol. 3, no. 1, 1975; vol. 6, no. 2, 1978.

Association of Headmistresses, *Towards Adjustment* (pamphlet) (AHM, 1973).

Atkinson, J. Maxwell, *Discovering Suicide* (London: Macmillan, 1978).

Barnett, Rosalind C., and Baruch, Grace K., *The Competent Woman* (London: Wiley, 1978).

Bassett, G.W., *et al.*, *Individual Differences* (Sydney: Allen & Unwin, 1978).

Becker, Ernest, *The Denial of Death* (West Drayton: Collier Macmillan, 1974).

Bettelheim, B., *Love Is Not Enough* (New York: Free Press, 1952).

Beynon, H., and Blackburn, R. M., *Perceptions of Work* (Cambridge: Cambridge University Press, 1972).

Bion, W. R., *Experiences in Groups and Other Papers* (London: Tavistock, 1961).

Blishen, Edward (ed.), *The School That I'd Like* (Harmondsworth: Penguin, 1969).

Blos, Peter, 'Character formation in adolescence' in *The Psychiatric Study of the Child*, Vol. XXIII (London: Hogarth Press, 1968), p. 245.

Brunner, Dr Guido, quoted in the *Guardian*, 20 January 1979.

Blos, Peter, *On Adolescence* (New York: Free Press, 1962).

Blos, Peter, 'The second individuation process of adolescence', in *The Psychoanalytical Study of the Child*, Vol. XXII (New York: International Universities Press), p. 162.

Bowlby, John, *Child Care and the Growth of Love*, 2nd edn (Harmondsworth: Penguin, 1965).

Brandon, Ruth, 'Father's girls', review of Hennig and Jardin *The Managerial Woman*, *New Society*, 30 March 1978, p. 731.

Bruch, Hilde, *Eating Disorders* (London: Routledge & Kegan Paul, 1974).

Byrne, Eileen M., *Equality of Education and Training for Girls in the Second Level of Education*, to be published in 1979 as a European Economic Commission study.

Byrne, Eileen M., *Women and Education* (London: Tavistock, 1978).

Cadogan, Mary, and Craig, Patricia, *You're a Brick, Angela* (London: Gollancz, 1976).

Cairncross, Frances, 'The Secretary Bird Trap' in the *Guardian*, 27 September 1976.

Caplan, G., and Lebovici, S., *Adolescence: Psychosocial Perspectives* (New York: Basic Books, 1969).

Carroll, H. C. M., *Absenteeism in South Wales* (Swansea: University College of Swansea Faculty of Education, 1977).

Cauthery, Philip, *Student Health* (London: Priory Press, 1973).

Cave, R. G., *All Their Future* (Harmondsworth: Penguin, 1968).

Cheetham, Juliet, *Unwanted Pregnancy and Counselling* (London: Routledge & Kegan Paul, 1977).

Clegg, A., and Megson B., *Children in Distress*, 2nd edn (Harmondsworth: Penguin, 1973.

Coleman, J. S., *Relationships in Adolescence* (London: Routledge & Kegan Paul, 1974).

Cox, S., *Female Psychology* (Chicago: Science Research Associates, 1976).

Dally, Ann, *Mothers: Their Power and Influence* (London: Weidenfeld & Nicolson, 1976).

Dalton, Katherine, *The Menstrual Cycle* (Harmondsworth: Penguin, 1970).

Dancy, John, *Curriculum choices in the sixth form*, talk given at Dartington Hall, Devon, January 1977.

Davie, R., Butler, N., and Goldstein, H., *From Birth to Seven* (Harlow: Longman, 1972).

De Mause, Lloyd (ed.), *The History of Childhood* (London: Souvenir Press, 1976).

Deem, D. R., *Women and Schooling* (London: Routledge & Kegan Paul, 1978).

Department of Education and Science, *Education in Schools,* Cmnd 6869 London: HMSO, 1977).

Deutsch, Helene, *Selected Problems of Adolescence with Special Emphasis on Group Formation* (London: Hogarth Press, 1969).

Douglas, J. W. B., *The Home and the School* (St Albans: MacGibbon & Kee, 1964).

Eliot, George, *Middlemarch* (London: Folio Society, 1977).

Elkind, David, *Children and Adolescents*, 2nd edn (London: Oxford University Press, 1974).

Erikson, Erik H., *Childhood and Society* (Harmondsworth: Penguin, 1965).

Erikson, Erik H., *Identity, Youth and Crisis* (London: Faber, 1973).

Esman, Aaron (ed.), *The Psychology of Adolescence* (New York: International Universities Press, 1975).

Fitzherbert, Katrin, *Child Care Services and the Teacher* (London: Temple Smith, 1977).

Fogelman, K. (ed.), *Britain's 16 Year Olds* (London: National Children's Bureau, 1976).

Fordham, Michael, *Children as Individuals* (London: Hodder & Stoughton, 1969).

Fraiberg, S. H., *The Magic Years* (London: Methuen, 1959).

Frankenburg, C. U., *Commonsense about Children* (New York, Arco, 1970).

Freire, Paloa, *Pedagogy of the Oppressed* (Harmondsworth: Penguin, 1972).

Freud, Sigmund, *New Introductory Lectures in Psychoanalysis* (Harmondsworth: Penguin, 1973).

Freud, Sigmund, *Introductory Lectures* (Harmondsworth: Penguin, 1974).

Freud, Sigmund, *Studies in Hysteria* (Harmondsworth: Penguin, 1974).

Friday, Nancy, *My Mother Myself* (New York: Delacorte Press, 1977).

Fromm, Erich, *The Art of Loving* (London: Allen & Unwin, 1957).

Gallagher, J. R., and Harris, H. I., *Emotional Problems of Adolescents*, 3rd edn (New York: Oxford University Press, 1976).

Gibbs, Lewis, *The Admirable Lady Mary* (London: Dent, 1949).

Goodman, Paul, *Growing Up Absurd* (London: Sphere, 1970).

Green, Hannah, *I Never Promised You a Rose Garden* (London: Pan, 1967).

Haigh, Gerald, *The Reluctant Adolescent* (London: Temple Smith, 1976).

Haim, Andre, *Adolescent Suicide* (London: Tavistock, 1974).

Harrington, Alan, *Psychopaths* (New York: Simon & Schuster, 1972).

Harrison, S. I., and McDermott, J. F., *Childhood Psychopathology* (New York: Transworld, 1969).

Harris, Martha, *et al.*, *Your Teenager* (New York: International Universities Press, 1972).

Haslam, M. T., *Psychiatric Illness in Adolescence* (Sevenoaks: Butterworth, 1975).

Hemming, James, *Problems of Adolescent Girls* (London: Heinemann, 1960).

Hennig, M., and Jardin, A., *The Managerial Woman* (London: Marion Boyars, 1978).

Hewitt, Patricia, *Rights for Women* (London: National Council for Civil Liberties, 1975).

Hoffman, Louis, 'Fear of success in males and females 1965–1971', *Journal of Consulting and Clinical Psychology*, vol. 42, 1974.

Holt, John, *Escape from Childhood* (Harmondsworth: Penguin, 1975).

Holt, John, *How Children Fail* (London: Pitman, 1964).

Home Office (P. Mayhew *et al.*), *Crime as Opportunity* (pamphlet) (London: HMSO, 1976).

Horner, Martina, 'The best girl loses', in *Psychology Today*, no. 8, November, 1975.

Horney, Karen, *New Ways in Psychoanalysis* (New York: Norton, 1939).

Horney, Karen, quoted in H. Kelman (ed.), *Feminine Psychology* (London: Routledge & Kegan Paul, 1967).

Hutt, Corinne, *Males and Females* (Harmondsworth: Penguin, 1973).

Illich, Ivan D., *De-schooling Society* (Harmondsworth: Penguin, 1973).

Irish Department of Education, *Research Report on Mathematics* (1977) quoted in Byrne, *Women and Education*.

Ireson, Carol, 'Girls' socialization for work', in Stromberg and Harkness, *Women Working*.

Irwin, E. N., *Growing Pains* (Plymouth: Macdonald & Evans), 1977.

Isaacs, Susan, *Social Development in Young Children* (London: Routledge & Kegan Paul, 1933).

Isaacs, Susan, *Childhood and After* (London: Routledge & Kegan Paul, 1950).

Isaacs, Susan, *The Psychological Aspects of Child Development* (pamphlet) (London: Evans, 1952).

Janeway, Elizabeth, *Man's World, Woman's Place* (Harmondsworth: Penguin, 1977).

Jephcott, Pearl, *Time of One's Own* (Edinburgh: Oliver & Boyd, 1967).

Jersild, A. T., *The Psychology of Adolescence* (New York: Macmillan, 1957).

Jones, Anne, *School Counselling in Practice* (London: Ward Lock, 1970).

Jones, Anne, *Counselling Adolescents in School* (London: Kogan Page, 1977).

Jones, R. M., *Fantasy and Feeling in Education* (London: University of London Press, 1968).

Jung, G. C., *The Integration of the Personality* (London: Routledge & Kegan Paul, 1950).

Kagan, J., and Moss, H. A., *Birth to Maturity* (London: Wiley, 1962).

Kahn, J. H., and Nursten, J. P., *Unwillingly to School*, 2nd edn (Oxford: Pergamon, 1968)

King, E. J., *Post-Compulsory Education* (Beverly Hills: Sage Publications, 1974).

Klein, Melanie, *Our Adult World and its Roots in Infancy* (pamphlet) (London: Tavistock, 1960).

Klein, Melanie, *Love, Guilt and Reparation and Other Works 1921–45* (London: Hogarth Press, 1975).

Klein, Melanie, *Envy and Gratitude and Other Works 1946–63* (London: Hogarth Press, 1975).

Klein, Viola, *Britain's Married Women Workers* (London: Routledge & Kegan Paul, 1965).

Konopka, Gisela, *Young Girls* (Hemel Hempstead: Prentice-Hall, 1976).

Larkin, Philip, *The Whitsun Weddings* (London: Faber, 1964).

Laslett, Peter, *The World We Have Lost* (London: Methuen, 1971).

Laufer, Moses, *Adolescent Disturbance and Breakdown* (Harmondsworth: Penguin, 1975).

Lessing, Doris, *Briefing for a Descent into Hell* (London: Jonathan Cape, 1971).

Liberman, R. P., *A Guide to Behavioural Analysis and Therapy* (New York: Pergamon, 1972).

Lister, Ian, *De-schooling: A Reader* (Cambridge, Cambridge University Press, 1974).

Lorand, S., and Schneer, H. I., *Adolescents* (New York: Hoeber, 1961).

Lovell, Mark, *Your Growing Child* (London: Routledge & Kegan Paul, 1976).

Lowe, G. R., *The Growth of Personality from Infancy to Old Age* (Harmondsworth: Penguin, 1972).

Lowenstein, L. F., 'The bullied and the non-bullied child', *British Psychological Society Bulletin*, vol. 31, 1978.

McCann Erickson Advertising Ltd, *You Don't Know Us* (London: McCann Erickson, September 1977.

Macdonald, Barry, *Accountability Standards and the Process of Schooling* (Norwich: Centre for Applied Research in Education, University of East Anglia, January 1978).

Mack, Joanna, 'The inequality of sex', *New Society*, 8 September 1977.

Mackie, Lindsay, *Women at Work* (London: Tavistock, 1977).

Maier, H. W., *Three Theories of Child Development* (London: Harper & Row, 1969).

Marchant, H., and Smith, H. M., *Adolescent Girls at Risk* (Oxford: Pergamon, 1977).

Marsden, Dennis, *Mothers Alone* (Harmondsworth: Penguin, 1973).

Maslow, A. H., *Towards a Psychology of Being* (New York: Van Nostrand/Reinhold, 1968).

Mayhew, Pat, 'Crime in a man's world', *New Society*, vol. 40, no. 767, 16 June 1977.

Mead, Margaret, *Coming of Age in Samoa* (Harmondsworth: Penguin, 1954).

Mead, Margaret, *Growing up in New Guinea* (Harmondsworth: Penguin, 1963).

Mead, Margaret, *Male and Female* (Harmondsworth: Penguin, 1970).

Mead, Margaret, *Culture and Commitment* (London: Bodley Head, 1976).

Midwinter, Eric, 'The professional–lay relationship', *Journal of Child Psychology and Psychiatry*, vol. 18, no. 2, 1977, pp. 101–13.

Miller, D., *The Age Between* (London: Hutchinson, 1969).

Miller, Derek, *Adolescence* (London: Aronson, 1978).

Miller, J. B., *Psychoanalysis and Women* (Harmondsworth: Penguin, 1974).

Miller, Ruth, *Careers for Girls* (Harmondsworth: Penguin, 1966).

Mitchell, J. J., *Human Life: The Early Adolescent Years* (Eastbourne: Holt, Rinehart & Winston, 1975).

Mitchell, Ross, *Depression* (Harmondsworth, Penguin, 1975).

Mardaut, Louise, 'Time to make it compulsory', *Contact*, 14 September 1977 London: ILEA.

Ministry of Education, *Half Our Future* (Newsom Report) (London: HMSO, 1963).

National Birthday Trust, (R. Chamberlain *et al.*,) *The First Week of Life*, vol. 1, *British Births 1970* (London: Heinemann, 1975).

Neill, A. S., *The Free Child* (London: Herbert Jenkins, 1953).

Neville, Richard, *Play Power* (London: Cape, 1970).

Nicholson, John, *A Question of Sex* (London: Fontana, 1979).

Oakley, Ann, *Sex, Gender and Society* (London: Temple Smith, 1972).

Oakley, Ann, *Housewife* (Harmondsworth: Penguin, 1976).

Oakley, Ann, *Becoming a Mother* (Oxford: Martin Robertson, 1979).

Offer, Daniel, *The Psychological World of the Teenager* (New York: Basic Books, 1969).

Office of Population Censuses and Surveys, *Married Women* (London: HMSO 1979).

Okely, Judith, 'Girls and their bodies', *New Society*, 7 December 1978.

Oxford Women's Services, *Fit Work for Females* (London: Croom Helm, 1979).

Palazzoli, M. S., *Self-starvation* (London: Human Context Books, 1974).

Parker, Beulah, *My Language Is Me* (New York: Ballantine Books, 1972).

Pizzey, Erin, *Scream Quietly or the Neighbours Will Hear* (London: Coventure, 1975).

Plath, Sylvia, *The Bell Jar* (London: Faber, 1963).

Powys, John Cowper, *A Glastonbury Romance* (London: Macdonald, 1965).

Pringle, M. K., *Deprivation and Education* (Harlow: Longman, 1965).

Rauta, I., and Hunt, A., *Fifth Form Girls* (London: HMSO, 1975).

Rayner, Eric, *Human Development* (London: Allen & Unwin, 1971).

Richards, M. P. M., *The Integration of the Child into a Social World* (Cambridge: Cambridge University Press, 1974).

Richardson, H. J., *Adolescent Girls in Approved Schools* (London: Routledge & Kegan Paul, 1969).

Ridgway, Roy, *Aggression in Youth* (London: Priory Press, 1973).

Rilke, R. M., *Letters to a Young Poet*, trans. M. D. H. Norton (New York: Norton Library, 1963).

Robinson, S. M., *Juvenile Delinquency its Nature and Control* (New York: Holt, Rinehart & Winston, 1966).

Rogers, C. R., *Client Centred Therapy* (Boston, Mass.: Houghton Mifflin, 1951).

Rogers, C. R., *et al.*, *Person to Person* (London: Souvenir Press, 1973).

Rogers, Dorothy, *Issues in Adolescent Psychology*, 2nd edn (New York: Appleton-Century-Croft, 1972).

Roland, A., and Harris, B., *Career and Motherhood* (New York: Human Sciences Press, 1979).

Rowe, Albert, *The School as a Guidance Community* (London: Pearson Press, 1971).

Rowe, Dorothy, *The Experience of Depression* (Chichester: Wiley, 1978).

Rutter, M., and Madge, N., *Cycles of Disadvantage* (London: Heinemann, 1976).

Rutter, M., *et al.*, *Fifteen Thousand Hours* (London: Open Books, 1979).

Sandstrom, C. I., *Psychology of Childhood and Adolescence* (Harmondsworth: Penguin Books, 1968).

Saunders, M., *Class Control and Behaviour Problems* (London: McGraw Hill, 1979).

Schaffer, Rudolph, *Mothering* (London: Open Books, 1977).

Schofield, M., *The Sexual Behaviour of Young People* (Harlow: Longman, 1965).

Schools Council, '*Cross'd with Adversity*' (London: Evans/Methuen, 1970).

Schools Council, (J. Ritche and R. Morton-Williams), *Sixth Form Leavers* (London: Councils and Educational Press, 1971).

Schools Council (A. S. Willmott and D. L. Nuttall), *The Reliability of Examinations at 16-plus* (London: Macmillan, 1975).

Schumacher, E. F., *Small Is Beautiful* (London: Blond & Briggs, 1973).

Schuterbrandt, J. C., and Raskin, A., *Depression in Childhood* (New York: Raven, 1977).

Seidman, J. H. (ed.), *The Adolescent* (New York: Holt, Rinehart & Winston, 1960).

Serbin, L., and O'Leary, D., 'Lessons in inequality', *Psychology Today*, vol. 2, no. 3, March 1976.

Sex Discrimination Act (London: HMSO, 1975).

Sharpe, Sue, *Just Like a Girl* (Harmondsworth: Penguin, 1976).

Shuttle, P., and Redgrove, P., *The Wise Wound* (London: Gollancz, 1978).

Singleton, C. H., 'Sex differences', in B. M. Foss (ed.), *Psychology Survey No. 1* (London: Allen & Unwin, 1978).

Spicer, Faith, *Adolescence and Stress* (London: Forbes, 1977).

Spock, B., *Baby and Child Care*, rev. edn (London: Bodley Head, 1979).

Stein, A., 'The effects of sex-role standards of achievement and sex-role preferences on three determinants of achievement maturation', in A. H. Stromberg and S. Harkness (eds), *Developmental Psychology*, 4, 1971, pp. 219–31.

Stengel, Erwin, *Suicide and Attempted Suicide* (Harmondsworth: Penguin, 1973).

Stern, K., *The Flight from Women* (London: Allen & Unwin, 1965).

Stevenson, Yvonne, *The Hothouse Plant* (London: Elek/Pemberton, 1976).

Stewart-Prince, F., *Teenagers Today* (London: Mind, 1978).

Storr, Anthony, *Integrity of the Personality* (London: Heinemann, 1960).

Stromberg, A. H., and Harkness, S., *Women Working* (Palo Alto, Calif.: Mayfield, 1978).

Suttie, I. D., *The Origins of Love and Hate* (London: Kegan Paul, Trench & Trubner, 1935).

Toffler, Alvin, *Future Shock* (London: Bodley Head, 1970).

Training Services Agency, *Training Opportunities for Women* (London: TSA, 1975).

Turner, Barry (ed.), *Discipline in Schools* (London: Ward Lock Educational, 1973).

Usdin, G., *Depression* (New York: Brunner/Mazel, 1977).

Waldman, Milton, *Elizabeth and Leicester* (London: Reprint Society, 1946).

Walkenstein, E., *Shrunk to Fit* (London: Coventure, 1975).

Wall, W. D., *Constructive Education for Adolescents* (London: Harrap, 1977).

Ward, J. P., *Social Reality for the Adolescent Girl* (Swansea: University College, Swansea, 1976).

Wattenberg, W. W., *The Adolescent Years*, 2nd edn (New York: Harcourt, Brace, Jovanovich, 1973).

West, D. J., *et al.*, *The Delinquent Way of Life* (London: Heinemann, 1977).

Wilson, H., and Herbert, J. W., *Parents and Children in the Inner City* (London: Routledge & Kegan Paul, 1978).

Winnicott, D. W., *The Child, the Family and the Outside World* (Harmondsworth: Penguin, 1964).

Winnicott, D. W., *The Maturational Processes and the Facilitating Environment* (London: Hogarth Press, 1965).

Winnicott, D. W., 'Adolescent process and the need for personal confrontation', *Paediatrics*, vol. 44, no. 5, Pt 1, November 1969.

Winnicott, D. W., *Playing and Reality* (London: Tavistock, 1971).

Winnicott, D. W., *Through Paediatrics to Psychoanalysis* (London: Hogarth Press 1975).

Wodehouse, P. G., *Mike* (London: Herbert Jenkins, 1908).

Wolff, Sula, *Children under Stress*, rev. edn (Harmondsworth: Penguin, 1973).

Wolpe, A. M., *Some Processes in Sexist Education* (London: Women's Research and Resources Centre, 1978).

Women's Studies Group, Centre for Contemporary Cultural Studies, University of Birmingham, *Women Take Issue* (London: Hutchinson, 1978).

Index